The Sea & The Snow

Major W M M Deacock
WARWICK
Leader

Major H W Tilman
SKIPPER
Skipper

Dr G M Budd
GRAHAME
Scientific officer

J R Crick
JOHN
Quartermaster

Dr M C Hay
MAL
Cine-photographer

A J de V Hill
ANTONY
Mate

Dr R Pardoe
RUSS
Medical officer

C K Putt
COLIN
Engineer

E J Reid
ED
Radio operator

R P Temple
PHIL
Entomologist

The Sea & The Snow

How we reached and climbed
a volcano at the ends of the earth

PHILIP TEMPLE

Lodestar Books

First published 1966
by Cassell Australia Ltd

Revised & enlarged edition published 2016
and paperback edition published 2022 by
Lodestar Books
71 Boveney Road, London, SE23 3NL, United Kingdom
lodestarbooks.com

Photos by Warwick Deacock except where indicated

A CIP catalogue record for this book is available from the British Library

ISBN 978–1–907206–59-7

Typeset by Lodestar Books in Adobe Jenson Pro
Printed in the UK by CPI Books
All papers used by Lodestar Books are sourced responsibly

The poem 'Fire and Ice' by Robert Frost is reproduced by permission
of Laurence Pollinger Ltd., from *The Complete Poems of Robert Frost*
published by Jonathan Cape Ltd., and Holt, Rhinehart and Winston.
The author also wishes to acknowledge the kind permission of
Mrs Rose Lindsay to include two verses from *The Magic Pudding*
by Norman Lindsay, published by Angus and Robertson Ltd.

Contents

INTRODUCTION

MORE THAN HALF A CENTURY ON, it is easy to forget that no-one had done it before. There had been expeditions to Ant-arctica and the sub-Antarctic islands, but these had all comprised substantial bodies of men on ships of a sensible size fitted out for ice and the Southern Ocean. They may have had sails, but they were mostly powered by steam or diesel engines. Even when sail was the only option, back in James Cook's day, his *Resolution* was 111 feet long and carried a complement of 112 men.

To most people in 1964, therefore, it seemed a preposterous pro-posal that ten men should undertake a sailing voyage of 10,000 miles across the Southern Ocean in a sixty-three-foot schooner to land on a harbourless, ice-covered island and make the first ascent of a 9000-ft volcano. Men in small ships had sailed to remote places before, alone or with small crews, but none with so much ambition.

But that was the point. As the expedition scientist, Grahame Budd, put it, its leader Warwick Deacock wished to demonstrate that, 'If one will only dare, one can actually do the most unlikely things that may come into one's head. For the hesitant, the diffident, and the many amateurs overawed by the experts of this world, this demonstration can't be made too often'. Warwick's vision captured the imagination of Sydney, from where the expedition began, and his energy drew enough support from its community, in finance and kind, to make it possible. That the expedition then succeeded in all its aims, exploratory and scientific, was a tribute not only to War-wick's leadership but also to the skills and dedication of his chosen crew, under the sailing direction of that peerless explorer and skip-per, H. W. 'Bill' Tilman.

It was a privilege to take part in the South Indian Ocean Expedition to Heard Island during that southern summer of 1964–65. It was one of the most important and memorable experiences of my young life. As, I think, it was for all of us, it helped shape who I was and went on to become. Ed Hillary wrote that what we undertook was indicative of our 'courage and imagination'. If that was true, the example offered by such adventurous enterprises cannot be made too often, for the value it renders to its participants and for the encouragement it gives to others to also try the 'most unlikely things'.

NOTES ON THIS FIFTIETH ANNIVERSARY EDITION

I wrote *The Sea and the Snow* soon after the completion of the expedition in March 1965. It was the second of my books to be published, in August 1966. I wrote it under some pressure, with a deadline of marriage in early June 1965, and then joining the New Zealand Outward Bound School as an instructor. In my haste, I scribbled corrections on the typescript, did not keep a copy, and airmailed the manuscript to the publishers in Sydney, expecting it to be professionally edited. It wasn't. I was horrified to find that the published work included some uncorrected bad grammar, omissions, and inappropriate word choices. So, 50 years on, it has been a pleasure to have the opportunity to clean up the text. This 50th anniversary edition includes many more photographs than the original, and there is also an addendum about what the expedition members have done with the rest of their lives. All of this has been made possible for this beautiful special edition by the generous Dick Wynne of Lodestar Books.

Although I copy-edited the text, I resisted the temptation to excise one or two cringe-making passages that an ingenuous 26-year-old wrote in the opening pages. But that is the way I was, and we were, in the ambience of the times and they should stay. Similarly, I was rather appalled at our cavalier attitude towards rubbish: plastic bags flying everywhere, gear dumped in a pristine environment, empty diesel drums thrown overboard. All I can say is that environmental awareness was in its infancy then and the dumping on the island was prompted by our simple desire to stay alive in one of the most hostile places on earth.

I enjoyed re-reading this story by a younger self whom I sometimes recognised. Skipper Bill Tilman, in his own account of this voyage[*], described me as one of the scruffiest members of the crew. Mmm. How he came to that conclusion remains as much a mystery to me as where his old bones lie now!

Philip Temple
Alexandra, New Zealand,
January 2016

---

[*]   *Mostly Mischief,* Hollis and Carter 1966 and Tilman Books 2016

FOREWORD

Even in our comfortable society there are an encouraging number of men who will sacrifice their ease and security in order to undertake a great adventure. Such a group were Warwick Deacock and the crew of the *Patanela*.

Their programme was a formidable one—to sail their small vessel thousands of miles over the stormy southern ocean to Heard Island; to make the first ascent of the ice-clad Big Ben; and then to sail right home again. Their first obstacles were met at home—ignorance, apathy, official opposition and the problem of raising the necessary finance. The grimmer moments of their long sea voyage and on the windy heights of Big Ben were tackled with determination, ingenuity and good humour.

That the *Patanela* party achieved all their objectives is a compliment to their organization and planning. That they set out at all is indicative of their courage and imagination.

Sir Edmund Hillary
1966

Budd Peak from Pass Camp

BEGINNING

What is an expedition? My dictionary explains—'(men, fleet sent on) journey or voyage for definite purpose'. There it is baldly, but the definition neglects to tell that some men enjoy sending themselves, and for a variety of purposes that often seem inexplicable to an onlooker.

The dictionary suggests that expeditions were military in origin, and the word was surely invented to label those great voyages and armed treks that had conquest or mercantile one-upmanship in view. Sir Francis Drake epitomised that old kind of expedition where incredible daring and courage, that still rings through the centuries, were the trademarks of adventures with the questionable ends of piracy and plunder. These expeditions of a golden age merged slowly with those of a later time that displayed a more perceptible aim of discovery. Exploration, which had been a slightly regarded value of Drake's voyages, began to achieve a clear status beside the claims of trade and colonial expansion. Science gave an added impetus and there came the great voyages of Cook and later such enterprises as the Royal Naval expeditions to Antarctica and in search of the North West Passage. Exploration even became a prime justification for expeditions, and Stanley crossed Africa for no other objective cause.

By the end of the last century the age of fundamental discovery was over. There was no new land to be found; most of it had been traversed, and man's channels for adventurous discovery were narrowed. Mountaineering began to provide a splendid basis for enterprising expeditions, and these grew apace as the influence of the new democracy gave the opportunity of personal adventure to almost everyone. The peak of these was reached ten years ago, when the world's three highest mountains were climbed in successive years, but they continue undiminished today.

All expeditions, old, new and whatever their aim, have been expressions of adventure and enterprise with their valued progeny of determination, courage and tolerance. Lately, to gain support and bring expeditions into being, there has been need of great scientific and commercial justification. Though the interests of science and commerce must be fostered, their demands and technicalities must not be allowed to overshadow this spirit of adventure, the zest for climbing a peak 'because it is there', for crossing a continent because no-one has before, that is essential to the survival of a strong society. 'Without the instinct for adventure in young men, any civilization, however enlightened, any state, however well ordered, must wilt and wither away.' The time has gone (we hope) when adventure must be provided by expeditions of expansion and conquest. It is a narrow attitude which holds that only the best of men's courage and endeavour can be brought to light by war. If we think that war is a bad thing, but courageous adventure a good thing, then we should be ever eager to promote those enterprises that provide it without killing. Training schools for youth have begun to provide the more desirable attributes of army training (and more) without the final design to kill. If these schools provide the training then modern expeditions provide the squadrons going to battle without the desire to conquer or slaughter. We hope that war will go but not the finer qualities it inspires.

The underlying aim of the South Indian Ocean Expedition to Heard Island was to demonstrate that a major private expedition was possible from Australia and that such an enterprise was worthwhile in the context of what I have written above. But the full nature of the expedition, its aim and even its name were not all derived from one sudden, succinct idea.

Major Warwick Deacock found, after fighting with the British Army in Malaya, that 'one might be more constructively employed than in destroying other people'. He left the Army in 1959 and moved to youth work which eventually led to his position as first Warden of the Australian Outward Bound School. His own adventurous background of mountain expeditions to Alaska, Lapland and the Himalayas, and his dedication to Outward Bound objects were ample qualification for administering an institution whose declared object for youth was 'Character Training Through Adventure'. After three years at the school, he determined to spread the philosophy further afield and in 1963 he undertook a round-Australia tour with his wife and two small children. Lecturing to clubs and associations, he paid his way by labouring, and even grave digging.

Before he went, he was invited by Dr Grahame Budd to be a member of an Australian National Antarctic Research Expedition to Heard Island. The Antarctic Division's base on the island was closed by Grahame's party eight years before and there was a need to secure current scientific information to supplement the older records. Grahame was leader of the new expedition of six men who intended to spend six weeks on the island. Three men would undertake scientific research from the old base huts on the northern end of the island, while Grahame, Warwick and Jon Stephenson were to make the first climb to the summit of Big Ben, 9005 feet. Although there was considerable enthusiasm in all three to reach the top, the small team laboured under the obligations of scientific research which, as they were public servants, was the only real justification for climbing a mountain. Warwick relates he was 'a sort of climbing public servant and nearly got my wife a widow's pension'.

The attempt was foiled by Heard Island weather. Precipitous retreat from a buried tent and a hastily dug, self-sealing snow cave resulted in the total loss of equipment and records while the trio were fortunate to reach sea level alive. There followed an arduous journey round the coast, without proper equipment, to rejoin the rest of the expedition. Grahame suffered frostbite of the fingertips and Warwick went down with appendicitis on arrival at the old base.

The ANARE expedition departed Heard Island in March 1963 with valuable scientific results—but the mountain was unclimbed. Stephenson expressed no desire to return for another attempt, but there were two scarred public servants who muttered different thoughts in their beards.

Warwick wrote the first letters about a new expedition as the

ANARE ice-breaker *Nella Dan* steamed back to Melbourne that March. He wrote to Himalayan and polar explorers Eric Shipton and H. W. Tilman. He later wrote to the director of the Antarctic Division about the idea of a private expedition, and Dr Philip Law told him that there was a small ship in Tasmania that had been to Macquarie Island (54°S) and might do the job for Heard. Her name was *Patanela*. The new expedition was barely stirring into life as the Deacock family set off around Australia.

When Warwick wrote to me first in June 1963 I was losing pints of sweat on the Sepik River and the idea of ice-cold mountains appealed to me immediately. Colin Putt was an early, enthusiastic starter and other people showed interest but nothing clearcut was undertaken until September when Warwick 'appreciated that if anything were to be done in the coming 64/5 season, planning must be got underway forthwith'. In Darwin he had printed 125 sheets of paper headed *The Australian-New Zealand Antarctic Expedition*. The enterprise was launched.

Not being a sailor, I was rather apprehensive of the whole project when it became clear that there would be no chance of reaching Heard Island in a large, modern ship fitted for Antarctic waters. The problems of making the first ascent of Mawson Peak on the island's Big Ben volcano became minor compared to Warwick's proposition of sailing to the place—a dot at 53°S and in the middle of the world's stormiest ocean. I found that it was more than 2200 nautical miles in a straight line to the nearest point of Australia, and just as far from South Africa.

The need to sail down in a small ship was dictated by the limitations of our budget and, although at first it may have seemed just a necessary evil, the prospect lent the expedition a much greater sense of enterprise and challenge. Free of governments and large companies we would show that the Antarctic could be reached in a small ship crewed largely by inexperienced, if willing, Australians (and others); that this could be done safely, chiefly under sail, in a summer season. We would also show that a party could be landed on an uninhabited, inhospitable island, climb a virgin mountain and carry out valuable scientific work—all as capably as within the framework of a large government-backed enterprise.

Bold objects indeed and at times only Warwick's unblemished confidence and sweeping enthusiasm saved us from wilting under their obligation. There were precedents to inspire us and we reflected that the early navigators had done even more, in ships no bigger than modern yachts, and with fewer technical advantages than we could call on. But it was not necessary to look to the sixteenth century for inspiration—only a few years before, a modern exploring navigator had sailed from England to Îles Kerguelen (300 miles from Heard) in a forty-five-foot cutter.

This was Major H. W. Tilman whose successful, long ocean voyages with mountain exploration at the end showed conclusively that our ambitions were well within the realms of possibility. An early suggestion was that Tilman (the Skipper as he became known to us all) could use his own *Mischief* to take us to Heard. But there were the problems of sailing her out from England and then beating into the westerlies from Australia. In the end, Tilman agreed to be skipper to our expedition if Warwick found the right ship in Australia.

Investigations and enquiries round Australia and further afield revealed that the earlier-suggested *Patanela* was the only ship that was offered or even worth considering. She was owned by the Hunt brothers who crayfished out of Strahan, Tasmania and, since she had made a trip to Macquarie Island, seemed capable of coping with the big seas of the Roaring Forties. She was sixty-three feet overall with a sixteen-foot beam and draught of eight feet six inches. She displaced forty-five tons, had an all-welded steel hull, and was theoretically a gaff-rigged schooner. But she had never been fully rigged and her owners relied chiefly on a powerful 165hp Rolls-Royce diesel engine. When Warwick inspected her at Point Lonsdale in December 1963 he said he 'looked over rusty "Pat" with an eye of faith and hopes that Colin could fill the part of a sort of engineering god'. The makings were there, the fine hull revealed her a thoroughbred, and with engineer Colin Putt to supervise, invent and improvise there was little doubt that *Patanela* was the ship we had been looking for.

The ship was there and the object clear: to climb Big Ben via *Patanela* and accomplish scientific research that increased in scope

Grahame Budd and Russ Pardoe join Patanela in Sydney

over the months to include marine biology, entomology, survey, zo-
ology, meteorology, geology and botany. Members began to sign on
and apart from Warwick and Colin, the provisional party included
Ed Reid, Malcolm Hay, John Crick, the Skipper, me and Grahame
Budd, if he could arrange leave. The Hunt brothers themselves were
to come as professional crew but they declined the pleasure at a later
date and the number of members was finally fixed at ten. Russ Pardoe returned from Russia and England to take on the job of medical
officer and Antony Hill, after months of hoping, jumped from reserve to full member when Chris Thomas, a marine biologist, could
not accompany us. The name of the expedition was changed to indicate the wide scope of our project and Sir Edmund Hillary kindly
agreed to become our patron.

It might appear that things went swimmingly, but there was always the problem of raising nearly £A20,000 which was enough to
keep anyone awake at night. A programme of sales promotion was
instituted, spurred by Warwick's almost full-time attention, and the
plans were turned into action. At an early stage each member agreed
to pay £300 and Rupert Murdoch's recently launched *The Australian*
newspaper generously gave £3000 for news rights. That took us a
third of our way to meeting the budget but was equivalent to only
two thirds of *Patanela*'s charter cost. The ship had to be fitted out,
fuel obtained, climbing equipment, clothing, food and innumerable
extras. A series of functions was arranged for fund raising, circulars
were sent out and dozens of businesses approached for loan or donation of equipment and goods. The Trans-Antarctic Fund, Mount
Everest Foundation, BP Bishop Museum, and NZ Alpine Club gave
money and equipment and, with the unstinting support of the Australian business community, the expedition slowly came to fruition.
Finally, in April 1964, our major sponsor George Sample gave us
£4000 in exchange for film rights and we could confidently say that
the trip was 'on'.

The mountains of paperwork and frustrating late nights of plan-
ning and labour can well be imagined. It must be said that under
Warwick's relentless leadership, the expedition members resident in
Sydney, with their innumerable friends and helpers, were the ones

who pulled the expedition to its feet. Planning an expedition can be exciting in itself but there is a tiring, worrying time with many set-backs and much unrewarded labour. Early in the year there was a scare when *Patanela* broke down in heavy seas off western Tasmania and the engine seemed badly damaged. But the ship came to no harm and later Rolls-Royce made a thorough overhaul free of charge.

Members of the public sent cheques, free food supplies mounted, equipment came together, begged, borrowed or bought at a discount. The Lord Mayor of Sydney sent £5 and a letter wishing us good luck, 500 'Big Ben' meat pies were donated, we received a message of faith from Cardinal Gilroy, and Mobil gave free fuel and oil supplies. Gifts and help were innumerable and a full list of those who made our expedition possible is printed at the end of this book.

We did not always receive messages of faith, and a distressing lack of faith in our abilities and motives was shown by the Department of External Affairs, which initially said we could not go to Heard Island. Under charter to the expedition, *Patanela* had been registered as a private yacht and fortunately there was no law which forbade yachts sailing from Sydney or ocean-going ships from calling at a glaciated island in the middle of the Southern Ocean. From higher quarters it was intoned that representatives of government 'could not be associated with anything that was not National'.

Opposition later moved to another department, which tried to put our noses out of joint with technical shipping regulations. Active opposition went no further although there were many pundits who averred we would never get off the wharf or that we would blow our sails out in the first decent gale. Such comments merely acted as a spur to our ambitions and fostered a useful determination.

With memories of his illness on Heard Island in 1963, Warwick had his appendix removed in March. Colin and Antony followed suit, no doubt appalled by stories of deep-sea operations on buck-ing ships. Russ, Grahame and Mal were appendix-less, too, because theirs had been removed before service as medical officers in the Antarctic. Ed, John and I may have had some anxieties in this re-spect but the figure of the Skipper with an appendix at sixty-six, having undertaken more outlandish journeys and exploration than the rest of us put together, bolstered some confidence in our guts.

A period of regular training began in June. There was no opportunity for raw members to learn how to sail and it was thought there was a sufficient nucleus of experience to see us through until we all shook down. It was essential, however, that as many members as possible learn the techniques of surf landing with the rubber boats and outboard motors we had assembled for landing on the harbour-less island. Its ring of freezing, hostile breakers could well prove our most serious obstacle. A letter from Colin to me in the Solomon Islands gave a brief glimpse of the fun they had during the weekend training at Manly. 'We have taken delivery of one US Rubber Co. inflatable 18 foot assault craft and have had good practice in medium to heavy surf. It is quite easy, even with paddles instead of motor, to get through the "smooths" between waves—and it is remarkably stable even when hit by a big breaker. We put her into one or two of these and the first time we did not realise the importance of holding tight. The boat stood up on her tail and the six others all fell on me as I was at the steering oar. I fell out over the stern, except for one leg which they were all sitting on and this got slightly damaged. The two doctors grabbed me and (take due warning) their conversation went like this: Russ—"I think his fibula is fractured don't you Grahame?" Grahame—"Yes, see how he jumps when I kick it."'

In September *Patanela* was brought from Victoria to Sydney for the final fitting out. D-Day was 1 November and preparations reached a feverish pitch as the deadline approached. Colin bore an enormous burden, being in charge of engineering and mechanical problems that seemed endless and time consuming. Scores of willing workers swarmed to the ship at weekends to lend a helping hand, and an itinerant Kiwi artist painted two anatomically impossible penguins on our stern.

By the end of October, all the expedition members but Malcolm Hay were in Sydney. He was finishing surgeons' examinations in London and would fly out to meet us in Western Australia. We were variously appalled, reassured or dismayed at the sight of the small, tubby ship, painted a nauseating yellow (the paint was free and the colour aided identification). It was an effort to move along the decks through piles of debris, while the tangle of ropes, wires, spanners, winches, hammers, bolts and pipes provided a mystery that took some time to unravel. But if not accomplished, we tried to help towards the end of setting sail, though on 1 November it seemed as though another two weeks would pass before we left Rushcutters Bay.

The Skipper arrived on 19 October and worked inconspicuously at the rigging and sails, refusing to be rushed into a sailing time until he had the measure of a strange ship and its state of readiness. The food came in truck-loads and amazingly it all fitted 'tween decks. Reluctantly we turned away three-quarters of a consignment of meat pies when 2000 were delivered instead of 500! On the morning of 5 November the Skipper said quietly he thought we were about ready to go. There was hurried last minute shopping, unwanted gear was piled on the jetty, and we cast off from a crowd of well-wishers at three o'clock in the afternoon. Colin and Grahame had work to conclude and were to join us with Mal in Albany. But we had three able substitutes for the first part of the voyage in Albert Rogers, Jim McCormack and Alex Theakston. We motored away but soon hoisted sail, despite exhortations from the press launch to go faster. A yacht with friends came out to see us off, scraping our side, but soon we were alone, dipping in the swell of the Tasman Sea. Grahame stood above us on the Heads to take photographs as the tiny yellow schooner with new, white sails set out across the untrammelled ocean.

Part One:

PATANELA

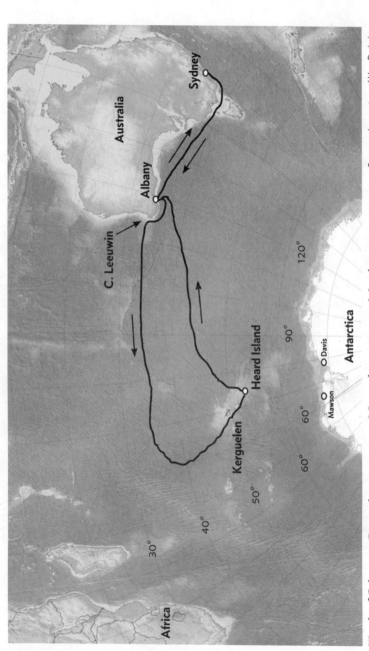

Track of Schooner Patanela   5 November 1964 – 14 March 1965

Base map by courtesy of Uwe Dedering

I

BASS STRAIT AND BEYOND

THE SKIPPER NEVER SPOKE TO EXCESS, and when we were on the early watch that morning his opening gambit was very English: 'Not very good weather is it?' A 'moderately rough sea' as he told me to write in the log book. We had a fresh southerly dead ahead so we could not hoist the sails and we pitched and bucked in the short seas with the engine at low revs. At times *Patanela* was awkward to steer at south or south by west as the stern lifted and the wheel spun freely. John and I were with the Skipper on the morning watch and we looked into a white, leery dawn with dirty brown muttonbirds circling and disappearing among the waves. But it was dry to start and only at six did the rain beat down and make life cold and miserable.

There were a few haggard and grey crew members at breakfast. We had not yet been at sea for a day, and frequently above the rumble of the diesel I heard the horrid sound of retching over the rail. Warwick was cook and his rushes to the side while doling out food were not conducive to good digestion. Russ looked ghastly. Gaunt, white, eyes staring glassily at the sea, he sat hunched by the rail in his foul weather suit as Jim twirled the wheel with professional ease and lit a cigarette: 'This is the best cure for seasickness!' Jim had come for the trip round to Albany, our only port of call before the sub-Antarctic. He proved invaluable in those early days when half of us could not tell a peak halyard from a bobstay. He was tall, redheaded, freckled and weatherbeaten from eleven years at sea in fishing boats off his native Tasmania. And he had served with the Beast of Bass Strait: a legendary skipper who preferred a rope's end to a reprimand. Jim's tales of him were hilarious and frequently, if one were steering a few degrees off course, his throaty voice would growl in imitation: 'Don't bother to call the next watch.' Though several would have welcomed missing a watch at that stage, we were all glad to be under way, that the expedition had become a fact and not a project. The apprehensions and worries were still there but now we could come to grips with them. Heard Island seemed lost in time and distance and for those of us who had not sailed before, the biggest challenge was the long voyage in our small ship. All our eggs were in its one basket and there could be no miscalculation that would jeopardise its safety.

At Rushcutters Bay she had seemed massive alongside the sleek and fragile yachts but on the open sea *Patanela* shrank to a toy, if a sturdy one. Only sixty-three feet long—it hardly seemed possible that ten men and all their accumulation of gear and food for five months had been jammed and hidden beneath the small decks. But she was beamy with spoon bows and we suspected her draught was more than eight feet six inches when she left in her overloaded state. The main engine tanks were full, the cray tank was chock-a-block with forty-four-gallon drums of diesel, the water tanks were full and every nook and cranny was overflowing with tins and bags of food.

Sleeping room for ten men seemed to have been allowed as an afterthought. The Skipper said that it did not matter where anyone slept since all the bunks were 'equally bad'. Allocation of berths was easy. Logically, Warwick slept in the galley next to the stove with the Skipper on the port side, handy to the charthouse and sextant. Both the lockers at their heads and the space beneath their bunks were full of food and Warwick adopted strange bedmates in the form of a mountain pack, kitbag and box full of papers which he insisted would stop him falling out when the ship rolled. There was nowhere else to put them anyway. The smokers were in the fo'c'sle, away from the fuel. That meant John and Ed in the lower bunks, port and starboard respectively, me and Jim, later Grahame, in the top bunks. The bottom bunks had lee boards to prevent us from rolling out but, curiously, not the upper ones. Jim and I did not have far to fall, however, since the deck was buried to a depth of three feet in cartons of bottled beer and cigarettes—a glorious cushion. It was appropriate that the fo'c'sle hatch was permanently labelled in blue paint: *Saloon and Bar*.

Amidships was a wide hold that was normally filled with sea-water for keeping freshly caught crayfish. We had cleaned it out, knocked away most of the rust and fitted in bunks made of rough timber above the lower layer of diesel drums. There were two long bunks, about ten and a half feet, so Russ, Antony, Albert and Alex (later Col and Mal) had to suffer an uncomfortable overlap and play midnight footsie until improvements could be made later in the voyage. But here was felt the least motion of any part of the ship, and the cray tank always seemed to remain snug and warm.

Colin wrote and told me in New Zealand that *Patanela* had 'flush decks'. This undoubtedly must be some technical term for, rather than presenting the streamlined aspect of a submarine that I expected, she was as cluttered on deck as she was below. The basic super-structure (see plan) consisted of a welded deckhouse in keeping with the rest of the ship, an engine-room hatch, a large cowling like a gun turret to cover the cray tank, a deep-freeze hatch and a small cowling to cover the fo'c'sle entrance. But apart from these there were a dozen large cylinders of propane gas for the stove, oxy-acetylene cylinders, a cluster of pipes to be used for a radio aerial, a drum of benzine, three eighty-gallon drums for water, a Beaufort life raft for ten men, two store lockers, two pumps, three winches, three air vents, engine exhaust, two escape hatches, anchor winches, anchors, a davit, two barrels of rum and a large tin of biscuits. Add to this the compass binnacle and main steering wheel for'ard of the deckhouse, the full heavy gear of a gaff-rigged schooner, and some other bits of para-phernalia which took several days to identify, and 'flush decks' became something of a joke.

Despite all our efforts we could not cram in enough fuel to feed the 165hp diesel for the round trip. Although we would refuel at Albany there were at least 4500 miles to cover before we returned there. The engine would have to serve as auxiliary, except when rounding Australia, and our main motive power lay in the seventeen-ounce terylene sails. Though she was eleven years old *Patanela* had never been seriously sailed and had spent most of her life pounding away

Schooner Patanela

Western Tasmania aboriginal word meaning 'Spirit of the Storm'

Built in Hobart, registered in Strahan as a crayfishing boat.

Patanela was re-registered for the expedition as a private yacht with the Cruising Club of Australia, Sydney. LOA 63ft, beam 16ft, draft 8ft 6in, sail area 2,000 sq ft, engine 165hp Rolls-Royce diesel.

1	Aerials	13	Fo'c'sle hatch	
2	Gaffs	14	Vegetable crates	
3	Jib	15	Cray tank hatch	
4	Staysail	16	Water kegs	
5	Foresail	17	Binnacle	
6	Mainsail	18	Wheel	
7	Reef points	19	Gas bottles	
8	Booms	20	RFD liferaft	
9	Ratlines	21	Wheelhouse	
10	Insect nets	22	Mainsheet	
11	Bowsprit	23	Log	
12	Anchor winch	24	Food stored in bilges	

25	Galley, and bunks of Skipper and Leader
26	Fuel drums, engine room
27	Radio in engine room
28	Fuel in cray tank
29	Bunks on fuel drums
30	Deep freeze
31	Fo'c'sle
32	Forepeak

under engine at high speed in competitive crayfishing. So even her owners could not tell us how she would handle under sail. With his raw crew, and no opportunity for working up, the Skipper was in for an interesting time. Not that this situation was new to him.

Although sixty-six years of age, the Skipper had not begun ocean cruising until 1954. Until then he had made a series of mountain expeditions that will live for ever in alpine history: Mount Kenya in 1931, Nanda Devi in 1934/5, Mount Everest in 1938. In 1950 he was the first to approach Everest from the Nepalese aspect and thus paved the way for the successful ascent in 1953. Added to this was service in both World Wars, the DSO, Military Cross and Bar, and fighting with Albanian partisans in 1944. Later he looked to a fresh challenge and chose to sail to his mountains. Since 1954 he had covered some 100,000 miles in his forty-five-foot cutter *Mischief*; circumnavigated South America and Africa; made four trips to Greenland and the Arctic; and sailed from England to Kerguelen, 300 miles north-west of Heard Island, in 1960. On all his trips he had trouble finding an experienced crew with the time and energy for a long, hard voyage. Raw hands were nothing new.

This time he had the added responsibility of a strange ship, and a steel ship at that, with 'iron things all over the place'. She was stiff and unbending compared to *Mischief* and, for him, there were too many mechanical contrivances on board. Before long the automatic pilot was banished, the echo sounder looked at askance and a suggestion that we motor and sail at the same time treated as sheer sacrilege. Clean, pure sailing was the object and there is no doubt that for unadulterated enjoyment and a comfortable ride the sails had it over the Rolls-Royce every time. Then the jerky unnatural motion and the noise would be gone as the ship, clouded in white terylene, dipped and slipped through the swell to the soft rustle of the sea, with the occasional flap, thump or creak of blocks.

We had little opportunity to sail on our way round Australia although the Skipper would make use of any favourable shift in the headwinds. On the second day out, as we neared Green Cape close to Bass Strait, a sou'wester freshened. The Skipper turned to Albert and said 'Can't we switch the engine off? Don't you want to look at it or something?' There was a twinkle in his eye at the prospect of a brisk sail. Soon we hoisted all plain sail—mainsail, foresail, staysail and jib. But our seamanship was poor and, as we held her bows into the wind while Albert braked the propeller, we swung on to the wrong tack and set off at a fast lick back towards Sydney. The wind was increasing and only by manhandling the staysail and jib were we able to bring her back to a southerly course. Absorbed in these manouevres, we had neglected the log line and our circling had wrapped it firmly around the rudder. To further complicate matters, the peak halyard became detached from the jib and ran to the masthead. While Russ hung over the stern and spent an hour disentangling the log, first Jim and then Antony went aloft until the halyard was retrieved and the jib hoisted.

All this time the wind strengthened, the swell increased and the crests were being whipped from the waves. It was exhilarating, forgeing ahead. 'B— the exhilaration,' said Antony. 'I'd like to lay back and sunbathe.' Even so he enjoyed his trick at the wheel and it was after noon before he let me take over on the new watch. Taking the wheel for the first time in a strong blow, I felt suddenly alarmed at the feel of a heavy, powerful ship fighting to pursue her own course. Feeling very small and inexperienced, I stood with my back to the midships wheel, eyes moving regularly from compass to the stiff sails and then to the lee scuppers, more and more awash as the sea and wind increased and an overloaded hull rose sluggishly to meet each swell. Spray began to fly, so that we blessed our rubberised suits, and metal became gritty to the touch from a growing layer of salt.

There was no warning. I looked to port and next, out of the corner of my eye, I saw to starboard a huge wave leaping over the rail. Instinctively I ducked and hugged the binnacle stand as it hit.

There was thick, green water, the sudden silence of immersion, and dimly I saw John dashed to the deck. Behind me the Skipper was thrown so violently against the deckhouse that he broke the wooden cleat for a lifebelt and damaged his ribs. Staggering up with a mouthful of water I was amazed to find we were still on course and that nothing of importance had been washed away.

The danger was increasing every moment and the sails had to be

A balmy day in the Bight: the Skipper splicing a rope

lowered. The minutes seemed to drag until everyone was on deck, and then began the excruciating labour of hauling in against a powerful wind. All our rigging was heavy duty: bulky terylene sails, full weight terylene halyards, heavy sheets and massive stays, designed to cope with the rigours of the Roaring Forties. But there were no mechanical aids for raising or lowering sail and all depended on manpower. Pulling in the main boom was the hardest task of all and three men were needed to haul on the mainsheet. The Skipper brought the ship into the wind to ease the pressure on the mainsail. But this would fluctuate and sometimes the boom swung back violently as we took in slack, once almost pulling John overboard. Finally we had it in, muscles and wrists straining and we lowered and lashed the sail. Russ knelt on the deckhouse and clung to the boom as he worked with the ship's violent rolls and I looked up to see a red stain on the white sail from a badly lacerated hand.

Then we were hove to in a buster and we drifted out into the Tasman Sea waiting for the gale to abate. It was a sharp lesson at an early stage that did us all good. It seemed hard at the time, fresh from the fleshpots and pubs, but we learned about the ship and sailing by having our noses rubbed into it. There was a distinct strain on everyone from the seasickness, the gale and an irregular timetable that demanded one be dragged out of bed at midnight or 4am to stand a four-hour watch, whatever the state of the weather, one's mind or stomach. Hands became blistered from the unaccustomed rub of rough ropes. It took time to become used to the coating of salt on one's face and clothes; the blankets sticky as one tried to sleep for an hour in the exasperating pitch and roll before the next call.

There was little conversation in the galley and Warwick snarled as he fought to produce meals on time, which he did without fail. But a tuna we had caught a day before hung untouched from the rail and the roll call for meals grew smaller and smaller.

The worst time of all was the middle watch, or the 'bastard watch' as it came to be known. This was from midnight to four in the morning, the only watch when we could be assured of no light, no dawn or sunset to alleviate the cold, grim hours of black night at sea:

Dressing for bad weather is quite a job and I'm not looking forward to it again. Especially on a night watch. I may have grabbed an iota of sleep, jerking and tossing in the bunk but wake easily at the watch's call—generally Russ. The light flicks on in the darkness, a friendly, dim glow and the whirring fan becomes more evident again among the swaying clothes and kit-bags. Below, it's dry and warm and quiet save for the engine and the only sign that the weather might be bad is from the movement.

Rolling out of the bunk like a circus tumbler, I take a firm grasp of something and try to keep steady on top of the beer cartons while I pull my trousers on. This is time-consuming with all the rolling and pitching and by the time I stagger into the forepeak, clipping my head on the iron, muscles are starting to ache again from the unaccustomed effort of trying to maintain balance. Then come the seaboots, easy over woollen socks, and the foul-weather suit, wet and sticky from the previous watch. For the trousers I lean back on the warps and yank them over the boots, then stand with head and shoulders into the cowling to pull on the parka. Now almost ready.

But make sure that all the lacings are done up well and, if there's any doubt, clip on the safety belt with its rope and karabiner though the latter is hardly big enough to clip on anything larger than a thin line. Cigarettes, lighter, knife, handkerchief and we're right.

Climbing up the ladder is easy enough but then one must firmly unlatch and swing open the hatch. Then the night is apparent. The spray and seas dash across the deck, the wind tugs at the foresail and all that one can see is the white of breaking waves, a dim rigmarole of rigging and the grotto-like red and green of navigation lights. Hauling oneself into the opening, an arm should be snaked out to find a grip, then a knee brought up to the step. When the roll is right the other leg can be swung cleanly through and a foot placed on the deck. A lift, a twist and one is standing upright, knees bent, hanging on to the hatch as the weather beats into one's face. Close the hatch, turn and stagger down towards the wheel, moving carefully from stay to halyard to rope to winch to drum, singeing one's fingers on the engine exhaust or rubbing grease from the wires.— *From my diary.*

By the afternoon of 10 November we had covered 460 miles, negotiated the bad corner of Australia at Gabo Island and reached the narrows of Bass Strait at Wilson Promontory. We pulled into Sealer's Cove on its eastern shore and spent our only night at anchor before Kerguelen, seven weeks later. There were spare drums of diesel on deck. Albert pumped this into the tanks and we could motor through to Albany without any more refuelling. A few repairs were made in the rigging and we had a welcome night's rest after the first tiring days of a strange voyage. The waters of the cove were calm and the shores rocky; worn slabs and huge boulders of granite with the inevitable gum trees, dead stumps sticking out like white telegraph poles from the dark bush. The beach at the base of the cove was a lovely sweep of deserted sand but we had neither the time nor the energy to go ashore.

We left early the next morning and two days later were well off the South Australian coast at the beginning of the long stretch across the Great Australian Bight. The weather became settled and warm and we shifted into a regular routine. People began to wash, beginning with Warwick and he had his bath in style. Jamming his tall, 14-stone bulk into a plastic baby's bath, he suspended a canvas shower bucket from a stay. But most of us made do with a rough wash and a final dowsing from a galvanised bucket which served the all-purpose job of washing us, clothes, dishes, vegetables (when we had them) and defrosting bloody bags of meat from the freezer. There were no toilet facilities of any kind on board so that we soon learned to brace ourselves securely against the stout iron rail that ran round the bulwarks.

From Sydney to Albany we had three watches made up of Antony and Russ, Jim and Alex, while the Skipper stood with the two most inexperienced sailors, John and me. We stood the regular watch times: first watch from 2000–2400, middle from 0000–0400, morning watch until 0800, forenoon until 1200, afternoon watch until 1600 and then first and last dog watches from 1600–1800 and until 2000.

Thus we usually had four hours on and eight off but every third 'bad' day we had to stand twelve out of twenty-four hours: the middle, afternoon and first watches. Warwick had his time fully occupied as cook and served up meals dead on time: breakfast at 0730, lunch at 1230 and dinner at 1930. We also had morning and afternoon tea and one of the Skipper's chief impressions of the expedition was that he had never been on any small ship with such an inordinate amount of food. In the freezer we had a whole Aberdeen Angus which was donated to us after we had already bought a huge packet of meat nicknamed Granny. Most of the contents of one rum barrel spilled throughout the freezer. It did not destroy the flavour of our meals but we wondered if we would eventually tire of rum(p) steak.

Albert did not stand watch because of his responsibilities with the engine and neither did Ed as radio operator. The engine room door had *Sauna* written on it and this succinctly described its steam-heat qualities. No-one save Albert went anywhere near its cacophony of noise and 100-degree heat unless it was absolutely necessary. But Ed had his radio there and though he was not seasick at the start of the voyage, the engine room finally turned him up. This plus some indefinable virus complaint kept him out of sorts on and off throughout the whole voyage, and he won the booby prize for most time spent bashing the bunk.

But above all of us Ed took the prize for good humour, kept the party in stitches and was a sure cure for bad temper. His experience in the Royal Australian Navy clung to him with outrageous nautical tales, bell-bottomed overalls and a magnificent beard which unkinder members said was grown in an effort to make up for his receding hairline. We all learned to take leg pulls and derision but none better than Ed. When Antony lambasted him with: 'Go on Reid. Admit it. You're just a b— hypochondriac. What's wrong with you today?' Ed with deadpan heroics replied: 'Nothing really. My leg's broken but it only hurts when I laugh.'

The engine pounded away, the sails remained furled for almost the remainder of the trip to Albany and we endured 'halcyon days' as Warwick described them. Lunch on deck became an established practice, under a fierce sun that melted the tarry compound and burnt our feet. On the engine room hatch Warwick laid out bowls of cold baked beans, potato salad, ham, paté de fois gras, Gentleman's Relish, biscuits, butter and cheese, marmite, jam, bread and cake, so that it began to look like a pleasure cruise and we could afford to be fastidious in our tastes and appetites. Warwick was always careful, however, that no food was wasted and rations were conserved against the rainy day we might encounter 'down south'. This led to increasingly thick soup. Any leftovers, whether porridge, unchewed bones or curry, were tossed in the soup pot as stock. The Skipper's favourite dish was curry and he must have been pleased with the hot, turgid mixture which the soup finally became. Ed capitalised on this when it was his turn to cook on Warwick's regular Sunday off. He served us soup, entrée and main course but we did not realise it was all the same stew until we asked for pudding.

How well off we were for food and equipment! I took a book with me by a Spaniard who had been with Cortés called *The Conquest of New Spain*. It told graphically of the first discovery of Mexico in the early 16th century, how they made their way in leaking barks, sometimes smaller than *Patanela*, and subsisted on an unappetising diet of salt pork and cassava bread. When their ships were wrecked they built new ones and a small band went into savage, unknown country with muskets and horses as their only source of strength when fighting the Aztecs. When I thought of our fancy canned food, engine and radio we seemed to have descended a long way in self-sufficiency.

On 14 November we ran a sweepstake, with Albany beer money as the prize, to see who could make the closest guess of the time we would pass the first 1000-mile mark. As 'entertainments officer' I ran this with great gusto and had to bear the brunt of acrimonious remarks for weeks afterward when I won it myself. At that stage we were about 130 miles south of Investigator Strait and the approaches to Adelaide. On that day, and the days either side, we covered 175 miles and with such good going we expected to reach Albany within a week. The Skipper took the smallest opportunity to raise sail. The slightest favourable wind change and he would have us up on deck, even if it meant that the sails would be up only for an hour or two.

Although some of us felt that this was unreasonable perversity, and a nuisance to be dragged away from a book or pulled from one's bunk, it had the effect of making us work together and gave us practice in time for the rougher days ahead. Though ten of us lived on a small schooner it was not often that we were all together. I wrote in my diary after ten days that we had not shaken down into a very convivial crew and that the discussions we expected to be such a feature of the trip had not materialised. But it had taken time to adjust to a new way of life and the steady strain of keeping watch and catching up on sleep did not contribute towards the formation of a club. 'In some ways this is good since it's going to be longer before we're all sick of each other.' Late one morning, Jim ran down the deck shouting 'All hands and the cook on deck!' as if the ship were on fire and within a couple of minutes there were a number of startled, bleary-eyed men with bare feet and flapping shirts fumbling at ropes as the Skipper gave the order to raise sail. With a mischievous glint in his eye and a slight smile he took the wheel and muttered inaudible imprecations as the main peak was hoisted too soon and a headsail sheet ran out with a rush. But eventually we had the sails up and set, the Skipper brought *Patanela* back on course, and we went back to our sleepy hollows all the better for the exercise and work as a team. An hour or so later the sails were furled again.

This jack-in-a-box technique of raising sail gave Warwick plenty of opportunity for filming. One of the main financial responsibilities of the expedition was to provide a colour movie and we had 10,000 feet of film to dispose of during four months. Since filming was largely restricted to our ship and a small, glaciated island it was necessary to film everything that happened, not only to make a complete story, but to use up all the film. So we could not eat, drink, sleep or even relieve ourselves without the danger of finding a whirring camera pointed at us. Since Warwick was a sun worshipper, the sit-

Malcolm (left) and Russ on bunks in the cray tank

uation was even more alarming. I wondered what people's reaction would be, when watching the finished product, if they could also see the stark-naked cameraman.

It could not be denied that the sturdy Rolls-Royce pushed us steadily and inexorably towards Albany whereas we would have been a month of Sundays if we had tried to sail against the prevailing westerlies. But it was an uncomfortable, noisy ride. Sailing on a fixed tack, one could anticipate accurately the movement of the ship and adjust one's sitting or standing position accordingly. The engine took us in a straight line, regardless of wind and waves, and the unpredictable roll, pitch or wallow was exasperating in the extreme. I almost screamed aloud in fury during my attempts to sleep and the Skipper slid off the bench in the galley so often that Albert placed a piece of sandpaper beneath him.

John took the ship's wild movements as a challenge and on night watches he disappeared towards the bows to keep his lookout. Vaguely in the darkness I saw him swaying backwards and forwards, from side to side, as he endeavoured to keep his balance without hanging on to supports. John was dark, thickset with heavy, sudden movements and 'quite a sight when he's all dressed up in a black shearer's singlet belted into his grey worsted climbing trousers and an Australian slouch hat turned down like a bell'. He seemed to come from a long way past the black stump. He heightened this impression with an astonishing repertoire of bush ballads sung in a mellifluous baritone, and later instituted a reading of the play *Ned Kelly* to resound in the leading role.

John was also the baby of the expedition at twenty-two and, much to his chagrin, had been labelled an 'apprentice expeditioner'. With Antony he enjoyed the vivid, once-in-a-lifetime experience of a first expedition. To the rest of us, reaching its ultimate pitch in the Skipper, the basic impressions and joys of embarking on an arduous, unusual enterprise had been dulled by familiarity. But John could indulge his senses to the full in a new, exciting situation apart from the round of codes and norms of everyday life. One of the cardinal points of an expedition is that sooner or later one is reduced to the position where only basic values remain. Under conditions of stress and difficulty a man's weaknesses are pitched against his resource-fulness and the interaction of the expedition members brings out and, if successful, strengthens in each one the fundamental tenets of a strong social group; among them tolerance, service to and sympa-thetic reliance on others. On a first expedition the experiences which show this are never more vivid, painful and memorable.

Though we had been at sea only a fortnight we were all looking forward to a break at Albany. So it was a happy moment at lunch-time on 19 November when Jim swarmed up the for'ard ratlines and shouted 'Land ho!'. For a while only he could see it but then we dimly made out a distant headland, sometimes lost to the eye in the hori-zon haze or when we dipped in the swell. This solidified into Mount Manypeaks, a few miles east of King George Sound, and slowly oth-er blobs rose out of the sea. Shipping increased and by late afternoon we had a view of uninterrupted coastline. Warwick had sent off a cable earlier informing Colin and Grahame in Sydney and Mal in Perth that our ETA was the 19th and they should come and join us. We were determined to meet our deadline but for a while it seemed doubtful that we would find our way into Albany by nightfall.

It was a confusing coastline with hills, bays, peaks and islands merging into one so that we could not define the entrance to King George Sound, which led down to Princess Royal Harbour. Every-one proffered advice to the Skipper as to where we were. But he stood patiently by the after wheel surveying the sea with sharp eyes beneath bushy, jutting brows, opening and stretching his mouth or forming a ring with his lips which was his habit when musing on a problem. Finally the entrance was positively identified and, as we motored in at a record nine knots, Albert and I leaned on the deck-house and joined each other in a couple of convivial beers. At the fifty-fathom mark off the coast we caught tuna from our trolling line and there was fresh fried fish for tea.

We came up to Breaksea Island where the lighthouse did not re-spond to our signals, and hauled in the logline which read 1835 nau-tical miles. So the first lap was over. In my mind I had divided the voyage into distinct sections: Sydney–Albany, Albany–Kerguelen, Kerguelen–Heard, Heard–Albany and then back to Sydney. Now the first was over and we had proved not only to ourselves, but to the many doubters back in Sydney, that we had a sound ship beneath us and, under the direction of our Skipper, could point it and take it in the right direction. Even so, the trip across the Bight was only a working-up and there were still a few kinks in the ship, and many more in the crew, to be ironed out before we could be entirely confident in ourselves. We had not been tested under hard sailing conditions or under difficulties in isolation. Until Albany we had been either within sight of land or near a regular shipping lane should anything go wrong. As Colin later remarked, it was only on the round Australia run that our Beaufort rubber life raft was of much use to us. The real test was to come when we ventured deep into the Indian Ocean, far from ships and land, when the success and safety of the expedition depended entirely on the performance and our handling of *Patanela*. Slowly it became clear how much we relied on and put our faith in the Skipper.

In the sound the ocean swell was left behind and we cruised effortlessly towards the town. At first we could see nothing, then a square-looking block resolved itself into a grain silo above the harbour. To port the whaling station belched smoke, while queer patches of limestone and white beach gashed the dowdy and dusty hills. The sound provided a glorious anchorage, with attractive islands and inlets, and one could well believe Captain Vancouver's statement when he said in 1791 that all the navies of the world could safely ride there at anchor. There were no other ships about, no cars on the distant road, but we had a fine escort in a school of porpoises cavorting round the hull. Blue-black above and pale green on the belly these graceful creatures always impressed us with their speed, grace and sheer enjoyment of swimming and jumping. They must have thought *Patanela* a jaundiced, unresponsive boor with her yellow hull and undeviating course. But they kept us company for a while and we leaned over the bowsprit to watch them. Until Warwick appeared with the movie camera, when they promptly disappeared.

We now had to make our first berthing. Princess Royal Harbour has an entrance channel dredged to thirty-three feet and we curved down this guided by buoys adorned with shags drying their wings.

There was no indication where we should berth so, for ease of manoeuvre, we chose the vast and empty overseas wharf. We swung round and tied up with little difficulty but felt lost with our masts topping the empty roadway by only ten feet or so. After we stretched our legs the harbourmaster arrived and told us we had a berth at the Town Wharf.

We cast off and moved across in a northerly wind that persistently pushed our bows away from the new berth. There was half an hour of jockeying, cursing and unhelpful suggestions from the crew and bystanders before the Skipper put her alongside. Colin stood on the wharf, incongruous in heavy mountain boots and shirt which he had worn to save excess baggage costs on the 'plane from Sydney; Grahame looked worried and Mal in a shiny grey suit greeted us exuberantly and finally jumped on board to vigorously shake the Skipper's hand.

The expedition complement was together at last. Alex was glad to leave the seasickness behind for his farm in New South Wales; Albert's annual holiday was at an end and Jim was already casting covetous eyes on the whale chasers moored at the end of the wharf.

Soon we would cast off for the wide blue yonder. In the meantime there was work to do.

2

ROUNDING THE LEEUWIN

ALBANY WAS A PORT OF TWELVE THOUSAND PEOPLE and 'a town with a past, a city with a future' as we were told by the tourist bureau. The main feature of its past was that it was the first settlement in Western Australia in 1827 when Major Edmund Lockyer took formal possession of the territory for Britain. Older than Melbourne or Perth, its slow growth was mainly due to its isolation at the southwest corner of the continent. But now there were visions of greatness and 'it is bound to grow into a city in the measurable future'.

Behind the waterfront is the railway terminus from which the Albany Progress will take you 250 miles to Perth. Behind that are the low hills of the main town with York Street leading through the shops to the residential area and the northern outlets. The main feature of this street is St John's Church, 117 years old and steeped in local history. It was also the site one morning for an alsatian to chase a kangaroo.

We encountered tremendous hospitality and a succession of late nights to the detriment of work on the ship. At a splendid reception by the Mayor at the town hall, a radio reporter taped the proceedings and during interviews found that one lady councillor thought us 'very noble' though another told him 'to go to b—'. He heard that we had 10,000 donated cigarettes on board with only four smokers and when asked what we thought of this, Warwick appropriately broke into a wheezing cough.

To cure Ed of his sickness, we went on a tour of the town's eight pubs and were pleased to report a complete cure. At lunchtimes we regularly gravitated to one immediately behind the town wharf, patronising the Taronga Park bar. The Skipper came up often, for a pie and a beer, his small figure unobtrusive in weathered jeans, grey moustache and hair tousled and smeared with paint. He had not visited Australia before and sat quietly at the end of the bar with his pipe, listening to the conversation round the dart board. One remark passed in the talk was: 'That must be the bo'sun' and another friendly seaman leaned over the bar as he passed him a free beer and said to us with a wink: 'This is the joker who shoul' look after the rum!' On the wall of the bar was a cartoon of two whale chasers hove to while their captains agreed it was time to return to the pub. The whaling station at Albany was the only one in operation in Australia and three chasers were kept occupied, hunting mainly for sperm whales. For filming, Mal and I rose at the crack of dawn one morning and went out to Cheynes Bay, a few miles south of the town, where the factory was sited. The previous evening seven whales had been brought in and were drawn up on the beach covered in voracious seagulls, the red rips from shark attacks scarring the carcases.

The equipment at the factory was still of the type that had been used for decades, and steam winches made for ease of handling. The flensers started early and in the harsh glare of floodlights we watched as a carcase was hauled up on a gently sloping deck for the first part of the operation. With sharp, curved blades the side blubber was sliced away as if it were butter. Strategic incisions were made and then a hole for a shackle tied to a wire rope which ran back to the main winch. At a given signal the winch clanked into life, the rope tightened and then ripped away great strips. When the blubber had been removed the main carcase was carved into two big chunks and winched slowly to the head of the deck. There the ropes were changed and what remained of a once sleek whale was winched up a steep ramp. At the top was a wide, slippery platform where the meat was cut, either by hand or with a violent, mechanical saw, until pieces were small enough to fit through manholes leading to the cookers. The oil extracted was stored in large tanks and we were told that it was used currently, not so much for soap, but mainly as a base for cosmetics and automatic gear box oil.

The most colourful character we met in Albany was a Yugoslav refugee who had established himself as a photographer. He was commissioned by the local press to take portraits of the crew and came along to the ship with great flourish and a broken accent, calling everyone 'junior', 'pal' or 'big boy' except the Skipper whom he called 'Old Man'. In town he stopped Antony and I as we passed his studio called *The Little Heart*, pulled us inside and showed us his pictures. We looked at shots of *Patanela* surrounded by wedding groups and twenty-first birthday parties. He had a sort of collie dog which barked enthusiastically whenever his master became excited, which was often. As we walked away, he erupted from the shop, chased us, dog barking furiously while he waved a print under our noses. 'Here is a photo I would like you to keep. It is a picture of me und mein father.' It was him alright—with his arms wrapped round a full-blood aborigine. It was pasted in a place of honour in the galley.

One morning he came down to the ship early and attracted the Skipper's attention as he worked quietly away at a fitting on the bulwarks. 'Hey old man! They tell me you go in Albynya in the war. Which way you come?' The Skipper removed his pipe and quietly replied: 'From Cairo.' 'Oh! You come with de British Army?' 'Yes.' 'I come from Montenegro—next door. You ever work with Yugoslavs?' 'No. Only Albanians.' 'Oh! What they like uh?' 'All communists.' With that, Little Heart walked off in disgust, fingering the scars on his face. The Skipper turned to me and said: 'Bloody good blokes too.'

There were a number of jobs to do on the ship before we finally left Australia and these, plus a strong westerly which blew unceasingly, kept us in the harbour for a week. We fuelled and watered, and loaded on some crates of fresh fruit and vegetables while Colin worked in the engine room, replacing injectors and engrossed in the interminable pottering which seems to occur with any complex of machinery. Before Jim joined the chasers I got him to erect a yardarm on the port side of the foremast. This was made from the straightest piece of gum we could find in the local bush and supported by a galvanised wire stay and some copper sheeting. From it were suspended two long wires tied to one horizontally on the deck and between

Repairs to *Patanela*'s rigging as she hangs off the wharf in Albany

them I could raise and lower four nylon nets in the hope of catching insects which had been blown out to sea. This was a small part of a programme aimed at finding out relationships between insect families on different continents, caused by wind distribution.

Grahame and Colin worked on a winch bolted to the cray tank cowling that was to be used for deep plankton hauling with a weighted net. A vital clutch piece was missing and Colin just finished making one when the legitimate part arrived from Sydney. It was also discovered, to the Skipper's dismay, that we had no chart for Kerguelen, our most important staging point on the way to Heard. Cables went back and forth to the Antarctic Division in Melbourne and after a new chart had been flown out we found another one under the Skipper's bunk.

The weather became worse and worse. The wind was so strong that when we moved *Patanela* to a new berth, where she lay north and south, the westerly buffeted her severely and banged the hull vigorously against the pilings. To save the paintwork we floated her off, bows into the wind, and were moored by a single bow line. This entailed some precarious tightrope walking to get on and off and was an effective discouragement to unwelcome visitors. Only Antony fell in.

On one of the best days we had surf landing practice. The biggest problem of the expedition was the landing plan for Heard Island. *Patanela* could not anchor indefinitely at Heard unless we were lucky enough to find unsounded Winston Lagoon a practical harbour on the south-east coast. There is not a single cove or bay on the island that will offer safe anchorage for any length of time. Right from the inception of the expedition it had been anticipated that beach landings, through the surf, would be necessary. This had been the case often with previous ANARE expeditions.

But ANARE expeditions went down in large ships with room for large pontoons, even DUKWs, with plenty of men to handle them. With only ten in a ship the size of *Patanela* we had to make do with equipment less pretentious but still effective—and safe. It was decided finally to take one eighteen-foot US Rubber assault craft as the main landing agent with an old ex-army Zodiac rubber boat as stand by.

Both would be powered by 18hp Johnson outboard motors. Our safety lay in the effectiveness of the Zodiac as a rescue craft if the USR upset—and in our clothing. The average sea temperature near Heard is never much above freezing and immersion without protection can lead to death within a matter of fifteen or twenty minutes. To combat this we had tailor-made wet suits: close-fitting rubber attire used by skin divers. Then we had an assortment of Mae Wests and US Navy lifejackets. There was also the danger of leopard seal attacks on any man in the water but we could not prepare anything to combat them.

Several practices were made in the Sydney surf, both with paddles and motor, but a number of us were not able to participate. Warwick decided that another practice was essential since Albany presented our last chance before Heard. There was a small surf at Middleton Beach at the head of King George Sound and we chose this as our venue. Warwick tried to keep a strict time schedule but this did not materialise. We found our inflating system slow and inefficient and fitting the motors from the ship's side was not as simple as we expected. Russ fell flat on his face in the water and Grahame jumped in to glory in the buoyancy of his suit while taking photographs with a watertight camera, and the impact spread green stains of shark repellent. When we eventually became operational, John and I as new chums were given the chance to practise driving the Zodiac and then we set off down the harbour with Mal following in a launch with his movie camera.

Russ drove the Zodiac with great gusto, drenching in spray a local pressman who had come along to scoop a story. In the USR Colin drove, John and I sat with him in the stern while Warwick and Grahame were in the bows. We motored down the channel, twisting and turning to test both boats' manoeuvrability and then swung in towards the beach. There we stood off while Warwick firmly laid out the landing plan and told each of us what to do. Since he had been a major in the Royal Marines, the situation was not new to him. Then, at a given signal, we went in to the beach as Russ circled round at a safe distance. The surf was slight and when we came into shallow water Col cut the engine and shouted an order and we hopped out, grabbed the boat handles and dragged it easily up the sand. Now for the take-off. This was the crucial part. Anyone left behind at Heard, as we went through the surf, would be washed back on to the beach and the craft would have to risk another landing to pick him up.

We waited in the shallows. When all was ready Warwick yelled 'Let's go!' and we ran in, waited with the motor running in neutral until Col was on, then jumped aboard, bowmen first. At the first practice our technique worked like a charm. But the second time Warwick drove and, without the feel for an engine that came naturally to Colin, he stalled it then drove off quickly with John and I still in the water. With lack of practice and an awkward life jacket I found it impossible to hoist myself into the boat while it moved at speed. A non-swimmer, I was eager to test the effectiveness of both jacket and wet suit so I let go, pushed myself off and bobbed around like the best of corks while the USR sped away. I was soon picked up, but this and the apparent slowness of our practice, put Warwick in a sour frame of mind. At a briefing afterwards he emphasised the importance of efficient handling and speed of movement when the landing day came. Apparently there were only two kinds of people on Heard Island—the quick and the dead.

We were guests at an Albany Rotary dinner. After an introductory speech Warwick asked each of us to stand and say our piece. Although the Skipper was generally shy and diffident about asserting his views he spoke quietly but with authority as he told the audience of his responsibilities on the ship. 'My job is to get the ship there and keep it afloat (which is important).' He warned that it could be difficult to find Heard Island, a speck in the Southern Ocean surrounded by foul weather, and there was a danger of being blown past it. Accurate navigation was all important. 'This reminds me of the directions given to a Newfoundland fisherman who wanted to go to Bermuda—go south until the butter melts and then turn to port!' Perhaps we should have to work in reverse.

The days dragged on and despite the hospitality and the good friends we made in Albany we were eager to get away. By November 25th our jobs were finished and the Skipper said that we would leave as soon as the westerly showed signs of relenting. Albert and Alex had gone back to Sydney and Jim was on the point of landing a job with the chasers. For the first time all the chosen expedition members were together and sleeping on *Patanela*. It was certainly a mixed crew.

In age we varied from John at 22 to Antony 24, me at 25, Ed 28, Mal 30, Russ 32, Grahame 34, through Warwick and Col at 37 and 38 to the Skipper at 66. Col, Warwick, Grahame, Mal and Ed were married, all save the last with children, while I was engaged. In professions we were equally varied. John was studying to be a teacher and during our Albany stay sat exams for the Wellington Teachers College.

Antony received news that he had passed some law exams and, just before we left, I had sent off the manuscript of a book on New Guinea in the hope of having it published. Mal, Russ and Grahame were all qualified doctors although Mal was half way through his studies to be a surgeon and Grahame specialised in physiological research at the School of Public Health and Tropical Medicine in Sydney. Col was works engineer for ICI at Botany, Sydney. Warwick had devoted a great deal of his time to youth work since leaving the army in 1959 and created the first Australian Outward Bound School; Ed had been his chief instructor. Finally the Skipper: one of the greatest living British explorers and author of many books on his many expeditions and voyages.

Even the chasers would not put out. After an attempt one morning that week they came back and said the sea was too rough for hunting.

This was disturbing but eventually valour got the better part of discretion and we started on the long haul to Kerguelen at 0900 on 27 November. We were anxious to make an impressive departure after the bumbling arrival. With the westerly still blowing we could sail off the wharf and present a graceful sight as we slid through the channel. A block came apart as we hoisted sail and the staysail fell in billows to the deck and we almost forgot to cast off the last stern warp. But, these minor mishaps apart, we were soon shipshape.

We leaned back to take our last look at civilization for over three months and were touched as cars jammed the road over the channel and the noise of horns and cheers drifted over the water. A dog barked noisily (Little Heart's?) and Col responded with a fanfare from his battered bugle.

Ever eager to take good movie film, Mal followed us in a launch. I raised the insect nets for his benefit and then he dived overboard in a frantic but unsuccessful effort to retrieve a camera part he dropped in the water. As we sailed deliciously down the sound he came on board. Then the launch left us and we looked up in surprise as the whalers' spotting 'plane zoomed over the masts and landed in front of us to take photographs. We passed the rocks of Bald Head within two cables and then tacked out to sea, our first problem before us: the rounding of Cape Leeuwin.

Our intention was to sail to Heard Island and this meant that we could not take a direct course to the south-west, against the strong westerlies of the Roaring Forties. The Skipper spread out the chart of the Indian Ocean and indicated that we would have to take advantage of the south-east trade winds. To do this meant sailing northwest to about latitude 33°S, slightly south of Perth, and then making a long westward leg towards Africa. At the Skipper's discretion we would turn south after passing the longitude of Heard and curve in towards it with the westerlies blowing on our quarter. We had over 4000 miles to go.

Continuing under sail, we went well out to sea on a southerly course, then came about on the port tack towards land. In the evening all sail was handed and we motored into a persistent headwind, following the routine of our trip from Sydney. The watch keepers were now changed and remained in the new order until the landing on Heard. The Skipper stood with John and Mal, Antony—now First Mate—with Grahame while Col stood engine watch, Ed radio and Warwick persevered as ship's cook. Russ and I had our 'bad day' on the 28th and on the middle watch we saw the Eclipse Island light dip behind us but nothing else until the clouds and showers moved away to reveal starlight and a waning moon.

Later that day we motored along parallel to the coast, past rocky Chatham Island rearing like a brown whale, and treacherous reefs which showed their presence by the pounding white of breaking waves.

The wind force increased, the seas became short and choppy and we lurched violently. Steering became abominably awkward as *Patanela* bucked like an unruly horse. After a trick at the wheel one's wrists ached from continual strain and movement and we began to develop sore patches at the small of our backs where we leaned hard against the spokes. There was the familiar line of sick men at the rail but the Skipper and I maintained our clean record.

When we rounded D'Entrecasteaux Point in the late afternoon the gale began in earnest. Dark grey clouds flooded the sky, we punched heavily into rising seas and the Skipper decided to heave to until the worst of the weather had passed. But we were only two miles off a coast bound with reefs and shoals and could ill afford to lose any sea room. In an attempt to keep the ship stationary under foresail he decided to try our parachute anchor. This was basically an ordinary parachute, in gaudy red and white, with a bronze shackle at the apex of the shrouds.

It was not until that moment, unfortunately, that anyone read the instruction leaflet so that our handling was less than expert. It was a slightly ludicrous situation as the Skipper, Antony and Russ—who was a trained parachutist—stood on the foredeck, backs to the beating rain and pored over the soggy piece of paper. While I kept away and photographed, the parachute was tossed into the water attached to a stout warp. It slowly filled and ballooned like some writhing sea monster but drifted aimlessly under the hull, obviously with little effect on the movement of the ship. After some discussion it was agreed that it needed weight to give it stability and the anchor chain would be more satisfactory than a warp.

But the trip rope had come adrift so that we could not spill water from the canopy. Pulling it in by brute force was an almost impossible task and the engine had to be started to manoeuvre the bows away. We tried to grab the billowing nylon as the parachute rose up with the heavy rolls of the ship and at one stage Russ was eager to dive over and attach a new tripline. But he was restrained as we finally pulled it over the rail and I sat on it with a thump to prevent it

Seasick blues: Colin, Grahame (centre) and John

blowing away.

By this time we had drifted closer to the coast. Behind the grey rain squalls and drifting cloud we could see the 400-foot perpendicular cliffs of D'Entrecasteaux Point and its complex of reefs and tiny islands. Between the point and Cape Naturaliste was one of the most inhospitable stretches of Australian coastline and the further away we stayed from it the better. We pounded ahead with the engine for a few miles until we had secured more sea room, hove to again until the wind dropped at nightfall, then laboured slowly on to our turning point at Cape Leeuwin. The visibility was so bad at night that I stood watch by the fo'c'sle hatch peering into the lowering clouds and heavy rain. The only light came from the eerie red and green of the navigation lamps. I could see only a few yards ahead and the waves suddenly loomed up, rushed at the ship and then, as the bows lifted at the crests, it seemed as if there was nothing beyond but an empty, black pit.

The Skipper's first log entry for 29 November read: 'Time–0400; Log–2010; Course–NW; Wind–WNW; Barometer–29.69; Several heavy rain squalls. Leeuwin light (loom) seen 0150. Two ships eastbound, one west. Altered course to NW 0400.' By breakfast time the Cape Leeuwin lighthouse was abeam. But with the heavy seas, head wind and opposing current it was hard to maintain movement away and break from the clutches of Australia's south-west cape. We must have looked a sorry sight for in the afternoon a big bulk carrier, the *Iron Yampi*, changed course on seeing us and passed within a cable's length. The anxious faces at the windows of the closed-in bridge were not rewarded by signals for help and the carrier provided a welcome diversion in the grim aspect of a stormy sea.

The deck was awash for most of the day and occasionally, as one stood at the wheel, a wave would jump over the port rail and give an icy clout on the back of the neck. The seas began to look mountainous and it was disconcerting, sitting in the galley, to see the scuttles regularly filled with windswept sea and a rush of flying cloud as *Patanela* rolled back and forth. Cooking was a gruelling task and as Warwick prepared the meals the pots slipped from side to side in the stove fiddles, slopping during a specially violent roll when the angle of the ship's tilt could be measured by the ladles and tin openers swinging from their hooks. He scalded himself, although it was asking too much of the ship's good nature when he expected to safely boil eggs in a round bottomed pan without a handle.

The galley was the only communal space on the ship. Twelve to fourteen feet wide and seven feet long it was reached by stepping down a short iron ladder from the charthouse. Opposite this on the for'ard bulkhead one passed through a watertight door into the engine-room. Headroom and light were provided by the vessel's main superstructure while the bunks were fitted against the hull and directly beneath the deck where it ran round the deckhouse. Between the engine room door and Warwick's bunk was a small bench and sink, cupboards beneath, the gas stove and a series of shelves above.

Jutting from the after bulkhead was a table supported by a stanchion, benches either side of this and another running alongside the Skipper's bunk. There was storage room underneath, and at the head and foot of each bunk, and access beneath the table to a small hold beneath the charthouse. But this was not enough. The space beneath the table was jammed with boxes, and a wooden crate was suspended with wire from the deckhead for storing utensils and current food—the 'Bred baskit' as it was called with Return to Albany painted clearly on it—apart from other, ruder suggestions.

The lockers were so jammed with food that at times the Skipper woke in the night with a sense of claustrophobia and found himself smothered in packets of gravy mix or instant pudding. He endured this stoically but was forced to keep most of his possessions in a brown suitcase. Shiny and rounded, this sat precariously at the foot of his bunk. It remained unmoved at the most violent pitching and rolling but without warning would suddenly fly across the galley with a resounding crash to catch any unwary occupants on the way.

Beneath the Skipper's bench was an open tin of cashew nuts. This soon detached itself from Warwick's home-made knots and one morning as I went down to wake him for breakfast I was treated to the glorious sight of a nut carpet on the black and red lino.

To reduce condensation and engine noise most of the galley and charthouse was lined with limpet spray. This proved a great boon but also lulled us into a sense of false security since the warmth and peace below often belied the true nature of the weather. It was sometimes frightening to step through the after doorway and discover that indeed a gale-force wind was blowing and waves were breaking regularly on the deck. The limpet also provided a good surface for inscription with felt pens. One soon learned to live with quotations from Lewis Carroll and Omar Khayyam or philosophies ranging from: 'The mind is its own place, and in itself / Can make a Heaven of Hell, a Hell of Heaven', to:

> Let us value if we can
> The vertical man
> Though we honour none
> But the horizontal one.

There was little run on our beer and liquor supply. There was little run on food at that stage and Grahame who, not unexpectedly, found the thrill of setting sail spoilt by chronic seasickness, spent his mealtimes eating lifesavers with Ed in the fo'c'sle. At the start we had 20 cartons of bottled beer, ten of canned, three cartons of whisky, one of gin and two four-gallon kegs of rum. This proved to be an accurate estimate of our needs save that we came back with one rum keg unbroached and half the contents of the other at the bottom of the freezer. It was potent stuff. Raw rum, straight from the sugar refining factory, no-one knew the proof. But we called it super overproof and found that one infinitesimal sip caused a searing burn in one's throat and indigestion at least. Continuous diluting made it more palatable but we found no flavour until we mixed in lime juice. It was strictly ruled that rum be taken only after a watch since we did not want to suffer the consequences of inebriated steering.

We promised the empty rum kegs to the Hermandad de la Costa (The Brotherhood of the Coast). In the times of Captain Morgan there had been a sort of pirates' trade union in Central America when mutual assistance had been given to cobbers in distress (such as being hunted by the Royal Navy). This died out with the treasure ships but it was resurrected some years ago in a different form in Chile. Now it is a club with elaborate nautical custom and etiquette whose members must have an association or interest in the sea. But it still carries out the admirable job of assisting members in distress through its branches all over the world, apart from supporting certain seagoing enterprises. The Sydney sept gave us a finely-bound logbook and the honour of flying their flag: black and decorated, not with skull and crossbones, but with white stars and crossed oars. We raised it at the mainmast on leaving Albany and flew it until in tatters on arrival at Heard. Warwick was a member of the Cruising Yacht Club of Australia and we flew their pennant too, to the furthest south it had ever been.

Later on Sunday the 29th the log still told of heavy squalls and a powerful wind. During the previous twenty-four hours we made only seventy-eight miles. Like tall mountains, prominent continental capes create their own storms and it was taking much of the ship's strength and power to round Cape Leeuwin. But at midnight, though it was blowing hard, the loom of the Naturaliste light was astern. Earlier a ship had passed eastbound. This and the light were the last signs of land or people that we were to see for weeks.

At 0800 on 30 November Russ wrote that the cloud was clearing. The barometer was slowly rising, the wind veered to the south and late in the morning the Skipper gave the order to hoist all plain sail.

At these times he invariably took the wheel and kept the engine idling until we were under way with sail. He usually held the bows into the wind until sufficient canvas was aloft and then slowly brought the ship back on course as the remainder of the sails were hoisted. Though there was no exact procedure or special job for each one of us to do, raising sail fell into a pattern and everyone had a favourite niche to which he gravitated.

First the staysail. This lay lashed in the bow scuppers and it was a simple matter to remove the rope, clip on the halyard from the foremast and secure the sheet for the chosen tack to a cleat on the cray tank cowling. One man hauled away until it was almost fully set then another would help him to bounce the halyards until the luff was tight against the stay. Then the jib. At first we lashed this to the bowsprit but bad chafing caused us to remove it each time we lowered sail and stow it in a bag on deck. Someone, usually Antony, Mal or Russ, went out to the foremost stay, balancing on the bowsprit with nothing for protection save a meagre net beneath and no security save the stay itself. This man clipped on the luff while the sheet was shackled to the heel, the halyard block was attached and when the bowsprit man was clear another hoisted away as the rest moved to the foresail.

Foresail unlashed, the sheet was eased by the mainmast and the topping lifts strained to lift the gaff and boom out of the cradle atop the cray tank cowling. With a yell of 'Haul away!' from Antony, two men at each halyard hauled up the throat and peak of the stiff terylene sail. Both main sails ran up the mast by means of a leather gooseneck and a simple rope lacing so that invariably the peak was easier to raise than the throat. Antony yelled: 'Ease off on the peak!' as it threatened to outrace the throat and the ideal was to raise the gaff horizontally until the luff was tight, then pull up the peak. Then the lee topping lift was detached, the sheet adjusted and we moved on to the worst job of all—the mainsail.

This was when we really felt the lack of winches and mechanical aids. Half the crew was needed to raise it and during our early puny efforts my arms stretched and ached with effort and the infuriating strain of keeping one's balance on an unstable deck. At least two were needed on each halyard to raise the mainsail in the same manner as the foresail. Then a third when they reached the limit of their strength. Two bounced down on the rope as the third held it firm against the cleat and then took in the slack as the others let go.

There were many red faces after hoisting the mainsail and, although my hands threatened to drop off in the early days, we soon grew to enjoy the vigorous exercise and the pleasure of making sail quickly and efficiently.

Not that we were ever completely efficient. We had our ups and downs. Mainly on the downs when we dragged a billowing mainsail in the sea or had its gaff swinging free of the topping lifts when the throat was lowered too quickly. Often we would heave with might and main to raise this sail, to no effect, until we discovered that the downhaul rope was still lashed to its cleat or the mast lacings had jammed against a fitting. But when all the sails were raised we liked a tidy ship. All the ropes were coiled and hung neatly, the sheets adjusted finely, the topping lifts tightened, an extra bounce taken on a throat halyard to smarten a sail. Then we retired to the charthouse to remove our oilskins and someone noticed that a dirty pair of drawers, trailing on a rope astern to be washed, had wrapped themselves round the logline.

Those of us who had not sailed before became justifiably, I think, proud of our ability to help in running the ship. It was a satisfying feeling to know that we could steer *Patanela* without broaching or gybing the mainsail, although the Skipper's course was laid with an eye to these dangers and we finally discovered that it was difficult to accomplish the latter even if we tried. Naturally we all took a keen interest in our daily mileage, noon position and course. Not merely from growing nautical accomplishment but because we were eager to see those little crosses on the chart move quickly towards our objective. Although the sea voyage formed such a large and important part of our expedition, its main purpose was to take us to an unclimbed mountain on a small island at the bottom of the Indian Ocean. By the first day of December we were free of Australia, our course due west towards Africa.

3

WESTWARD HO!

O UR FURTHEST NORTH WAS 32°33'S but despite the low latitude and high barometer the temperature was low with a cur-
tained sky and a fresh south-easter which brought a bitter spasm
of the Antarctic. We had left the land behind. Near the coast there
had been flocks of birds feeding off the rich waters of the continental
shelf: seagulls, gannets, shags, petrels and albatrosses. But now there
were only a few of the ubiquitous muttonbirds, brown and silent,
gliding in and out of the swell, sometimes disappearing for hours so
that there was not the faintest sign of life across the wide, unlimited
horizon.

Warwick told me before we sailed that the biggest problem of the
voyage would be boredom. I began to dread the long days of inaction
on a dull ocean, but these never came. The basic requirements of our
life, sleeping, eating and standing watch, took two-thirds of the day.
In the remaining eight hours we had diaries to keep, scientific work
to maintain, preparations to make for the island and, in the last resort, a library of two hundred books to read ranging from Bobby
Charlton's *My Soccer Life* to Thucydides' *Peloponnesian Wars*.

The two hours of a watch when one was not steering was the
most boring time of all. Then one had to rely on thoughts or dreams
and the conversation of one's partner. The drag in time was more intensified during poor weather when everyone else was below. Then
one stood holding the deckhouse rail, stamping one's feet against the
cold, staring at a grey sea for the ship or rock that never appeared.

The best time was the morning watch. This ran into breakfast
and after it one knew that the rest of the day was free save for an

hour at the wheel during the first dog. There was always the chance of a brilliant dawn and watchmen felt deep pleasure at being the only two on board to witness a majestic sunrise while the others slept.

Though mostly it was a grey dawn, Russ and I drew one morning when the cloud pattern was open and steady with a developing mural of colour. Away from the sun were two cloud layers, the upper of pastel purples and pinks while the lower puffed against it in white. As the sun came there was an indescribable number of yellows and pinks with streaks of irradiating cloud like the proverbial Japanese Rising Sun. It seemed an inordinately long time between first light and the sunrise but when it appeared it was caught between the purple sea and the lower cloud like a squeeze of molten steel. The initial fire was soon lost behind the scarves of mist but returned higher to glorify and gild the upper cloud until the sky was diluted in the wash of full daylight.

After sunrise there was the never failing entertainment of watching the others emerge for breakfast at 0730. On a typical morning, before I took the wheel for the last trick, I would go down to the galley, moving slowly and quietly to avoid waking the Skipper, and slide across to Warwick's bunk, taking a firm grip of the rail which was my only security against the slippery floor of the rocking ship.

Warwick's dark, tousled head would be half buried in blankets, eyes shaded against the depressing light of early morning as it filtered through the scuttles. I would give him a gentle shake on the shoulder and, after a few seconds, one eye opened and its expression silently showed recognition and awareness that it was nearly seven o'clock. Each time, after this, I turned and made my way back to the deck, tapping the barometer on the way, oilskins rustling loudly.

Below it seemed stuffy but above there was fresh, cold air and Russ glancing over his shoulder to see if I was coming to take the wheel.

I lurched up to him, carefully, keeping a firm hold of the rail and said: 'Righto.' He told me the course and I repeated it in confirmation as I took the wheel and braced my legs apart on the matting before the binnacle.

There would be a pause in activity as I steered into a warming sea then Warwick tottered on deck, relieved himself, staggered to the row of gas bottles, hair dishevelled and looking as though he had been on an all-night jag. He turned the valve of the current bottle, released an inane pleasantry, beat his chest and disappeared. Later there was the whine of the water pump and a furious clicking sound as he fired his flint gun. Twenty minutes passed before a tantalising aroma of bacon and toast wafted up the stove ventilator to mingle with the smells of the sea and diesel.

Next came the Skipper at about 0715, his presence preceded by a sharp tapping as he emptied his pipe on the top step of the companionway. He came up quietly and one would turn to find him staring out to sea or up at the set of the sails, eyes puffy and full of sleep. Satisfied that all was well he stripped off, uttered a terse 'Mornin'' if one caught his eye, and threw a bucket over the side. Quickly he dunked two buckets of cold seawater over his head, gasping and once, as I watched the goose pimples, he spluttered: 'Don't know what you're missing!' Russ went through a similar performance and often Grahame would ask to be called before breakfast for his shower. Once he came up to find the Skipper in possession of the sole bucket and said with a disgruntled look that it was a bit poor when it came to having a lock on the bathroom door. He pulled off his string vest, the pattern firmly pressed on his back and to our chortles replied: 'Crocodile skins are in this year!' When breakfast was ready Warwick rang a small bell, jangling it against the aperture of the ventilation pipe which ran right through the ship and through the scuttle if the weather permitted. Its noise died away and soon there were signs of movement in the cray tank.

The heavy hatch on the cowling was open unless the weather was bad and from the wheel one could look down to the small platform between the bunks. Colin usually rose first. He looked and moved like a sleepy possum, slowly pulled on his clothes and deliberately climbed up the ladder, pausing halfway to sniff the air outside his hole. He grinned sheepishly, finished climbing out and made carefully for the urinal which was on the lee side of the deckhouse. As more people emerged, the scene became à la Clochemerle with men lined together, bellies pressed against the taffrail.

Col always moved slowly and I thought that it no doubt explained his survival through years of hard mountaineering. Deliberate and careful, his daily routine was to go around the ship with oilcan and grease, lubricating winches, steering chains and anything else which appeared as if it might creak or seize. Even oneself if one stood still too long, and I was reminded of the old service maxim, 'If it moves salute it; if it doesn't, paint it!' Col's forte was the ceaseless production of fertile, inventive ideas based on an immense chemical and engineering knowledge. These were generally in the genre of Heath Robinson. But he produced double charging power for the batteries by using a welding generator instead of the standard type attached to our Lister donkey engine.

He was eager to make an impression on the French when we arrived at Kerguelen and proposed an ingenious type of bow chaser for firing a salute. He suggested filling an empty porridge tin with the correct quantities of propane gas and air and firing a spark plug fitted in the bottom. But his most valuable contribution to the expedition concerned our spiritual welfare. On the flywheel of the Lister diesel he inscribed the words *Om Mane Padme Hum* as if on a Tibetan prayer wheel and at 400 revolutions per minute one could almost feel the virtue pouring into the ship.

Mal came next, often bleary eyed, but he took to bursting from the cray tank naked and running into a vigorous performance of calisthenics. He led the way in this with pressups, pullups, jumpups and running on the spot. This slowly became a fetish with some members as they feared losing fitness during the sedentary life on board ship. Morning and evening we were treated to Mal, Grahame and Warwick hanging from the ratlines or bouncing at the rail.

Finally, Antony emerged from the cray tank. Flaccid, stunned and foul in the mouth he lumbered on to the deck, gave a shuddering look at his surroundings and ducked into the deckhouse, unable to coordinate his thoughts until our rude remarks and jibes had stirred him. After the Skipper he was the most experienced sailor in the crew. He had ocean cruised before, participated in the Sydney-Hobart race, and was best qualified to hold the position of Mate. With his past acclimatisation to the sea he stood at the wheel with less

If it squeaks or moves, oil it; Colin in the engine-room

clothing than any other. Though it transpired that he brought very little with him and had to conserve his shirts and sweaters to make them last the trip. But often I would admire his asceticism as he braved bitter wind and spray dressed only in a thin shirt and shorts while the rest were muffled in sweaters and oilskins. He had a magnificent head of curly hair and it was a sad day when this was shorn, for like Samson he seemed to lose his strength and appeared on the next watch clad with balaclava and scarf.

Ed rose reluctantly, at five or six. As radio operator it was logical that he be meteorologist too. He squirmed through the fo'c'sle hatch, tripped down the deck with a polite good morning and looked every inch a seaman with bare feet, trousers rolled up, nautical beard and a casual regard of the sea around him. His meteorology involved air and sea temperatures, wind speed and direction, state of the sea, cloud formation and so on. Most of his observations were made from the security of the charthouse but he ventured out for a bucket of sea water and to twirl a thermometer round his head. His weather log written up, he descended to the bowels of the engine room and spent up to two hours making contact with Perth, Sydney or Mawson in Antarctica in order to send his information out. This was a gruelling process. Although we had a high-powered transmitter, our aerial length was very short and Ed needed all his perseverance and technique to establish morse contact.

Lastly John rose, darkly, loathfully leaving his bunk and surly until the day had eased his temper. Then the ship, which had been so still half an hour before, came alive. Waiting impatiently for eight o'clock when I was relieved, I stood alone at the wheel listening to the rumble of muffled laughter in the galley and perhaps Warwick would shout up the ventilator and pass a cup of tea through the scuttle. As I sipped and stretched my legs, cramped from the same standing position, I planned my activities for the rest of the day.

It was 5 December and a notable day. It was a month since we left Sydney. It was also Saturday and to celebrate our first anniversary, a sports afternoon was scheduled and a ding for the evening. Warwick issued the first progress report which showed that we had come only 630 miles in the week after leaving Albany but 2465 miles altogether at a daily average of 117. Slow by modern standards but satisfactory for a small ship often sailing in light airs and round stormy capes. Warwick continued: 'Present intentions are to sail west and north above Amsterdam Island to a point where we can sail south to Kerguelen and Heard. This is based upon the necessity to use the best sailing route with motor as auxiliary and the conclusion reached that *Patanela* will not "economically" push into head seas. Economical motoring is approx 7 knots at 1300 revs. Economical sailing is 3-plus knots with an expectancy of 7-plus knots in best conditions.' At that rate we could expect to see Heard before the middle of January.

It was a brilliant day with an oily calm at the beginning tempered later by the ripples of a cool westerly breeze. We were under power again but it was a gentle ride in a smooth sea and it created the pleasant sensation of making plenty of ground in fine weather. Late in the morning we hove to for swimming. All save myself cavorted in the water testing waterproof watches and cameras while Russ used a snorkel to have a look at the hull which had a surprising lack of weed or barnacles. Warwick said that the sensation was frightening.

They swam in the deep, inky blue of 2000 fathoms with no firm, sandy beach behind but only one small, garishly yellow ship riding on a slight swell. It was then that the expedition seemed to achieve complete synthesis: all of us, our food, our water, our equipment, our aims, ambitions and hopes; all the months of effort and planning, all our £20,000 budget, our safety, our success lay enveloped in the sixty-three-foot yellow hull of *Patanela*. Her name meant Spirit of the Storm and we hoped she remained the spirit and did not become the ghost!

The 'sports' consisted of four events: eating the carrot, putting the tail on the donkey, a race up the ratlines and round the deck and a beer and biscuit boat race. The teams were Fo'c'sle versus Cray Tank while the Skipper slept and Warwick took John's place since he was on the wheel. Carrots were hung from a rope tied between the foremast and stay and there was the inevitable cheating when Antony used his shoulder to keep his carrot steady. Ed drew a donkey on the deck and the race caused hilarity when Warwick lost his footing descending the ratlines, lost the lap-lap which was his only covering, and slid down with hands only, in danger of losing his manhood. Eating a dry biscuit was hardly alleviated by a bottle of gassy beer but Russ produced a hidden skill in downing one without pause. The evening ding fizzled out since two men were on watch, others sleeping in preparation and it was clear that we could never hold a complete party until we were at anchor.

About this time the scientific work settled into a routine. Twice daily Ed made his meteorological observations and I checked the insect nets. Russ kept a detailed bird and whale log but the main onus of science rested on Grahame. He undertook daily plankton hauls and hydrology stations for the CSIRO. The initial requirement was for plankton samples from a depth of 200 metres. This entailed lowering a large net weighted by a 100-lb. lead, but our only source of power was a small electric winch which wound in a thin, inadequate-looking wire rope. The first trial was almost the end of the whole programme. The wire led out through small blocks attached to the foremast, then along the spare staysail boom to a special block over the water that also acted as a counter. The net, its weight and a special sample bottle suspended from the apex was lowered away. But before it was out of sight Col called out in alarm that the clutch was slipping. Even with the winch in reverse the net relentlessly pulled the wire off the drum, faster as the ship rolled away, pausing when it rolled back. Quick action was needed before the net went too far and became irretrievable. Colin tried lashing the wire with a rope but it bit through. Then he tried reversing the winch during the slack period while Russ held the wire with a rope during the adverse roll. But nothing would stop the inevitable, steady descent of the net. In desperation Grahame grabbed a big marlin spike. With the danger of the thin wire suddenly snapping to flail the crew, he waited for each slack period, then twisted it around a projecting mast fitting.

The net came to a halt. Colin tightened up the clutch and with careful manipulation we were able to wind the apparatus back on board. But this proved that a deep haul was impractical even in the calmest weather and the project was finally discarded on discovering a serious drain on our limited battery power. Grahame cabled

Hauling in the plankton net

Sydney and the CSIRO suggested surface hauls instead. He finally evolved the ideal method of trailing the net astern while the ship moved at two knots but initially found that he collected far more plankton than would fit in his small sample jars. Another querying cable brought the not unexpected reply that he should reduce hauling time.

The plankton hauls were part of a wide Indian Ocean programme to find out more about the minute animals and vegetable life in the sea. We had no financial support for this work but Grahame, conscientious and meticulous, was determined to make a good fist of the programme. Despite watch fatigue and mediocre weather he made regular hauls after sunset when the plankton were most prolific, the whole operation involving up to two hours' work. Generally with Warwick's and Colin's help he would take in the logline, trail the net, haul it back after a few minutes, then carry it down to the foredeck for hosing. Often the haul meant reducing engine revs, changing course or shortening sail to achieve the right speed. By the for'ard decklight the net was suspended by the staysail halyard and as someone worked the hand pump amidships— or the power pump if the engine was running—he would wash scattered plankton down the net into the metal receptacle at the apex. If the wind was fresh the fifteen-foot net flew around with drenching spray and in the darkness it became a miserable pastime. After washing, the sample was preserved in small jars of formalin. Then Grahame took the sea temperature, a salinity sample, filled in his data sheets and made off to bed, often only an hour before he was roused to stand watch.

I was made entertainments officer at Albany and though there was little to organise—the crew made up of independent people who did not like being organised—I arranged a few more activities to help kill boredom before it developed. There was a weekly sweep in which each member was asked to guess the average daily mileage for the forthcoming week and the prize was a tin of anything the winner cared to choose. This spurred on the favourite pastime of eating, as Warwick served us great quantities of food in an attempt to build us up before the Roaring Forties and the Furious Fifties.

The Skipper found the plethora of meat, fruit cake, nuts and chocolate a welcome change to the austerity rations on his own *Mischief* where the menu rotated round curry, bangers and mash, spaghetti, curry, bangers and mash and spaghetti. Nevertheless his favourite dish was curry and he liberally laced all the non-curry dishes with hot Tabasco; *olé!* we used to add.

On anniversary night Warwick served up a mammoth curry that kept us all awake and I was still in some distress the following morning. I mentioned my stomach ache to Russ and pointed to the lower regions of my abdomen. He showed an abnormal interest, his eyes brightened and seemed to flicker quickly like a poker machine coming to the jackpot. Then I remembered. Russ, Mal and Grahame had all had their appendixes removed as a matter of course before serving as medical officers in the Antarctic. The Skipper, John, Ed and I were the only ones on board with their stomachs still intact. Curry was the ideal irritant and in his professional capacity Russ was eager to detect the first signs of illness.

If we had gone without a doctor, there is nothing surer than someone would have gone down with a serious illness or injury. But apart from Russ, our official surgeon barber who had won the MBE for outstanding surgery in the Antarctic, we had Mal, halfway to being an FRCS and, with Grahame, a fully qualified and experienced general practitioner. The result was that the three of them spent a good deal of time treating each other—of rashes, boils and wounds which never affected anyone else in the crew.

This is being a little unjust since Russ did fix Ed's bad toothache. Reclining in Antony's deckchair on a day of brilliant sunshine, Ed submitted warily to Russ as he probed around his molars and finally filled the objectionable cavity after due consultation with his colleagues. There was a lot of palaver and I finally suggested from the wheel that to save time and trouble they tie a piece of string to the offending tooth, with the other end fastened to the main boom and I would gybe it.

Ed's toothache probably derived from eating too much fruit and nut chocolate. Warwick had issued each of us with packages of this. With money a currency of no value the chocolate became a valuable item of exchange and Ed charged one bar for a haircut and by special arrangement would send cables at a charge of one square per word. In fact, personal cables were severely limited. With the difficulty of radio contact, a great deal of extra work devolved on Ed if there was unlimited personal communication, and Warwick felt that morale and team spirit were all the better without undue preoccupation with home.

I also ran a sweep with a special prize for the one who correctly guessed the day we sighted Heard Island. There was a wide range of estimates—from optimistic Mal's 2 January through my 7 January to the considered pessimism of Warwick's 12 January. The odds fluctuated as each day's mileage became known, but there could be no accurate forecasts until after Christmas.

This was now little more than a fortnight away and we wondered if we would spend it in a comfortable anchorage at Kerguelen or stormbound in the Forties. There was little time for wondering as we ploughed our way through the monumental task of signing thousands of postcards. To raise more money for our high budget, Warwick had designed a printed postcard which was sold to any member of the public for five shillings. On one side was a photograph of Big Ben and *Patanela*, on the other a list of expedition members and space for their signatures. The postcards were considered a good idea until we came to signing them and spent day after day developing writer's cramp on the confined spaces of the galley table. Later we had them franked at Kerguelen but posted at Albany since mail was collected only annually in the Antarctic.

Other activities which filled the long, sultry days on the Indian Ocean included weekly lectures ranging from Col's 'Dieseline and Old Boots' to the Skipper's talk on Arctic Bylot Island and Antony's 'Law and its Vicissitudes'. But undoubtedly the tour de force was SOS—an apt abbreviation of *Spirit of the Storm*. This was the ship's magazine with John as editor, me as publisher and Ed as its accomplished illustrator. Typed on fine, heavy paper it opened with an appropriate poem—*Landfall in Unknown Seas* by Allen Curnow—and was followed by articles from each member of the crew. These had no signature but the author was depicted by Ed's brilliant caricatures. There were other cartoons by him and photographs were cut from picture magazines and labelled with new, ludicrous captions. The publication of SOS was heralded by John's imaginative posters in good, yellow rag style. Russ's tale of his trip on the Trans-Siberian Railway was headlined *Aussie commo in Siberia tells all in shocking report*; my New Guinea story yielded *NG natives exploited, mocked* and Grahame's scientific article *Plankton exposed*. There were fictitious headlines and a report that the winner of a new competition would gain a free return trip to Heard Island for two.

Ten days out from Albany wildlife suddenly increased. We watched two or three species of albatross relentlessly circling the ship, dominated by the great Wanderer. Unless there was dead calm they never flapped their wings but soared and glided over the swell with the air currents, their wingtips almost touching the water as they banked. Sei whales appeared, rising and spouting to within thirty yards of the ship, and causing alarm when they surfaced close beneath the bows. A few porpoises examined *Patanela* but on 8 December we were treated to an unforgettable display of swimming. We were sailing west-north-west under full sail, a steady northerly pushing us along at over four knots. Suddenly someone yodelled with excitement and shouted: 'Come and look at this!' There was a scramble to get on deck; then we climbed the ratlines, stood on the deckhouse or leaned over the rail as a gigantic school of porpoises closed with the ship from the south east. There were scores, travelling at 15–20 knots, and a brace would leave the water together to jump in graceful, curving leaps, followed by more and more so that there was a continuous spectacle of flying porpoises and white water where they returned to the sea. Albatrosses and muttonbirds appeared from nowhere, circling and watching the porpoises or landing amid them to pick up scraps of food and disturbed fish which they left behind in their wake. Abreast the ship many paused to swim around the bows in glorious marine acrobatics, sometimes surfacing with a snort, crossing each other's tracks. Then they outstripped us, disappeared, taking the birds with them and once again the ocean became desolate.

The Skipper's noon sight on Tuesday 15 December showed that

Ed Reid cuts the Skipper's hair

we were about 180 miles due north of the French islands Amsterdam and St Paul, small volcanic outcrops around latitude 38°S. There was a research base on Amsterdam and at one point the Skipper had considered calling there for an anchorage when Col could have a steady ship for pumping diesel from the cray tank drums to the main tanks. During calm weather a week earlier, however, he had been able to transfer fuel from drums in the engine room wings and there was enough in the tanks to see us through to Kerguelen if we used sail for the better part of the remaining 1700-2000 miles. Within the following forty-eight hours we could expect to pass Heard Island's longitude. Kerguelen was three degrees further west and we knew that soon after that we would turn south into the strong westerlies and could expect to sail full time.

Over the previous ten days we had covered 1125 miles, equally under sail and engine. The wind came from every point of the compass, never reaching great strength while the prevailing weather was calm and overcast, and the barometer remained high, fluctuating slightly between 30.11 and 30.43. There was an increasingly high humidity which did not relent until rain came on the 11th. Though there was no rain or spray during the night we often woke to find the ship saturated in dew; washing took days to dry despite sun and breeze.

With the rain came more wildlife and, despite the grey skies, fifty or more pilot whales, a type of dolphin, created an exciting interlude as they swam behind us, surfacing and diving rhythmically in apparent slow motion after the jubilant energy of the porpoises.

On the morning of the 15th a whale shark appeared to starboard, flopping and lolling near the surface until it drifted astern, quite unperturbed by our presence. The little book we had describing ocean fish and whales said: 'They are quite harmless unless bumped' when they are known to take bites out of wooden ships. Other sharks, however, were described as a 'perfect nuisance' if caught in fishermen's nets.

We had a surfeit of brilliant sunsets. One night there was little cloud in the sky to the west save for a long, low bank which we sailed into later to find misty rain. The sun dropped behind this to leave nothing but a frill of gold along its edge and diffused pink and a rare violet over the open areas of the sky. To the north a pile of cumulus varied in levels of grey-blue and cream while above a half moon silvered ripples in the swelling, glassy water. The stars and planets showed themselves slowly—Jupiter, Canopus, Sirius and the red twinkle of Betelgeuse. Most striking of all were the stark silhouettes of rigging and people against the violet sky and the smooth water. Colin, Warwick and Russ were all making pushups or pullups on the ratlines and they seemed to move in sequence. For a while their stiffly-moving silhouettes irresistibly reminded me of the clockwork figures on a German exhibition clock.

For that moment I brought our little tape recorder on deck and from the small selection of tapes played Handel's *Water Music* and Greig's *Solveig's Song*—both seeming to flow and mingle with the beauty of the scene.

On the calm nights that followed, the time passed quickly for Russ and I. We had a book of star charts and, with a pair of binoculars, whiled away hours fixing the positions of different constellations as they slowly wheeled across the sky. Jupiter was ever dominant, we could see four of its moons, though Venus ruled the morning and the regular star pattern was enlivened often by earth satellites or the bright green flare of falling meteors.

There were always little jobs to do. The Skipper's work seemed never ending as he pottered around the ship, splicing this, whipping that, tidying the sheets or replacing the rungs of the ratlines. The bobstay became slack so he and Antony hung over the bows to remove links in the chain and tighten it up once more. Over the weeks at sea, water slopped through the hawse pipes into the forepeak and the fo'c'sle crew had to buckle down and pump out the bilge. Regularly Colin emptied the main bilges with the motor pump and increased revs to maximum for a few minutes while we were motoring, to clean out the exhaust. At top speed, *Patanela* glided across the calm sea without rolls or bad temper, but for this the price was heavy fuel consumption which we could ill afford.

Patanela's character changed with the weather and depended on whether she was under sail or engine. Sailing she was firm and purposeful though sometimes contrary, especially before the wind, and she was still heavy in the gut though the paunch slowly disappeared as we used more fuel. She sailed well close-hauled but responded best with the wind abeam or slightly for'ard of the beam.

With the wind abaft there was the ghastly risk of gybing while a following sea gave one the ultimate feeling of helplessness at the wheel. I wrote in my diary on 20 December: 'Well—we had a bit of wind and sea so that *Patanela* sailed well close hauled, then poorly so that we covered only 60-odd miles on yesterday's noon and this brought the week's daily average down to 114.5 so that John won the sweep again. But the weather's clear and sunny now, the wind's dropped and the only nuisance is a long swell rolling up from some storm in the south west. I expect that we'll turn in that direction tomorrow, then we'll cop the lot for Christmas and, you never know, we might reach Heard when the Skipper estimates: January 3rd.' At the middle of December our thoughts turned increasingly to the key months of January and February. During those months we expected to reach Heard, attempt our objectives and at least begin the return voyage to Australia. Somewhere there lay the high point of the expedition, the attempt on Big Ben. There was growing awareness that the real tests were not far away; the balmy, sub-tropical days were coming to an end. Grahame brought out equipment—crampons and boots for fitting and modification, and Warwick could not put off any longer the invidious task of provisionally selecting those to land on the island should *Patanela* be unable to remain at Heard.

To begin with he gave each member a distinct job, a part in the overall organisation on arrival. Antony as Mate was put in charge of people and operations on board the ship under the Skipper's ulti-mate authority. Russ was responsible for inflation and preparation of landing craft and safety gear; Col, the outboard motors and fuel; Grahame was to look after climbing and camping gear and still pho-tography. I was in charge of scientific gear, Mal cine photography, John food, cooking gear and fuel; Ed, radio equipment.

We were told this around 14 December and began preparing lists of requirements. Meanwhile Warwick had to sort out the expedition aims and priorities and decide who could best fulfil them.

Although it was planned for, and would have solved all personnel problems, the prospect of a good anchorage in Heard's Winston Lagoon was always a vain hope. From the beginning the odds were that only half the number of members would be able to land while the rest sailed *Patanela* back to a safe harbour at Kerguelen; the Skipper needed at least four men with him to safely manoeuvre the ship back and forth over 300 miles of stormy ocean.

The main objective was clear: an attempt to climb Big Ben. This meant that the five who landed must be experienced ice mountaineers.

Such a requirement gave Warwick seven members from which to choose the landing party. Grahame had climbed in the Himalayas, Antarctica and had led the 1963 attempt on Big Ben; Colin had climbing experience over twenty years in New Zealand and Europe; John had climbed for three seasons in the Southern Alps; I had climbed in New Zealand and New Guinea while Warwick himself had been on expeditions to Alaska, Lapland, the Himalayas and was with Grahame on Heard in 1963; Russ and Mal had both been in Antarctica while the former had limited experience in the Southern Alps.

Next, responsibilities to our sponsors were considered and which members could best cope with them. News and photographs for *The Australian* newspaper were best covered by Warwick; colour photography by Grahame or myself; insects for Bishop Museum by myself and movie film for our main sponsor, George Sample, by either Warwick or Mal. Also to be taken into account were members' other abilities to fulfil a broad scientific programme. Warwick was experienced in botany, Grahame in biology and he had the added advantage of being the most knowledgeable man in the world on Heard Island. Colin was an experienced surveyor.

On the 20 December the die was cast. Warwick, Colin, Grahame, John and myself would go ashore, with Russ and Mal as first and second reserves should one of the basic party fall ill or the opportunity arise to include another member. It was hard on those left out. It was implicit virtually from the start that the Skipper and Antony would stick with the ship but Ed, Mal and Russ had pinned high hopes on landing. But Warwick's decision was accepted with equanimity, its

Decanting the rum: The Author, Russ and Grahame

logic and reason recognised. And everyone realised that the task of sailing and safeguarding *Patanela* would be just as hard, and just as important to the expedition as a whole, as the activities on the island.

On 18 and 19 December the barometer dropped below 30 and a westerly brought the first mediocre weather we had encountered since leaving Cape Leeuwin. These days showed how quickly the mood of sea and sky could change. Together they were a mess of paint, chiefly blue, black and white, and it was easily stirred into a variety of violent contrasts. Swells rose and diminished, bad weather threatened to develop, then faded away. One moment the sky was cloudless but within two hours it could be covered; with light rain came blank grey clouds intersticed by great arcs of cream.

After the poor weather, an annoying swell beset the ship, tossing waves haphazardly over the decks. Warwick seemed to have a jinx for, wherever he sat, he received a splash of water. When one bad spell seemed to have spent its fury he went to open a scuttle for ventilation and enquired of Antony at the wheel: 'Do you think it's safe to leave this open?' Antony assessed the sea and replied: 'I wouldn't if I were you.' Warwick paused, cogitating, there was a sudden splosh and a jet of water shot through the scuttle into his eye.

At the direction of some sixth sense the Skipper ordered a practice reefing of the mainsail on the 15th. We had been at sea for five weeks but had not undertaken a reef! The operation went smoothly enough, everyone was eager to show that they could tie reef knots, but it was found that the leach cringle could not be securely tied to the after part of the boom. Since both cringles were the main points of attachment, and failure of one could cause reef points to tear through the sail in a blow, it was important to devise a strong and foolproof method of attachment. Col's inventive genius rose immediately to the challenge. He fastened a block to the boom at the foot of the leach, a downhaul rope was passed through this from the cringle. During reefing the strain was taken from near the wheel by three hands, the rope finally lashed to the mainmast.

By 20 December some of us had grown restless and irritable. It was not a product of boredom since there were more than enough activities to occupy our time. But we seemed to be spending far too long in a meander across the Indian Ocean. We were nearer to Madagascar than Heard Island but after weeks of empty ocean it seemed unreal that such places existed. Briefly I felt we were the ship of the Ancient Mariner, upon a painted, lifeless ocean, water, water everywhere and though the crew were not dead we had all descended into varying degrees of torpidity. For days I barely saw Antony who sought his bunk at the end of each watch and rarely appeared save for this and meals. The Skipper seldom spoke now, favouring sleep to conversation and I became more and more disgruntled at our slow progression. I wrote: 'So far the belching symptom of this expedition has been overeating and an uneventful cruise on the world's most uninteresting ocean. I shall probably eat my words before the month is out but for the time spent one could expect to see a bit more at the end of it than a couple of windswept islands. Today marks three weeks since we last saw land or a ship.' Grahame groaned: 'Roll on Kerguelen! Life at sea consists largely of monotony interrupted by periods of nastiness.' The longest day of the year produced a stiff blow from the north-west. We rattled along in fine style under all plain sail, touched six knots before we made our first serious reefing and looked most expert and seaman-like as we lined the main boom in blue foul-weather suits taking in the points. Later the jib had to be lowered as the seas rose. It was a frightening prospect to go out on the bowsprit with no protection as it dipped close to the big waves. But the Skipper set the example, went out himself and grimly pulled down the luff as Russ and Grahame hauled the sail inboard. I was at the wheel and could find nothing but admiration for this incredible man as I eased *Patanela* into the wind. He came off exhilarated, puffing but grinning slightly, a typical, mischievous look in his eye. Life was full of worthwhile challenges—even for a man of sixty-six.

When were we going to turn south? The Skipper's sight on 22 December showed we were at 34°24's and 64°10'E—already nine degrees west of Heard. His use of the sextant was a model of speed and accuracy. He took sights at every opportunity and from his expression of confidence we never had any doubt that he knew where we were. There was a standby sextant on board that others used to practice navigation and it could well have been regarded as a talisman—it had belonged to Fletcher, third mate to Mawson on the Aurora when he had taken the Australian Antarctic Expedition to Adélie Land in 1911.

The blow went as quickly as it came and we motored again with slight, contrary winds. The night of the 22nd was fine and clear with a dropping swell, the Skipper noted a satellite in the log during the early morning of the 23rd, and by breakfast the wind had freshened again—enough to hoist sails. The Skipper often waited until everyone had finished breakfast before hoisting or shortening sail and that day was no exception. Russ and I were on the forenoon watch as he took the wheel and we went to help others with the halyards. The wind came steadily from the west, the swell slight, the barometer still high. The log read 4720. When the sails were set I came back down the deck from tidying ropes and relieved him at the wheel. Quietly he gave the course: 'South west by a half west.' A new course. We turned south, trailed by twelve wandering albatrosses.

4

SOUTH UNTIL THE BUTTER FREEZES

DECEMBER 23 WAS ALSO WARWICK'S 38TH BIRTHDAY, the first on the expedition, and it provoked him to reflection. 'This time last year I was just in Melbourne without a job trying to piece my thoughts together after the tour of Australia. The expedition was a "perhaps" and now it is for real. The initial urge is unchanged and seeing the crew around me I see how valuable such experiences can be (how much will the outlooks and future actions of one or two of these chaps be affected?) Whether my grandiose idea of a "demonstration" in Australia will in fact affect many I doubt. I suspect two values: what we do as individuals and what builds out of the expedition.' Instead of taking on Sunday cooking I cooked the evening meal that day in celebration of Warwick's birthday and Mal produced a bottle of brandy. I jammed myself by the stove, hanging on to a rail for support, and after spending the whole afternoon preparing spaghetti bolognese I realised what an atrocious job Warwick had given himself. There was very little room to cook, let alone prepare. All the time one had to combat the movement of the ship, standing on rubber tiles which had degenerated to a skating rink after repeated spilling of concentrated detergent, grease and salt water. Warwick was exhorted by the rest of us to bake cakes. He produced fine sponges though the ship was always against him. Now that we began to sail full time, *Patanela* heeled steadily on one side or the other, the cake mix ran in the tin, and Warwick proudly announced that we had either a port or a starboard cake.

Food was still a favourite topic and preoccupation. As the temperatures dropped Warwick plied us increasingly with duffs. We had a book called *The Magic Pudding* and Antony, Ed or Warwick took to reading a verse from it before each heavy mound was cut up and served. At the presentation of an early duff the Skipper told this traditional tale: 'The new cabin boy is always asked if he likes the middle or ends of treacle duff. Middle! says the boy. Me and the mate likes ends, says the Skipper, promptly cutting it in half.' And then as Antony replied with some rude retort: 'What I want from you Mr Mate is silence—and not too much of that.'

Now the engine really became the auxiliary as we chose a course that moved us into latitudes where the steady westerlies blew favourably on our starboard beam. The compass course hovered around south-west but, with the magnetic variation now in the order of 35–40 degrees, our true course was almost due south. Every hour of sailing meant a few more miles directly towards Kerguelen and Heard. Now we were at the nub of the expedition and this was emphasised as the barometer dropped below 30 early on Christmas Eve, to stay below for nearly two months.

On Christmas Eve the Skipper tossed a plastic bucket overboard for his morning bath and, as it was snatched and torn away by a violent sea, he took the hint and declared that baths were off for the duration. We were still not past 40°S but the wind gave us a taste of things to come, and first we reefed and then lowered the mainsail altogether. This was the first time we had done so in a strong wind and sadly I misinterpreted the Skipper's instructions as I stood by the peak halyard. As the throat ran down I held the peak up until the gaff swung merrily through the air, threatening to come out from the topping lifts, and only a great deal of muscle power on the vang, and black looks from Antony, finally got it down.

Birdlife increased. Apart from albatrosses there were Wilson's storm petrels (Mother Carey's Chickens), Schlegel's petrels and prions but the whales and porpoises were gone. The storm petrels were delightful little birds, dancing and fluttering over the waves, their long legs reaching down to touch the water in a curious manner of feeding. But the huge wandering albatross was ugly, well-named Goony Bird, with a heavy body, bulbous head and lumpy neck, be it sooty, black-browed or shy.

On Christmas Day they provided a feast of entertainment. If the ship was not sailing fast the wanderers' habit was to fly past, land in the sea ahead, wait until we had passed by, then take off in their lumbering ungainly run and fly past to repeat the procedure. But for Christmas Day the wind dropped away into a flat calm and the ship slowly lost all way. The wanderers became disgruntled at our lethargy, stopped flying altogether and paddled alongside. Plainly curious, they pecked with their huge bills at *Patanela*'s hull, unabashed as we leaned over to take photographs. When several crowded round the stern, they vied for a favourable position as we tossed them titbits. The older birds shooed the immatures or protested against rivals by arching their necks, spreading their magnificent wings and croaking or grunting in curiously unbirdlike tones. They landed like a seaplane but their takeoff as they ran energetically over the sea was a certainty for filming although Warwick could not persuade them to take off when he leaned over the taffrail with a movie camera. They were more interested in watching us strange animals—they could fly any day. He thought that noise might chase them away. Col brought out his bugle, Antony took a deep breath and as several of us roared and shouted, a cacophony of strange noises burst over the poor birds' heads. They cocked their eyes at us, regarded each other, swam slowly to one side as if to say: 'Good Lord Mabel. One finds such uncouth people in this part of the world.' So Christmas Day was spent 900 miles from the nearest land at Kerguelen. But the weather had produced its miraculous period of calm and both Russ and Mal were determined that the atmosphere of Christmas would not be lost despite our alien watery surroundings.

Late on Christmas Eve they went round the ship exhorting us to hang up our stockings. They seemed to be half joking, half serious but there was obviously something afoot so we followed their instructions. The foc'sle crew hung their stockings in the forepeak, left and right and at the levels appropriate for each bunk. But the Skipper outdid everyone by suspending a pair of longcoms.

On Christmas morning there was no-one absent from breakfast and it was a curious sight as men climbed out of the hatchways, dishevelled, half-dressed but with stockings clutched in their hands.

There were marzipan bars, cigars and small plastic toys appropriate to each member. Col was given a tiny hammer and saw, the Skipper a pair of binoculars and, in view of my impending marriage, I was given a baby's dummy. Each of us had an articulated toy depicting a famous cartoon character—Donald Duck, Pluto, the Flintstones— astride some monstrous steed. If placed on an angled surface the toys ran and we had hilarious horse races on the galley table, using the ship's roll to set them off. The toys never ran the same way twice though the results were almost as inevitable as the Melbourne Cup since the New Zealand-owned horses generally won.

It was also Friday and each week on that day a special pro- gramme was beamed from Radio Australia in Melbourne. This was *Calling Antarctica* and after the theme tune of 'Limelight' the melodious voice of Jocelyn Terry came on the air, sending messages and news to Australians on and around the Antarctic continent. It was broadcast at 1920 Australian Eastern Time but now we were five hours behind this and we tuned in at mid-afternoon. The pro- gramme was our only firm link with home. Ed's fluctuating morse contact with distant radio stations gave little room for personal chit- chat, and although Warwick allowed each of us to send a Christmas message, the warmth of home, the contact with loved ones was only felt through this programme. Several of us received messages, our progress was broadcast and we heard news of other Australians at Mawson and Macquarie Island. The Antarctic relief ship *Nella Dan* had just left Melbourne and a certain measure of our loneliness was lost when we knew that another Australian expedition ship would soon be in similar waters.

In other respects Christmas Day was not ideal. Russ and I had our bad day of long watches and it was my turn to be slushy. All, apart from the Skipper, Warwick and Col, took their weekly turn at washing up, piling the cutlery, plastic bowls and cups into a baby bath.

With the tiny sink and restricted room in the galley it was best to wash on deck. We sat on the bulwarks, backs firmly braced against the rail, and washed the pots in a bucket of salt water with a dash of highly concentrated detergent. This procedure was quite satisfactory until the sea became so rough that bowls were scattered all over the deck and the wind picked up cups and blew them over the side. The colder water was an added excuse to pamper ourselves so that eventually we turned to washing up down below with seawater boiled in a saucepan.

Boxing Day gave us a notable milestone. We clocked 5000 miles on the log and passed 40°S. Now the Forties should start to roar and I naively expected the sea and winds to increase rapidly after crossing this imaginary line. They did, but slowly, steadily so that it was difficult to say exactly when we were embraced by the Southern Ocean. Early in the morning of 26 December we made sail after twelve hours of motoring in a brisk wind that caused us to reef the mainsail by nine o'clock. The staysail was lowered soon after but, contrarily, by noon the wind had dropped and when we came about at 1220 we hoisted it again and shook out the reef. The wind was predominantly southerly and we were forced into wide tacks, first at west by north and then at south by west. Overnight we had drizzle but a similar pattern followed with a rising wind which caused a shortening of sail. On our morning watch we found the staysail sheet almost frayed through from rubbing against a stay and one of my insect net wires. The Skipper's jaundiced view of science was not improved by this incident, especially since my nets had not caught any insects since leaving the Australian coast—except a big green caterpillar balloon which Mal had put in the top net on Christmas Day.

We could not change course or alter sails without the Skipper's authority. This was a safeguard against prejudicing the ship's safety by the faulty handling of his inexperienced crew. But this left us with a feeling of helplessness should anything go amiss during the night when there would be an inevitable time lag before the Skipper was roused. That same morning the wind had got up so fast that within an hour *Patanela* was rapidly sailing beyond our control as she creamed along under full sail at seven knots. The lee scuppers were dipped in the sea and occasionally waves of water swept over the bulwarks and down the deck. Fortunately five of us handed the mainsail before the weather worsened more. But by noon of the 27th we were

The Author at the wheel, Roaring Forties

under foresail and jib only, still maintaining four knots.

The biggest physical danger was now upon us—man overboard. In the calmer, warm seas it would have been an easy matter to come about to pick up a man in the water. But under sail with a fierce wind and high waves a sudden emergency turn could have endangered the whole ship—in a broaching or gybe—for the sake of one man. We took to wearing life jackets and, in very heavy weather, safety lines which could be fastened to a rail, or to the boom if the mainsail was not in use. We also had a buoy with a flag that was to be tossed over to mark a man's position and a floating light for use at night. There was no doubt in our minds, however, that prevention was better than cure and that no-one could afford to fall over. The further we sailed south the smaller became the chances of survival. The water temperature steadily fell through the fifties, the forties and finally to little above freezing in the waters around Heard. There a man could die of exposure within fifteen to twenty minutes.

Though the seas roughened and the weather grew colder, Grahame persevered with his plankton hauls, anxious to preserve a full record of the change in marine life during a southerly progression. It became an increasingly unpleasant task as *Patanela* dipped and rose heavily in the bigger swells and a steady cold wind cut into fingers constantly soaked in salt water. Grahame noted in his diary: 'The colder the hands, wet in the wind, the more like steel terylene ropes feel.' Shortly before the start of the expedition he had completed a paper describing the acclimatisation to cold of men in Antarctica. While most of us succumbed to gloves Grahame remained at the wheel with bare hands, determined to be fully conditioned for Heard Island. There was an increasing reluctance amongst others to assist him with his hauls but his meticulous determination carried the programme through. His samples were rich and valuable to marine science and on one day we observed long, pale green lines in the water that Grahame attributed to plankton—despite Antony's facetious assertion that they were lines of latitude.

Hauling plankton, however, invariably meant reducing the speed of the ship. Now under sail full time we always had to shorten sail in the darkness, an awkward and even hazardous task in any kind of bad weather. One night we handed the mainsail altogether and Grahame went ahead with his haul. Russ and I were on the bastard watch so that we retired early. As I drifted away into my short spell of sleep I listened to the thump and rattle on the deck above my head as Warwick and Col manhandled the plankton net in a strong wind while Grahame hosed it down. The water splashed over their storm suits and occasionally played full force on the fo'c'sle escape hatch, to squirt through where the bolts did not fasten efficiently.

At midnight Russ and I went up to relieve Antony and Grahame and at 0100 I took the wheel, to steer into a sea and night that was utterly black. For three weeks now we had done without all navigation lights save that at the stern.

There was an odd clunking noise as *Patanela* bucked in rising seas.

We were always alert to any strange or new noise since it could indicate a loose or parted line or a piece of deck cargo coming adrift. In the middle of a pitch black, stormy night it was particularly important to find the cause before something broke loose and created a dangerous situation or at least the loss of gear overboard. There was the familiar squeal of a metal block, the creak of others as the ship rolled, the thud of a lead weight in the scuppers and the rattle of cups and thermos flasks in a box behind the wheel. But above these usual sounds, the familiar noises of a watch that mingled with the swish of the sea, there was a sharp, jerking thump.

After a few minutes I had traced its rough direction and looked up to see the main boom jumping a few inches each time the ship rolled leeward. I had tightened the sheet earlier but with the more violent motion it was trying to jump out of the crutch. Russ went back and found that the boom was not properly seated. I waited anxiously as he clung grimly to the deckhouse rail trying to shift the huge boom single handed. But to no avail. Finally he loosened the sheet for easier manipulation but with this greater freedom the boom jumped clean out on the next roll and swung heavily back and forth, held by a slack sheet and the topping lifts. I ducked as it threatened to clout me on the head and began to visualise what would happen if either the sheet or one of the topping lifts gave way. There was a muffled, negative reply when I asked Russ if he wanted any help.

Laboriously over the following half hour he brought the boom under control, timing its swing, and finally dropped it back into the crutch. He lashed the sheet firmly and the danger was over.

This incident illustrated how threatening situations could develop from discrepancies in attention to the rigging: the evening before the boom had been inadequately seated and lashed after lowering the mainsail. The crutch in any case had always seemed of bad design. After this, Col's ingenuity came into play, wooden shoulders were added to the metal cradle and a lug to the boom so that it would latch firmly into place.

Russ and I seemed to be fated. Three nights later we were on the middle watch again and the wheel jammed. When we took over *Patanela* before the voyage she had two wheels—one inside the charthouse and another outside at the stern. When the Skipper saw these he had the internal wheel removed and asked that a new one be placed almost amidships. There were a few groans of dismay since this meant we would steer in the open, exposed to all weathers. But the Skipper was right in his judgement when he said that one could not feel the motion and attitude of a sailing ship if one steered too far aft. So the new wheel was bolted to the fore end of the deckhouse and a long shaft connected both wheels with a chain and sprocket at either end. This was never ideal since there was a great deal of play in the for'ard wheel and delay before the ship responded to the helm.

In the heavy seas before Kerguelen, an unexplained thud arose in the stern compartment and though Col asserted that it was vibration from fuel slopping in the unbaffled tanks, there was a lot of talk about trouble with the rudder and that it was coming adrift. There were horrible forebodings about diving work at Kerguelen or worse if the rudder broke down at sea. That night, as Russ and I shivered our way through black, wet winds, the thud from the stern was more than apparent. We walked around the deck, trying to locate its exact position but were no further ahead than before. We only hoped that whatever it was would stay intact until we reached a good anchorage.

The mainsail was down again but *Patanela* slid along nicely at three and a half knots under the other three. The wind was right on the beam and she held the course beautifully. At about 0130 I corrected as she swung slightly and then the wheel stuck firmly, refusing to move more than an inch either way. Fortunately the ship was in the right attitude to the steady wind and she continued on without deviating but we could do nothing if she began to gybe or luff.

Quickly we tried the after wheel. That was stuck also. The rudder! Russ dived below to wake the Skipper and then shoved our emergency handle into the blunt tiller fitting beneath the chart table. I lowered myself into the cray tank and woke Col: 'Quick! The wheel's jammed and God knows what she'll do if we don't get her back under control!' Col stumbled sleepily on deck clutching a torch as the Skipper poked his head over the deckhouse. He shone the beam up and down the shaft, then to the chain, behind the wheel and put his finger on the trouble. Pulling out a dirty handkerchief which had wrapped itself round the chain he said: 'This looks like the trouble. Try her now!' Sheepishly I took hold of the wheel and it moved as freely as before. The only thing Russ and I could seek compliments for was prompt action!

Sailing in heavy weather at night was an exhilarating experience, especially when the seas came from behind and swept past like surf. One could tell the bad waves from the increased hiss and roar so that there was ample warning to take a firmer grip on the wheel and brace oneself for shipped water. The sea was full of plankton and when the deck was washed by the sea, glistening, glowing particles were scattered around our feet like a sprinkling of sea jewels.

Shipped water was now an accepted occurrence and an added advantage of the midships wheel was that the helmsman was protected by the deckhouse should a 'green 'un' come aboard abaft the beam. The Skipper laid his course expertly so that not only was the wind chiefly on our beam, but the prevailing swell hit the ship on either quarter. Not directly aft so that *Patanela* could be pooped, not on the beam when she might broach, nor for'ard when our speed and progress would be seriously impeded. Over the days from 27 to 31 December we descended into the depths of the For-

Reefing the mainsail, Skipper at the wheel

ties, the strong westerly lived up to its reputation and the skies were grey or blown clear by its force.

At sometime on Tuesday, 29 December we crossed the Antarctic Convergence, the meshing point of cold polar water with the sub-tropical. This was at the 45th latitude and the sea temperature dropped from 57°F to 43°F within a few hours*. The air temperature was not much higher. Marine life changed too and on the 30th Grahame hauled red krill for the first time—the chief food of the sperm whale and other sea mammals. On that day I wrote: 'Nearly everybody has now changed into winter woollies and vapour barrier boots. Some of us have even looked hopefully for ice. The weather has deteriorated slowly. At lunch-time yesterday the mains'l was handed and has been down ever since. Even so with a steady gale wind we have maintained 5 knots. The seas have been growing bigger and bigger so that it is an alarming sensation to steer the ship, roller coaster, down the swells and into the troughs. There is a definite pattern in the wave movements and the huge, nasty ones arrive about every ten minutes in groups of three or four.' Two came on board at breakfast. The first one sent Warwick cannoning across the galley to break the port bench and to bash the base of his spine on the large teapot. From the deck this wave was spectacular in that it seemed to collide with others and caused a confusion of broken water and troughs that swirled into a dark, forbidding hole. Immediately after this sea subsided a porpoise popped up on the starboard beam, surfaced a few times apparently not so much in its usual joy of living, but in protest at the coldness and disturbance.

Half an hour later there was an even greater crash of water. It swamped the deckhouse entirely and all those below having breakfast said the scuttles looked like the glass of an aquarium as green water washed past and carried away a lifebelt and jerrican. Fortu-

---

* The effect of the Antarctic Convergence on the temperature and weather in general is illustrated by the following figures. The midwinter sea temperature around Campbell Island (52°S) south of New Zealand, where the Convergence does not extend so far north, averages 45°F. Around Heard Island (53°S) the midsummer sea temperature is about ten degrees lower.

nately its force was broken by the deckhouse and although I was briefly immersed to the chest at the wheel I was not harmed. Its impact had been so powerful below that John rushed up a few moments later to see if I was still safe.

On that day there was no washing up on deck and everyone stayed below unless on watch. But the call of nature could not be denied and there was fierce competition to see who could pick a spell when it was safe to lower trousers and sit on the bulwarks. Col and I were unlucky and we received our crossing the line (i.e. Convergence) baptism. We thought we had timed the waves so that we would fit in between the groups of big 'uns. But we were the centre of much hilarity when we returned cursing to the galley, trousers sopping wet after a wave had jumped the rail and dunked us at the crucial moment.

With the cold, rum came into favour and at night we crept down quietly into the galley to take a tot before going to bed. By that time, also, we had an established club hour when most of us congregated in the charthouse before the evening meal to partake of beer and nuts as an aperitif. We had enough supplies for one bottle each but a warm atmosphere was created, and bonhomie at the only time of day when we were all together. Empties were thrown over the stern and we said that any rescue ship could find us easily by following the line of empty Miller beer bottles. Though, as Russ remarked, there seemed nothing more incongruous in the middle of the Southern Ocean than half a dozen beer bottles floating away in the vast swell.

Ed, in his position as meteorologist, claimed that the waves were no more than twelve feet high. Ever mindful of salty sea stories about the Forties and thirty-foot waves we shuddered at the thought of one that size hitting the ship. On watch we hung to the deckhouse rail and measured each one with our eyes as it came up astern. Since Ed was largely below decks we were sure he missed the bigger ones ('definitely twenty feet Ed!'). As they reared up, we ducked as they seemed sure to crash on to the stern, only to relax when the ship lifted over them and the crests raced past bearing her along.

Only on deck did one realise the true extent of the sea and weather. In the insulated galley playing chess, or in one's bunk safely wrapped in blankets, there was steady movement, little noise and our relaxation was only broken by the freak waves which thumped the sides of the ship and caused her to stagger. Even though our ship was small we had two distinct worlds aboard: the dark warmth and stillness below and the cold, windy storm above. These, with the alternate night and day watches gave us an atmosphere of stark contrast, a picture of black and white. I had never encountered a life more vivid than this. With no alternative one had to climb into the weather at the prescribed time, whether it was good or bad, away from the cosy security of bed. At times one would go off watch, weary to the bone, water streaming down one's foul-weather suit as another gale built up in the evil wrack of a feeble dawn. Then, rising at noon for lunch, one was astounded on swinging open the fo'c'sle hatch, to find brilliant sunshine in a wind-blown sky, dry decks and Antony in shirt sleeves once more.

But shirt sleeves rapidly disappeared beneath sweaters and there was no time now that we could forego our waterproof parkas, and even trousers, when going up on deck. Our log entries were models of modesty and John's 'Cloudy and cool' at 2000 on 30 December meant stiff, frozen fingers and a leaden sky as the days were at their longest in slow, grim sunsets. The southern summer was reaching its height and the next two months would provide the best time for activity on the cold islands to the south. The position on the chart showed that we were on the final curving run to Kerguelen. The Skipper estimated New Year's Day for our landfall but unforeseen bad weather or thick fogs which were common around the island could delay us for days. The possible winners of the Heard sighting sweep were reduced already and Mal and the Skipper with 2 and 3 January were no longer in the running.

On 29 and 30 December clumps of kelp floated past from the south to corroborate the Skipper's sights and birds increased in number as we approached their home. It was just as well that we were near Kerguelen since our main water tank suddenly ran dry. Warwick's careful calculations of water consumption offered no explanation since we had been told that it held 240 gallons. Then we remembered the hot water tank which had been removed in Sydney and guessed that its capacity had been included in the total. Fortunately we had three large drums of water on deck, carried for such an emergency, though it was an awkward job to climb on deck with a jerrican and pump them out.

Living conditions grew progressively worse as the high winds persisted and the piles of wet clothing increased with no opportunity for drying. Sleep became a kind of dying in damp blankets after an exhausting watch. Now we could not read in our bunks. Col announced that while the engine was not running we had to conserve electricity and avoid draining the batteries which must be kept at a high level for the radio and restarting the engine, which could not be cranked by hand. The small generating engine was only powerful enough to provide extra power for two lights and to maintain the freezing level in the refrigerator. Without the engine the elaborate hot air system was inoperative also. I wrote sardonically in my diary that under the difficult cold conditions when we needed them most, we had neither light nor heat.

Grahame summed up the situation well in a description of a morning in the galley: 'What with me mending the set, Ed washing up, the Skipper trying to read a book, Warwick standing about in assorted painful attitudes with his sore back and Col periodically emerging from the engine room with grease gun, oilcan and so on— and the galley floor a greasy flood, the ship rolling merrily—life was rather cramped and sordid.' There was still room for fun and celebration. We could not allow New Year's Eve to pass without some traditional recognition. It was Saturday night—ding night—but a proposed party fizzled under the exigencies of watches and it was left to the midnight watchkeepers to see in the New Year. Russ and I were on from 2000 until midnight, followed by the Skipper with John and Mal so that half the crew would be on deck. Appropriately John was awake for, as the youngest member, he circled the deckhouse sounding sixteen bells with the little dinner bell. We sang *Auld Lang Syne* and persuaded the Skipper to drink a capful of Scotch, breaking the unwritten rule of no drinking before a watch. So it was 1965 and we wondered if its first three months would support the strength of our resolutions.

Landfall at Kerguelen

It was a hectic New Year's night. At midnight the sound of John's bell was carried away by a force six wind and we were running under jib only at two and a half knots. The Skipper entered in the log at the end of his middle watch: '0400; 5571; Course S; Wind WSW; Barometer 29.75; Two rain squalls. Hoisted foresail and staysail. Mainsail at 0400.' So we moved into the New Year's first light under all plain sail. The barometer rose steadily and the day developed into fine sailing weather with a fair measure of sun as the wind veered round to the south and blew away the clouds. I rose for breakfast, bleary eyed but with a sense of excitement as more kelp drifted past the ship and there was the prospect of seeing our first land for five weeks. The Skipper was on deck quickly at the sun's first positive appearance and took a careful sight. Soon after the start of our watch he came up and told me to change course to south by east—a fine alteration of the long curve we had followed since leaving the 40th parallel.

The ship's routine followed that familiar to every day; but as I held the wheel I was particularly careful to hold the exact course and for the two hours between 0800 and 1000 I stared ahead, straining my eyes to see through the pall of white cloud that mantled the horizon. Suddenly a little red lacquered head popped up from the lowering waves and disappeared just as quickly. A moment later I shouted out to the others as the penguin reappeared, alternately swerving through the water like a porpoise and then resting to regard the ship, looking like a low-slung duck.

At 1000 my watch was rewarded. Dimly off the starboard bow a dark shape appeared in the cloud. After ten minutes of watching it had not changed configuration or colour and excitedly I waved to the Skipper in the charthouse and pointed ahead. Antony would not believe me at first but half an hour later there was no doubt. It was an island, one of the Îles Nuageuses, the north-western outliers of the Kerguelen archipelago. Our immediate reaction was one of admiration—for the Skipper's navigation. After five weeks of sailing across an ocean without a ship or island, with no radio or radar aids, he had brought us safely into Kerguelen at exactly the prescribed point. We could not have had a better New Year's present.

The echo sounder read off ninety fathoms as we sailed over the archipelago sea shelf and new species of birds appeared in greater numbers. Shags swept past, low over the masts with their frantic beat of wings and long, craning necks. The course was changed again to south-south-east as more islands came into sharper outline. At midday, twenty miles from land, the wind dropped right away and we handed all sail to start the main engine for the first time since Christmas Day. It became overcast and warm, the swell slowly diminished and at seven knots we moved quickly to reach a secure anchorage before nightfall. It was a great joy to see land again and for those who had been to the sub-Antarctic before—the Skipper, Warwick, Grahame and Ed—it was a nostalgic return to a fascinating world.

Our feeling at the landfall, and at the success of our first objective of reaching the sub-Antarctic in a sailing schooner, was well described by Grahame. 'Essentially the surprise and pleasure, and no doubt salutary instruction, is at this renewed demonstration that, if one will only dare, one can actually do the most unlikely things that may come into one's head. For the hesitant, the diffident, and the many amateurs overawed by the experts of this world, this demonstration can't be made too often. So Warwick's concept of the purpose of this trip gains in strength as we proceed.'

5

ÇA VA?

Early in the afternoon we passed a high rock which the French called Îlot du Rendezvous. But Captain Cook originally named it Bligh's Cap after his mate who achieved such notoriety later in the mutiny on the *Bounty*. The islands had been discovered by the French navigator Yves Joseph de Kerguelen-Trémarec in February 1772. To quote from *The Antarctic Pilot*: 'Thinking that he had discovered the great southern continent he hurried back to France and in the next year he was dispatched with three vessels, *Rolland*, *L'Oiseau* and *Dauphine*, to explore the continent. He reached Îles de Kerguelen again on 14th December 1773, but though he remained over a month in the vicinity he himself never landed.' A circumnavigation of the islands soon revealed his mistake and in despair he returned to France, calling them Îles Desolation.

Cook was the second navigator to reach Kerguelen, on his celebrated third voyage in 1776. He arrived on Christmas Eve at the same point we approached and anchored at the bottom of Baie de l'Oiseau which is now known at Port Christmas. The Skipper considered this for our anchorage but thought it too exposed and chose instead a small bay off a deep fiord which ran into the island about ten miles further down the coast. Soon we passed the Îles Nuageuses which rose to 1500 feet, their summits made attractive by saucer-shaped clouds. In the channel between them and the main island were thousands of prions and pintados wheeling and fluttering over the sea like the flakes of a snowstorm. Occasionally penguins cavorted past and a strong wind picked up from the south-west, roaring past the great cliffs and towers of Kerguelen's ferocious west coast.

We reached Cap d'Estaing and found the steep boulder slopes beneath crowded with penguins. Rounding the cape we motored across the entrance of Baie de l'Oiseau, thankful that we had not chosen Port Christmas on seeing a cluster of black clouds at the head. On the southern side of the Baie was a feature known as Pointe de l'Arche, two fine rock pillars with a debris of rock between where their bridge had collapsed since they were first discovered. We were all on deck, crowding the rails and the ratlines as we watched each new feature come into view, and rested our eyes on the green grass that adorned the gentler slopes of the headlands. We looked out for the entrance to our fiord, Baie de Recques, and were particularly anxious to ascertain the position of the huge beds of kelp that adorn the island's coast. A fouled propeller and we might be stuck on a dangerous point for the night. Long streamers of the weed began to appear so that Antony or I stayed up in the for'ard ratlines and shouted warnings to the helmsman so that he could deviate.

I pulled down my insect nets for examination then paused as the engine seemed to change its note. Above the heavy rumble and pound of the powerful engine there was an unfamiliar whine. In astonishment we looked up as a glittering shape swept past the masts. It circled and came back and Russ exclaimed that it was a jet 'Alouette' helicopter of the French Air Force. Excitedly we waved as the small helicopter zoomed past and Antony quickly pulled out the red ensign to establish our nationality. There was no doubt that the aircraft was French as it was flown with the verve and elan that might be expected of them and we identified the red, white and blue roundels of the Armée de l'Air. There were six men jammed into the perspex bubble at the nose and they gave friendly waves, obviously as surprised to see us as we were to see them. After a few minutes of circling the helicopter levelled off and headed for the black clouds of Port Christmas.

We were a little anxious about this unusual meeting. The main French base, Port aux Francais, lay sixty or seventy miles away at the southern end of the island and we had not expected to meet its personnel until *Patanela* returned from Heard. Although the Antarctic division in Paris knew of and authorised our visit they had no idea

Watering and testing equipment at L'Anse du Jardin, Kerguelen

of the date of our arrival and we had not been able to contact the base by radio. Our sudden, unobtrusive arrival seemed discourteous at least.

Especially since the French had asked that we make no land expeditions on Kerguelen and it might appear that we were going to make a sneaky attempt on their unclimbed Mt Ross, the highest peak on the island. Not knowing quite what to do next, or where the helicopter had come from, we continued on as a bitter wind swept through the shrouds, and turned into Baie de Recques.

A wide bed of kelp guarded the entrance but we safely rounded this and took in the log line. On watch, I steered the ship down the fiord, past the steep, horizontal layers of rock that rose up in cliffs to make table top hills. The nasty sou'wester blew the freezing wave tops into my face and constantly the shags whirred round and round *Patanela*, working hard to fly into the strong wind, necks stretched out, their heads cocked or turned to observe us. On the port hand, five miles down the fiord, we picked up the entrance to the anchorage and at 1900 the Skipper took the wheel for final manoeuvring. The side bay was called Anse du Jardin and when we passed through we saw the reason for its title in the attractive terraces that rose from the water to the hills; the clumps of azorella, grass and moss decorated with brown boulders, streams, waterfalls and pools. The southern end of the bay was closed by aptly named Mont Lignite and a square ridge that rose to 1500 feet with patches of drifted snow. The water was deep and clear with little kelp and since the shore fell steeply we were able to anchor close in at the south-west corner.

The anchor rattled down, the engine stopped and for the first time in five weeks we enjoyed an aura of peace and quiet. We were sheltered from the wind, the sky was crystal clear and over the gentle ripples on the Anse the only sounds were the steady drum of a waterfall, the shrill cry of a tern and the distant chatter of penguins. It was strange as conversation carried clearly throughout the ship. From the foc's'le bunk there was a soft lap of water near my head and occasional laughter floating down the ventilation pipe.

Then I thought delightedly: 'We'll be able to sleep right through the night!' But before sleep, and two days' work, came our long-delayed Christmas-New Year's party. With calm anchorage and a still, cold night we had no better opportunity. Balloons, hats, streamers and paper bugles made a sudden mysterious appearance and repartee was brilliant from the start. We opened a big, green goodies tin that Russ's mother had given us and found it full of nuts and cakes.

Warwick served up a huge meal—his pièce de résistance we called it as French phrases became popular. Ed prepared a menu which read:

NEW YEAR's DAY MENU

The *Patanela* Puddin' Shoppe

Fruit Juice

Les Petits Deecox

Receiver Soup

Rosbif and the lot

Christmas Pud and Wow! Sauce

Bikkies and Cheese

Coffee and Marzipan

Cigars and Liqueurs

Gluewine

…and at the bottom were two verses extracted from

The Magic Pudding:

> We've Puddin' here a treat
> We've puddin' here galore
> Do not decline to stay and dine
> Our puddin' you'll adore.

> Our pudding, we repeat,
> You really cannot beat,
> And here we are its owners three
> Who graciously entreat
> You'll be at our request
> The Puddin' owners' guest.

We found that ten was a crowd in the galley after the accustomed nine and one at the wheel. Despite this, Mal brought out his movie camera, floodlights were set up and he filmed the proceedings from cramped positions on the bunks. We sang songs, retold jokes and the small feathered inhabitants of the bay must have opened their eyes slowly and suspiciously at the muffled noise floating over the water.

We woke next morning to begin work under a plan that was carefully worked out some days before. At breakfast we had a final briefing and, as we made our way to it, Russ and I remarked that the eastern shore of the Anse appeared strangely close. A few minutes later the Skipper thought the same and roused us out on deck when he realised that the anchor had dragged. Fortunately the weather had been fine or we might have found ourselves beached on a rocky shore in the early hours of the morning. We raised the anchor and motored back to our old position with the Skipper's firm decision that on the remaining two nights we would institute anchor watches.

In the eastern shallows of the Anse was a grim reminder that we should not take the island too lightly. Half buried in sand lay a small wooden ship which we ascertained had been a French sailing schooner about the size of *Patanela*. It had been wrecked some fifty years before so that Colin looked with interest at the remains of a primitive single-cylinder diesel engine. Some of the other parts were labelled *Renard St Malo* (in Brittany) and its mainmast had been in a tabernacle, capable of being lowered for canal work. We learned later that Kerguelen was well endowed with wrecks, especially on the south and west coasts. Sealers and whalers had flocked to the island when they heard of its richness at the middle of last century, and the French told us that up to 400 ships and whaling boats at a time had been anchored in its bays. Incredible as it seemed, the fiords like Baie de Recques had been teeming with whales, the beaches overflowing with elephant and fur seals. But the former had gone and the seals represented only a fraction of their former number.

There was a great deal of work to do in our final preparations for Heard Island. The main tasks for the first day, Saturday 2 January, were refuelling and food packing. The cray tank was torn apart. Forty-four gallon drums of diesel were pumped dry to fill up the main tanks and the drums in the engine-room wings, and then the empty drums had to be hauled out, punctured and dumped over the side so that room could be made for better sleeping accommodation. John dived into all the holes and corners, dragged out food and began packing it in polythene bags. Ed checked the shore-to-ship radios, Grahame pulled out the climbing and camping gear while Russ prepared to take the Zodiac ashore for repairs. I had the day for insect collecting. As I helped Russ to launch the Zodiac at 1000 the ship had regained the look of disorganisation which had been its main feature in Sydney. Boxes of food, pump lines, paddles and bedding smothered the decks and halyards tumbled down as the Skipper and Antony prepared to reverse them through the blocks.

Just as we lowered an outboard motor into the Zodiac we heard a distant, combined chatter and whine and looked up to see the Alouette helicopter flying low over the eastern hills of the bay. It flew a straight course for a while then, obviously sighting our small yellow hull, it banked sharply and flew across the water. It circled the ship quickly then abruptly came to a halt as it hovered over the shore a

Port Christmas, Kerguelen *(Grahame Budd)*

hundred yards away. The whine and roar of the turbojet was now deafening as it carefully dropped and with precision touched down with its skids on a mossy bluff directly above the water. The rotors jerked to a stop and four men climbed out, colourful in flying suits and red lifejackets, and we self-consciously called out Bonjour! to their greetings.

Russ and I went ashore to bring them on board and Mal's camera whirred as I stepped ashore to shake hands, promptly slipped on a slimy rock and fell into the arms of a waiting Frenchman. We took all of them back to the ship and there learned that they were from a survey base established at Port Christmas. There was the pilot and engineer of the helicopter, the senior geologist and his assistant.

They told us that two Alouettes were operating from the base which had been established only a week before. Several surveyors, geologists and biologists were being flown over the island by personnel of the French army in a programme aimed at detailed mapping and survey. There was much conviviality as we brought whisky out and Antony astounded us with his fluent French. They showed great reverence for the Skipper after his voyage there in 1960 and announced that on their new maps a peak in the Crozet Islands was named Mont du Mischief after his ship and a glacier on Kerguelen, Glacier Tilman. They had work to do, we had work to do but they left only after extracting a promise that we would visit their base before we departed. Then they took off and roared away over the bare, inhospitable hills.

Russ deflated the Zodiac on the beach so that it resembled a small, flabby whale and spent the whole day patching and sealing the worn-out surface with Neoprene. Its patchy appearance did not generate much confidence in its ability as a rescue craft and we were thankful that the big USR was in fine condition. I collected many insects near the beach and then climbed higher over the sparsely-vegetated slopes, trying new localities and plants. Apart from the azorella and tussock there were other grasses, moss and a plant known as Kerguelen Cabbage. Looking like a cross between a cabbage and a seedy brussels sprout it was a useful anti-scorbutic that the old sailors had used and when eaten raw tasted remarkably like water cress.

There should have been whole fields of this plant but the depredations of rabbits and sheep introduced by the French had seriously affected its growth and I could find only isolated clumps. The denuded vegetation affected insect life too and the higher I climbed the less I found.

I climbed up past an impressive waterfall and the wind rocked me on my heels when it shot in bursts through a gap in the hills. At the limit of my climb I leaned into its blast and looked out over the Anse. The ship looked tiny and forlorn in a wide landscape of flat-topped hills, swampy margins littered with tarns and, beyond, the congealed waters of the Baie and the Southern Ocean. In its barren silence with no sign of man save *Patanela*, the island stirred a strong feeling of history in me. It was changed little since its first discovery, and I could imagine easily Cook's square-rigged Resolution sailing slowly through the islets off Port Christmas. I was brought back to the present when I returned to the shore at dusk. Russ and I prepared to launch the Zodiac but stopped as both Alouettes spun out of the valley at the head of the Anse and skimmed towards the ship. Their navigation lights were on, flashing red, white and green and in a scintillating display they weaved and manoeuvred round the ship like glittering Christmas trees.

During our stay it was very plain how tame the birds were from a lack of predators and no molestation by man. Though we saw only one Gentoo penguin in the Anse there were many shags, skuas, terns, ducks and storm petrels although we did not discover any nests. The shags often flew past the ship, waddled on the bluffs or paddled near the shore, upending suddenly to catch fish. The terns were the most graceful and delicate, flying daintily over the littoral, heads cocking and dipping to watch for fish, hovering in the strong wind if there were signs of food, then dropping into the water until half submerged to catch their prey. They evinced a strong dislike for the skuas—scavengers to the extent of raiding nests—and the air was filled with the terns' shrill cries as a pair swooped down and dive bombed the dark-brown bogey men. We saw two ducks, small, delightful, grey pintails which hunted for food amongst the shore rocks at our feet. Then at night the air was filled with a strange croaking which we found was a medley of seal and penguin calls filtering through the crags.

On Sunday we practised loading and manoeuvring the USR. It poured with rain all day and violent katabatic winds swept down from the hills, once rocking *Patanela* to the gunwales. Under Grahame's expert supervision, the packs, tent bags and kerosene drums were well lashed into the assault craft. With a sail cover to protect the loads against rain, Russ drove it out over the choppy bay while Grahame, Mal, John and I clung to the ropes with paddles. It was the last trial we could make with the USR before reaching Heard.

Grahame, with his past experience, was eager to ascertain the craft's manoeuvrability and stability with a load. We went on as far as rough water near the entrance to the Anse where crosswinds met and stirred up the waves. Russ turned the boat backwards and forwards, round and round, sharply and gently and we returned confident that it would not capsize—at least not on the open sea.

Watering was accomplished by driving the USR in the mouth of a large stream and filling it with a bucket. Then it was driven back and the water pumped over the side into the main tank. Fuelling was finished and there was room to fit extra bunks in the cray tank. Partly using timber salvaged from the French wreck, bunks were hammered in fore and aft so that the four non-smokers had full sleeping room for the first time on the voyage. Sleeping across the ship had its disadvantages. Antony and Colin who drew these positions preferred sleeping head up as the ship heeled over on tack. But sometimes in the middle of the night when the Skipper ordered the ship brought about not only the booms but the two of them were forced to come about in the dark, confined spaces.

Despite the pouring rain, Grahame, Ed and I erected all the tents on the beach to fasten new guys. The Pyramid and Bechervaise tents were heavy and sturdy, well fitted for the atrocious weather on Heard but the others did not come up to our expectations. There was one tent erected by pumping air into its four rubberised corners. Though it might have been satisfactory on a milder scene, the wind buckled the green sides and it flopped down repeatedly so that we named it, ironically, the Kerguelen Cabbage.

On Monday we woke to a perfect morning. During anchor watch at dawn, the sharp, crystal air reminded me of the start of a climbing day in the Southern Alps. By 0900 it was so warm that we stripped off sweaters and worked in shirt sleeves. We put everything back in place, the Heard Island loads handy in the cray tank and the tents were dried out. Mal paddled to the eastern shore in a little two-man dinghy for movie photography but the Skipper warned him that we would leave at ten sharp. He came back just in time as we brought in the anchor and at 1300 revs we motored out into the placid fiord. It was a magnificent day of still sunshine that hardly seemed credible in the wild wastes of the sub-Antarctic. The birds took advantage of the calm conditions and littered the sea in feeding. The shags, with a still-insatiable curiosity, followed us in scores and as *Patanela*'s bows parted the sea, blue for the first time in many days, the Sooty albatrosses, Wanderers, penguins, pintados and skuas flew or swam away in alarm.

In two hours we retraced our course and rounded Pointe de l'Arche into Baie de l'Oiseau. To our left a huge rock called Mont Havergal reared over the Port Christmas cove and the vegetation steamed dry so fiercely in the powerful sun that we mistook the clouds for hot springs. In 1840 Sir James Clark Ross's famous Antarctic expedition in the *Erebus* and *Terror* had spent some time at Kerguelen and, on the level beach of fine, dark sand ahead, he had erected astronomical and magnetic observatories. First Cook, then Ross and now the French. Far above the beach we picked out two red huts and two tents. Ed swung the lead as we motored smoothly to a halt one hundred yards from the shore, and a red smoke bomb exploded in greeting. We began to inflate the USR. Before we could finish, two Frenchmen paddled out on a raft made from 44-gallon drums, crate sides and paddles of four by two. It was hard work to propel the raft on a straight course but they finally made it and were enthusiastically hauled aboard. It was made especially for our benefit, and Antony and John went back with it while we launched the USR.

The Alouettes were parked a few yards from the water and next to them we looked in astonishment at trestle tables with cloths, dishes of nuts and crisps, bottles of wine, Scotch, Cognac, West Indies rum and Anis. There was fresh bread, as crisp and wholesome as only the French can bake it, and from the huts drifted the aroma of cooking in wine. The skuas and sheathbills sensed a feed afoot and hovered fearlessly round the tables. We were shown the huts with utmost courtesy and on one a signpost had been painted. It gave the mileages of Paris, Sydney, Port aux Francais and on one side was inscribed *Heard Island 300 miles—20 minutes by jet, three months from Sydney by Patanela. Ça va?* Their stores tent was stacked with good food and supported by huge barrels of *vin rouge*. They told us that one barrel was sufficient for the ten men for one week. The leader of the party shrugged and said: 'Without wine a Frenchman will not work.' Each week they made a special flight to Port aux Francais for fresh victuals but sometimes earlier if the wine ran out. Some of the Frenchmen spoke English, a few of us stammered in French and the gaps were filled with gestures. First we were given a drink of Scotch or Anis and they looked in amazement as we all chose the latter for a change.

But the Skipper made a mistake and muttered next to me: 'Tastes like damned aniseed balls.' Then came fresh, plump rabbit cooked in wine, glass after glass of red wine that was called Louzoù—a Breton word for medicine. It certainly cured any low spirits and soon, in the astonishing hot sun, the luncheon developed into a zestful party. The army NCOs at our right taunted the skuas with meat tied to a string and after much interplay and flapping of wings, caught one with the bait halfway down its gullet. To our alarm Scotch, brandy and anis was poured down the poor bird's throat and it was released. The alcohol went straight to its legs and as it reeled and staggered down the beach, the other skuas looked on in suspicion, sensing a cannibalistic meal. To save the bird from attack by its mates we shooed it into the air and it flew away with the right wing permanently dipped.

The party slowly became hilarious and reached its climax when Grahame expressed unbridled enthusiasm for Louzoù. The Frenchmen challenged him to drink it nonstop from the large plastic jerrican and without more ado he placed a funnel in his mouth and leaned back. They poured until the wine ran down his chin and neck and he could take no more. Then he produced his daughter's recorder, jumped on his seat and exhorted us all to join in the *Marseillaise*. As Grahame rocked unsteadily from side to side, piping out the thin notes, we sang lustily but the return anthem of *God Save the Queen* sounded horribly flat and ponderous.

The Skipper thought it was about time we left before the situation grew out of hand. We made regretful au revoirs, took signed photographs of King Penguins and addresses in Paris. Grahame continued playing, fell flat on his back for no apparent reason and the French carried him aboard the USR with roars of laughter while he gave the Churchillian V sign ('It seemed like a good idea at the time'). John and I caught a Gentoo penguin with a rugby tackle then tossed it in the sea to watch it speed away in the clear water like a startled torpedo. We were given gifts of French food, jerricans of wine and we towed the drum raft back to the ship with some of the research workers who wished to see below.

We timed our departure exactly. Over the low hills to the west, grey clouds appeared and by the time we hoisted sail, damp fog dogged the Baie. We tried to make an impressive departure but our co-ordination seemed strangely lacking, Grahame was still eager to celebrate and we made slow progress towards the open sea. Some of the Frenchmen lined the shore and as Very lights were fired, *Auld Lang Syne*, sung in French, reached us faintly over the water. An Alouette took off, buzzed *Patanela*, and then we were enveloped in a cold curtain of fog.

It was the evening of 4 January. As the sails flapped in windless, misty conditions we knew that there were no more than 350 miles left. Three days, if nothing went wrong. The foresail gaff lacing broke, and we had trouble with a mainsail halyard so that it was an hour or two before the sails were set. We settled back into regular watches and the Skipper laid a firm course of south-east by east. It was an anxious night as we groped in the fog, hoping that the compass read truly and we were moving clear of the Îles Leygues and their foul ground of kelp. The wind was negligible and over the first sixteen hours we covered only twenty-seven miles. It would take a long time to reach Heard at this rate.

At 1110 on 5 January the Skipper judged we were clear of Îles

Partying with the French at Port Christmas

Leygues and altered our course to south-south-west so that we would clear Cap Digby, Kerguelen's easternmost point on the Presqu'île Courbet. The wind increased after noon and by the first dog the cloud had lifted to allow us occasional glimpses of snow-drifts and mountains off the starboard beam. The contrary weather changed rapidly and at 1810 we were forced to hand the mainsail when the wind reached gale force, and *Patanela* knocked along at eight knots.

Then we rounded Cap Digby. It created an effective lee, cut away the wind entirely and we ghosted in a calm sea under a clear sky and settled sunset. A crescent moon hung over the low hills and little volcanic cones dotted the surroundings of Baie du Morbihan where Port aux Francais lay. For the first time in days we played music on the tape recorder and Eine Kleine Nachtmusik proved a fitting accompaniment as we gently sailed on the last lap with Kerguelen dropping into the night.

Patanela seemed primed like a gun, ready to go off when she found her target. The first climax of the expedition was near—landing, and with Warwick's penchant for military planning it appeared at times that we were making a sneak raid on an enemy bastion: *Patanela* running quickly into the Fifties to drop us then scampering away to safer latitudes until it was ripe to return and take us away for good. There was tension aboard as we passed 50°S and the relative security of Kerguelen. There was nothing ahead save Antarctica, a base of Australians 1200 miles away, and in between the pinprick of ice gathered in folds of the worst sea known to man. We and *Patanela* had come through well to that point but now we ventured to a wild realm where the ship and its crew would be tested to the utmost. Was the landing really feasible or would we be blown past it—not even find Heard—as the Skipper had warned in Albany? The ship was in full working order, fuelled, wa-tered, repaired, spick and span, streamlined, as it were, for the main op-eration. The rudder was pronounced in good order by Col and he had fixed an extra stanchion in the galley to stop Warwick careering from one side to the other when cooking. But we had not fixed any extra slats to the shelves over the stove. A huge tin of Marmite slid relentlessly backwards and forwards along the top shelf but it did not fall out until no-one was looking when it did its best to knock out Russ.

There was also a danger seat that we could not alter. This was on the port side of the galley table at the fore corner. The wooden rim was broken at the corners to facilitate cleaning but these provided good gutter spouts and it became established practice to wear waterproof trousers if unlucky enough to draw one of those positions. Especially on the port side where tea was poured—sometimes into Col's lap.

Colin suffered long from the jibes that unmechanically-minded members cast on his engine room. He was always at pains to explain any mechanical contrivance or chemical reaction in profound detail, and we often goaded him with puns and a humorous analysis of his latest invention. Warwick in particular took hold of the technical jargon with glee and when Col described the working of a jury rudder with scientific exactness and appropriate gestures, Warwick suggested that it would be better 'if we tied a bowline on the bobstay, ran the mizzen along the pintle and spliced the mainmast with a luff on the for'ard marlin'. Never dismayed, Col appeared, two days from Heard, with his newest piece of homemade protective clothing.

Basically it was a padded waistcoat made from calico stuffed with foam plastic and tied with strings at the front. Of course its use went further and it could be spread out as a hip mattress for use in a snow cave. White and bulky, it looked as though it had been crossed with a mongrel kitchen apron. Underneath he wore a black jersey and black trousers and a balaclava on his head that looked like a yellow bonnet. He was the image of a belle of St Trinian's and his willpower was finally broken when he received such rude remarks as: 'Ow yer goin' luv?' and 'Crikey! Yer get some real old bats on this bus!' It was never seen again.

Warwick continued to stoke us with heavy, fatty food and by 7 January we were all about a stone heavier than when we left Albany. We never became tired of food with the invigorating climate and the endless variety. But there was one type of vegetarian meat that we could not stomach, particularly Colin and me. We had subsisted on the food in New Guinea in 1961 during a period when I lost a stone and Colin two, so that we had an ingrained aversion. Later we all offered comments and criticism of all the products we used on the expedition for the manufacturers' information. I called the meat a 'good emergency ration' but when Warwick asked for one good sentence describing each item, Col remarked: 'I'd like to give that meat one good sentence—a hundred lashes!'

The middle watch again on 6 January and at 0400 I wrote in the log: '5772; Course SSW; Wind SW × W; Barometer 29.5; Clear, cold; moderate seas. Strong southerly until 0245 when wind dropped and veered. First light 0130.' Last light was in the order of 2300 so that now we endured a maximum of three hours total darkness. There was plenty of light for activities at Heard and then I grimaced on realising that it also meant long, hard working days. Nevertheless, excitement rose during that day because Kerguelen was now well behind. The log and chart told that 150 miles were all that remained if our course and position were true—which none doubted with the Skipper's quiet confidence. His sight on the sixth showed us at 50°43'S and 71°15'E. The top peninsula of Heard lay across 53°S, and 73°30'E ran right down the centre. All sorts of calculations ran through our minds. Since Big Ben was 9000 feet high we should see it from at least 60 miles away on a clear day. That meant we should sight it, with luck, only 90 miles further on! At the speed we were going, about five knots, that meant another eighteen hours. Some quick mental arithmetic and the general prediction was that we would sight Heard on the morning of the seventh. But the Skipper made no comment.

The weather was almost moderate after the Forties. The seas were not as high, the wind steady but not violent and there were even belts of sunshine to relieve the increasing cold. It seemed remarkably tame and I began to suspect the stories we had heard from Warwick and Grahame about the Heard climate. At midnight it was overcast but by breakfast on the seventh the sky was clear again and Grahame called out that penguins were swimming past. A few eyes met but excitement was well controlled. I was constantly keyed up, could concentrate on no task, as the island came nearer and nearer hidden by a thick pall of cloud on the horizon. My heart leaped when I tore it away in imagination and pictured the mass beyond.

Russ and I had the forenoon watch and I wondered if again I would be the one to sight land. But at noon I could only report that the sky was overcast, the sea still moderate, the wind still steady and that we came about on a new tack. Just before lunch the Skipper came on deck, braced himself between the deckhouse and bulwarks and with pipe still in his mouth squinted through the sextant at a brief flash of sun. Ruler, pencil, glasses, plotting chart, tables, log, time, dead reckoning, mathematics, eye at the sea, sixth sense and he wrote 52°51′S, 71°40′E. He seemed a bit concerned since his sight did not tally with the log reading. The line showed that we had covered 112 miles since the previous noon but the sight showed that we were a further dozen miles on—only some ten miles north of the island. But we had made little leeway and were about eighty to ninety miles west! The wind came from the north-east, of all directions, and our true course was near enough to east. The Skipper grinned and removed his pipe: 'Looks like we'll have to sail back to the island if we don't watch out.'

Heard Island first made its appearance in the guise of lenticular clouds rising through the low mass of horizon fog. Mal, at the wheel, stared for fully half an hour until he brought himself to believe that something solid lay beneath them. The Skipper said he could not see a thing and the vague presence only became acceptable as an island when the South Barrier ridge began to sharpen the cloud. The great, white mass slowly hardened in shape, aloof above the querulous mist and wind snapping at its feet, a shrug of cold shoulders in the sky.

Although the island became clear, the sky was dominated by wide, windswept curves of whipped-cream cloud. There was high cloud, low cloud, thin and wispy, thick and black, grey and white; each giving the short, steep seas a different shade—once sharp, brilliant jade green, later insipid grey. We were never sure what the sky would present next and, as the evening approached, we grew anxious.

Directly in our path, somewhere due west of Heard, lay the McDonald Islands: a small group little more than vicious rocks and an ideal trap for unwary ships. At about 1600 they appeared, sharp and warning, appearing and then disappearing like the Cheshire Cat. We climbed the ratlines, stared from the bows, because they were just a few miles away, dead ahead.

We were favoured, for the low cloud lifted and we sailed past the McDonalds within two cables' length. It was advertised that one of the expedition's objectives was to make the first-ever landing on the McDonalds and raise the Australian flag. One look at the precipitous, volcanic cliffs with pounding surf and our enthusiasm waned dramatically. The main islet a mile long rose to nearly 700 feet, cindery, fissured with a meagre skin of grass on its gentler slopes. But the most spectacular was Needle Island, a spire rising sheer from the water for 400 feet. Here we reefed the mainsail among seas troubled by conflicting currents, forsaken even by the birds.

Twenty miles away, Heard Island appeared flat and white as the sun disappeared, nothing to alleviate its ghostly configuration against a white sky, its beaches and unglaciated cliffs hidden by spume and surf. It was monumental. From an empty sea it swept up in regular curves to a height unbelievable for its thirteen miles diameter—1600 feet higher than any point in Australia. Slightly to the left in our view was the symmetrical cone of Mawson's Peak, the summit we had come 6000 miles to attain. Below, the glaciers tumbled in unbroken lines to the sea. The cliffs of the main crater, Big Ben, were decorated with bulges and terraces of ice equal to any in the world; but thankfully we saw breaks, lines of least resistance, whereby we might reach their crest.

I shuddered as Grahame said the water temperature was 35°F and the air temperature little more. There was snow in the air as Big Ben cast a huge, frozen shadow on the sea. Only the birds thrived as we stamped round the deck to keep warm, anxious to observe every detail of the icy coastline. Warwick seemed unconcerned, a study of stiff upper lip. Grahame repressed the urge to talk too much but was eager always to answer questions about the island he knew so well.

The Skipper was preoccupied about the night as we closed with the south coast, John was silent with shining eyes, Mal was excited as a schoolboy, Antony conferred with the Skipper on watches, Ed and Russ exchanged views on the sub-Antarctic and Col pottered in the engine room. I took a lot of photographs and suddenly realised that I had won the sweep.

6

CAPSIZE

T HE SKIPPER STAYED ON DECK as we sailed till midnight and hove to a few miles off Long Beach. The next morning I went on watch at 0400 to find a north-west gale blowing, the ship moving slowly to the east under foresail. To the west pitchy black cloud bellied over the sea though the island between Cape Arkona (see map) and Spit Point, up to about 5000 feet, was generally clear. Everywhere, everywhere there were birds. Prions, pintados, storm petrels all in great numbers with giant petrels and albatrosses joining in. Macaroni penguins appeared, diving and swimming underwater like porpoises, occasionally popping up their comical heads to take a quick, astonished look.

At 0715 the wind dropped suddenly and there was flat calm beneath a sullen sky. It was freezing cold as I jumped around, partly to keep warm, but impatient to move before the weather deteriorated further.

The barometer was the lowest we had ever seen it, 29.25. Grahame nonchalantly said that this meant nothing since at Heard Island it blew on a rising barometer, a falling barometer or a steady barometer. After breakfast the Skipper said we would go and have a closer look and we motored off with the foresail to hold us steady.

Our first objective was Winston Lagoon which might offer a safe anchorage or, if not, a good place for the USR landing. Warwick would make no immediate decision as he watched the weather and summed up our prospects. But half an hour before *Patanela* came to a halt, two cables off the lagoon entrance, he gave the order for the shore party to don wet suits and prepare for landing. The fo'c'sle was a scene of sweaty confusion as Grahame, John and I struggled into our rubber skins: the air like a ladies' boudoir with the stink of talcum powder. There seemed a tone of grim finality in the sound as the anchor chain rumbled through the hawse pipes and the coil diminished in the forepeak.

When I emerged on deck the USR was ready for inflation, the engine was revving hard for the pump and loads were appearing everywhere. The sea was like a millpond, the island in thin, grey mist and on the beach elephant seals seemed to rear up at the sight of the ship. Beyond, a snarl of crumbling crevasses revealed the Winston Glacier where it dropped to the lagoon, while up and to the west its nevé rose into the South Barrier ridge. Below its alpine towers, the Barrier splayed into wide, unglaciated bluffs and cliffs a thousand feet high.

The USR was inflated, over the side, outboards screwed to the rail and loads were almost ready. But I looked round nervously as the wind suddenly, within a few seconds it seemed, picked up from the north. The Skipper halted the landing operation and said we would wait to see how the weather developed. The barometer was touching 29.00. Grahame could not keep still. 'Now's the time,' he said. 'We should go before the weather changes. This is good weather for Heard. We'll never get a chance better than this!' Warwick said nothing and stared reflectively at hideous Dovers Moraine to the right.

The wind increased at a frightening rate and within half an hour a full north-west gale had developed. There was discussion, anxious looks, procrastination. Grahame became silent and then the USR began to fling about in the rising sea. The decision was made. Get the USR inboard and secure the loads. Russ in wet suit, parka and life jacket climbed into the bucking craft. Its movement became so violent as the wind twisted it, and *Patanela's* hull lifted so steeply, that we tied him to a life line. He removed the wooden fittings, passed them back, came back himself and we had a tense time pulling the inflated rubber boat, like a big, black sail, over the rail. The wind threatened to blow it away like a kite and not until we clipped it to the staysail halyard did we bring it under control.

There was trouble raising the anchor. Firstly the strain was too great for the electric winch so that a fuse blew and both Antony and John were forced to winch the long, heavy chain by hand. Then a fluke of the fisherman's anchor jammed beneath the bows and Antony hung over the side, held only by his legs, to free it while the ship's rise and fall dumped him frequently in the icy sea. As we motored away from the lagoon rocks, the loads were stacked on the engine-room hatch, draped with a sail cover and securely lashed.

Then, two miles offshore, the parachute anchor was thrown over and we tried to heave to. But by 1700 the wind was force eight, the bronze parachute shackle broke and we moved inexorably southeast under the savage blast of the nor'wester. The barometer reached an all-time low, 28.78. Heard Island disappeared in the furious cloud and we were swallowed by the storm.

There was nothing we could do but ride it out, hope that we stayed in one piece, that we did not drift too far and that though we ran away we could return to land another day. The wind was violent but the stout foresail blew stiff and firm and we realised that finally we had hit the foul weather we managed to avoid earlier. With Warwick in the throes of landing, Ed had taken the job of ship's cook. He could not have chosen a worse day to begin. Seawater insinuated its way into the galley and to crown his cooking efforts, the wind blew hard down the stove flue and showered charcoal over him, the stove, the food and eventually the entire galley.

That was 8 January. On Sunday, 10 January, I wrote in my diary: 'It is sometimes miserable since the only ways we can generate heat are by either crawling under damp blankets or hanging around the galley for mealtimes when the effect of food and stove heat combine to make a cheerful prospect. Condensation is the worst of the whole trip so that all the bare metal parts below are decorated with beads of cold sweat. The galley scuttles have begun to leak, people descend with dripping oilskins so that the floor is continually awash. All the loads brought up for landing were left on deck and it was not until yesterday afternoon that they were put back. I suffered in makeshift clothing, mainly Ed's, until I rescued my kitbags from the sodden pile. Now the fo'c'sle is a mess of wet kitbags, damp blankets and clothes, condensation and a draught that freezes our heads.

The engine room is a cold dank hole without the motor running and both the hot-air system and wide lighting become more and more of a joke under these conditions when they are needed most.' Even the galley was as cold as charity and that morning I helped Ed with breakfast so that I could make sure the oven burned for a while. Morale in the storm seemed good though each one showed some signs of wear and tear. Hove to, with everyone but the cook on watch, we stood one hour on, eight off and this gave us plenty of chilled sleep. Off watch we congregated in the galley, silent with books or chess until someone provoked Ed or Warwick to brew another cup of tea. It was so bitter on deck that we tried to save all outside tasks for one time: excretion, fetching a book, the watch. Then all the nastiness was bound in one hour and we could return to our quiet, if cold, cocoon.

We began to feel a sense of confinement for the first time. Before, we travelled to a distinct objective, now we drifted, and the ship became poky and squalid. Grahame wrote: 'I have the feeling of living in an unstable snow cave—either you're in someone else's way or someone is in yours.' The Skipper had not seen the sun for forty-eight hours and we merely estimated that we were seventy miles south-east of the island. The barometer was still low and there were no signs of the storm abating. In fact the wind gusted to force ten and fifteen-foot waves were common in a sea half white from the gale. The helm was lashed hard over, the foresail firmly sheeted and *Patanela* rode the sea with a strong confident motion. The Skipper had offered scant praise earlier for this jaundiced-looking steel ship but at the height of the storm he remarked: 'Thank goodness we have a good, sound ship beneath us.' A potent statement from him.

Sleet followed rain, and snow the sleet. It plastered the rigging to be blown off with splashes into the waves. It was hard to see for the cutting wind in one's eyes but there was nothing to see anyway but cloud, another huge wave and occasionally—a seeming antithesis in nature—a tiny, fragile storm petrel swooping over a crest of the huge swell. We began to expect drifting ice but none appeared.

As the hours passed, the wry joke went round that at the rate we were going we had better plan on a climbing season in Antarctica.

The Skipper muttered that if the nor'wester did not let up we would have a hard job sailing back and might have to descend to the Sixties for a favourable easterly. At this Warwick grew visibly worried! The mid point of *Patanela's* charter time was 15 January. We had to leave for home by 15 February, at the latest, so that every day lost now meant a day less on the island, a day less for climbing Big Ben.

By 0300 on 11 January the weather decided to relent. Antony persuaded the Skipper to start the engine and we lurched ahead at low revs. The foresail was our firmest friend, giving stability and extra push while the thick, terylene fabric never gave under the strain, though boom and gaff lashings were replaced in the course of the day. It was still bitterly cold as the wind swept icy spray across the ship. We did not return to four-hour watches but compromised with two, one hour each at the wheel. It was impossible to stand at the for'ard wheel for more than a few minutes before one's hands and face became frozen, eyes closed in the spray and the compass was covered in running water. So we took to steering with the aft wheel because the course was clear. With the wind now west to south-west we sailed close-hauled and the first quiver of the luff gave us the cue to fall away.

On the afternoon of the 11th the Skipper began to work out our position from two lucky sights. I looked out through the charthouse window to see a great raft of prions on the water, then back to the Skipper's puzzled frown. I went on deck for the watch and a short time later he came up. He peered ahead, wiping the cold tears from his eyes then said: 'There it is isn't it?' In astonishment I followed the lie of his finger and picked up a wild, glaciated coast. It looked nothing like Heard, too big. With a twinkle in his eye the Skipper said: 'Maybe we've discovered a new island!' It was Heard alright but it was some time before we discovered that we were off the north coast—seeing the full width of the island from Laurens Peninsula to Spit Point. The wind was still gale force but we put it to good use now and rapidly closed with the shore.

It was obvious that the storm had neither blown us south-east nor as far as we thought. By some quirk of the weather we had gone slightly north of east and at the limit of our drift had been about thirty-five miles off Spit Point. The Skipper laid his return course at north-west true, expecting to make landfall south of the Spit. Instead we sighted land well north and a due west course was necessary finally to bring us in to Compton Glacier. Since it was late in the day we pulled in to the first anchorage away from the sou'wester. This proved to be in seven fathoms off Gilchrist Beach, the tongue of the glacier in the sea to port.

The weather improved and the face of Big Ben cleared. North Barrier rose gently before us, then reared into a dyke of ferocious spires and gaps. There were coxcombs all around—one aptly named Little Matterhorn. They all fluted up to the great crater rim of Big Ben which occasionally showed itself through the rolling cloud and snowdrift. It was a spectacular anchorage, only a few cables off crumbling ice cliffs. Melt water surged out in a green spate to merge with the sea and the little storm petrels found the distinct demarcation line a lucrative zone for feeding. This was the Antarctic, with ice in the sea, wide snowfields, meagre life, the cold and, above, a massive, unclimbed mountain.

There was nothing sure about the next day, or even that night. We kept a sharp anchor watch since we dragged at our first attempt and a regular rumble of chain over the boulders gave a disquieting sense of instability. I marvelled at seeing stars again, enjoyed the luxury of a sleep at anchor but became suddenly afraid at the morning's prospects. The weather had changed so quickly before. What would happen if we were caught half way through the landing operation? I shuddered, not entirely from the cold.

Grahame woke me at 0400 after a shout from Warwick that seemed to sound in a dream. We had motored for half an hour, towards the Spit. The island was very clear, in bright sunshine, and the barometer rose fast—too fast. Within an hour cloud layers approached over the sea and the white cake of Big Ben was sandwiched between a dark sky and a dark sea. The wind was back to north-west, cold, and I was glad to go below as again the order came to don wet suits. The same claustrophobic struggle then down to the galley, my stomach writhing at the sight of breakfast as I sat stiffly on the bench in my strange attire. In a streamlined, skin-tight

Tilman the Navigator

covering, approaching a dangerous climax in a deliberate count-down, I felt curiously like an astronaut before blastoff. But being a non-swimmer I did not feel as well prepared.

We passed Spit Point within a mile and it was only later that the Skipper realised we had crossed a badly-known line of shoals that extended several miles beyond the Spit's long finger. But we did not ground and soon our attention was taken by the pounding breakers on its southern shore. The sea was rough but the Skipper pushed up the engine revs and the ship leaped quickly but uncomfortably towards the stand-off point. The loads were hauled out and, as we closed with Winston Lagoon, we were completely ready.

The engine idled as Warwick, Col and Grahame scrambled up the ratlines to observe the lagoon entrance and the state of the surf. After a few minutes of shouts and questions they decided that an entry to the lagoon was impossible with a line of rocks and surf breaking on a distinct bar. The rocks, old erratics from a withdrawn glacier, extended down the whole length of the low spit which hid the calm waters of the lagoon. To the west, however, before the beetle-browed cliffs of Cape Lockyer, there was a vegetated gully running down to a wide beach. There were no rocks and the surf seemed innocuous compared to the heavy cascades of foam that shot into the air each time a wave hit the shore elsewhere. There was a deep, heaving swell from the late sou'wester but the wind was still.

The decision was reached. 'Go?' I queried. Warwick nodded: 'My word!' *Patanela* moved gently to a point half a mile from the chosen landing and this time the CQR anchor was thrown over. The ship rolled far enough to dip her scuppers but the USR was launched in good time, outboard on, and loads in order of priority were stacked against the bulwarks. Three trips were planned if the weather behaved. The first load, of basic camping, climbing equip-ment, clothing and food was essential; the second desirable and the third luxury. There was little speech as we seemed to race against time. But now I cannot remember how long the preparations took, when we started; it is all lost in an aura of intense, nervous activity. At the time I felt how small we were, taking on the hostile island with its ring of treacherous surf and nothing behind but a sixty-three-foot schooner with five men and a sorry-looking Zodiac that would probably sink if it came to our aid.

Grahame sat in the USR, received the loads and lashed them superbly. It was a task full of strain as he combated the bucks and jerks of the boat, clutched heavy packs, all in the chafing discomfort of a wet suit. I held the bow line and fished the craft, pulling it in as each load was passed over then letting it out to minimise friction against *Patanela*'s hull. No loads were dropped but my heart lurched as the Zodiac outboard, screwed to the taff-rail, suddenly tipped and swung upside down after a heavy roll. It was saved and soon we could put the final covering on the USR. I jumped on board with a paddle, ready to go.

There was infuriating delay. The Zodiac was inflated and overboard but the motor was not fitted. Rightly, but annoyingly, Warwick insisted that the outboard was fitted and tested. The rescue craft had to be in a state of immediate readiness. Over went the motor, Russ screwed it on the transom, pulled the start toggle, then there was an awful din as the Johnson picked up in gear and shot forward. Clouds of oil smoke and spray surrounded his head until the motor was neutralised and tested more sedately. Then Colin reckoned we should move to the lee side for others to board the USR. We manoeuvred it round by hand but almost came unstuck as *Patanela*'s stern rose in the air, came down heavily and threatened to jam us under the counter.

Nervously I adjusted my Mae West as Warwick and John shook hands with an effusive Mal. They climbed over the side, we pushed off, the motor burbling, and with a bloodcurdling yell from myself we droned away from our source of security. The Skipper walked down the deck, there were a few waves, then we turned to regard the island. Warwick and Grahame were in the bows, port and starboard respectively, John and I behind, while Col drove. The swell seemed slight on the assault craft and after the first tense seconds I released my tight grip on a lashing rope, raised myself and took some photographs with a waterproof camera. Grahame photographed also and Warwick whirred with a movie camera. Making myself more comfortable I regarded the shore anxiously and remarked to Col: 'Just by those yellow rocks looks a good spot to land.' He said nothing. They were elephant seals.

After a few hundred yards Colin said that he would test the craft's manoeuvrability before we went in. He ran in a tight circle and it remained completely stable, weighing half a ton with load. We continued on, the surf breaking slightly on the black sand. The technique devised in Sydney required the assault craft to make the beaching on the back of a breaker. We would wait for a wave to pass us, gun the engine, chase it and hit the beach after the power of its break had dissipated. Conditions seemed ideal for just this. Now only a hundred yards from the shore Colin called out: 'Hang on tight. We'll have a go now.' Warwick tucked away his camera, pulled down his balaclava and joked: 'Mind now, don't want to get me titfer wet!' Col took us at the same steady speed, looking over his shoulder as the swell rolled in from the south-west. *Patanela* was a toy boat now, often lost to sight as we dipped in a trough. The beach was close, I suddenly saw the line of penguins and then as a hissing wave swept past Col yelled: 'Here we go!' Grahame responded with 'Beautiful Col!' as the engine roared and we chased the breaker. It exploded into foam before us, the bows of the craft touched and I made to leap ashore. Then all hell broke loose. Hardly aware of what happened, too involved to be frightened, I felt myself thrown violently forward in a melée of foam, green water, tumbling black figures and the big, black boat that rose behind, tossed like a child's duck in a bath, threatening to hammer us into the sand.

First Colin was above, the motor's propeller still racing as it swept past his head, then the craft enveloped me, twisting my shoulder and leg as the elemental power of the surf kicked us up the beach. As the shingle roared with retreating water I frantically wriggled myself clear and bent down to grab Grahame who was completely pinned. But barely had I moved when the sea attacked again. Another breaker smashed into the boat and we surged relentlessly up the beach. Struggling free, I grabbed Grahame again to stop him sliding further under the boat. But I seemed to have no strength and sagged over the USR's flat bottom as it lay half on its side, dead motor sticking in the air.

Eventually we regained our breath and strength as the sea left us alone. We helped Grahame to his feet and then leaned under the craft in an attempt to right it. Due to Grahame's expert lashing nothing came adrift save a few plastic mugs which we salvaged before they floated out to sea. The paddles were gone, the motor in a questionable state, but Colin had thoughtfully loaded extra paddles at the bottom of the boat and a repair kit for the Johnson. Miraculously no-one was injured, although my knee sometimes inexplicably gave way after the twist of the first capsize.

Righting the USR was beyond us and we resorted to unloading from its upside down position. Everything was saturated though most of the vital equipment and food survived through careful packing. But a reflex camera was full of salt water and Grahame discovered that his underwater camera had gone where it belonged. We were wet, the loads were wet and it began to rain. Black sand clung to everything as we heaved the packs and bags to a safe spot higher up the beach. Though we often struggled for breath in the tight suits we kept incredibly warm with movement, and chafing behind the knees and elbows could be endured in exchange for protection against exposure.

As the first clamour of the capsize subsided in my mind I dimly became aware of our surroundings. Above the beach was a terrace of rocks and shingle that led to a gully of azorella and tussock. Down the beach to the west were a great pile of boulders beneath the majestic edifice of Cape Lockyer; to the east was the lagoon spit and a huge wallow of elephant seals, snorting and rolling over each other. Clouds of steam rose as the rain beat on their hot, hairless skins and a mixed smell of oil and manure drifted over the neutral tang of cold seashore. The penguins were both curious and bored. A line of marching Macaronis paraded steadily along the water's edge, paused to watch our movements, scratched their armpits and moved on. Gentoos were more friendly, circled the Pyramid tent as we raised it on the sand while one jumped on the righted USR to examine the outboard. Skuas stalked beady-eyed but we scared them off when they grew too attentive and bounced rocks off an elephant seal which insisted on slummocking its way through our camp to the sea.

Col took the outboard down to a creek, poured a special 'de-watering' liquid through the motor, checked the propeller, ran it up and pronounced it fit for work. The USR was undamaged and the extra five paddles intact. We could go back for another load. I think it was about one o'clock when Warwick resurrected the army field radio and found it working despite the ducking. I helped him set up the equipment on the terrace and soon he was in contact with Ed on the ship. He briefly informed the Skipper of events and said the USR would return for another load if the surf was negotiable. The Skipper replied that he would wait until late afternoon but would be gone the next day.

John stirred up a hot feed in the Pyramid while Warwick strode up and down the beach with Col and Grahame, discussing the surf. Was it safe to go back? Could we make do with one load? The answer to the last question was—barely. Grahame argued strongly for another trip. The second and third loads could be rearranged into one, leaving reserve supplies and luxuries on the ship. Colin was dubious about taking another risk and I stood helplessly to one side, sorting my thoughts.

Before a decision was made, the surf was analysed. There was a deep swell but this was not sufficient to explain the tremendous break that was hidden from the seaward aspect. The beach was not steep but from the pattern of the surf we guessed that it shelved steeply at the water's edge. Nothing else could have caused the sudden dump and fast retreat of the waves: there must be a ferocious undertow. The bad dumpers came in series with a few minutes pause between. Grahame was positive that we could take off during this relatively calm period, and land the same way with the aid of hand signals from the shore.

Warwick decided that John and myself would remain on shore while the three of them went back for another load. The Skipper was duly informed and we moved the USR at two o'clock. John and I stood at the rear to give the craft an extra push then, as Grahame gave the commands, the three raced into the sea with the boat, jumped aboard and paddled furiously. Quickly the motor sang into life as a big wave tossed them dangerously, then they picked up speed and I watched as Warwick and Grahame thankfully shipped their paddles, free of the surf. They moved away steadily towards *Patanela* which occasionally showed its masts above a lurching horizon.

With a sigh I looked around the desolate black and white landscape, relieved by occasional colour from the penguins and the scum of green where sparse vegetation clung to the unyielding rock. I quickly grew stiff and cold as a gusty wind made the black sand hiss past the tent and swept rain into my face. There were two alternatives: sit down and become more gloomy or move, become warm again and get some work done. Warwick and Grahame had made a quick trip into the gully which ran up for quarter of a mile. Looking up it John and I saw the bluffs of the South Barrier to our left. There was vegetation to its crest, several hundred feet higher, and snow which fell in a steep slope almost to the stream in the gully's head. To the right was an old lateral moraine which formed the southern bank of Winston Lagoon and this curved upwards to enclose the gully when it met the South Barrier. Two streams rose on opposite sides and joined half way down to form an icy torrent through the wallows of elephant seals. There was little flat ground but all was well covered with tussock, azorella and Kerguelen Cabbage except where the seals or Gentoo penguins had worn it away. Above the junction of the streams there were no seals or penguins and the triangle of ground between the fork offered a good campsite. It was almost flat and the water was clean.

John and I hoisted the heavy packs which were to dominate the whole of our stay on the island, and began to move them to the chosen Base Camp. Occasionally we looked out to our only view—the sea with incongruous *Patanela*—but could see no signs of activity which would show that the USR was returning. Warwick wrote in his diary: 'The return to "Pat" was made well enough and I enjoyed a rum back on board. There Bill Tilman was grinning like a Cheshire Cat and Mal Hay kept dashing round to shake hands in the best British tradition! Finally away amid much rhubarb and Churchillian signs from me.' I was supposed to radio the ship at three but guessed that the USR was about to return and, sure enough, a few minutes later a small, black blob detached itself from the yellow hull and the second, final, load was on its way. John and I ran down to the beach and waited apprehensively as the low craft seemed to crawl towards us over the sea. They came to a point well outside the surf then Warwick half stood up and gestured that I should give them the landing signal. I swallowed hard, summing up the surf, flinched as a particularly violent breaker threw rocks into the air, then vigorously waved them in as the sea settled. Col turned on the power and the craft surged along in calm water. But either my signal had been ten seconds late or Col's application of speed had been too slow. The USR shot over a small wave, touched the beach and, just as the three made to disembark, a wave shoved a shoulder beneath the boat, tipped it sharply and threw them all out. John, who had gone to meet the USR, joined the flying legs and arms in the foam. The raft broached but did not capsize, straightened out and, as I stood ankle deep in water, the bows came to meet me. The others staggered out before another wave came and we all gave a yell of relief.

As prearranged, we made our way to the terrace over the beach to show those on *Patanela* that we were intact and uninjured. We stood in a line, waved, spread the Australian ensign as a signal and watched as *Patanela* responded with the Blue Peter on the mainmast.

Shortly the anchor was got and the graceful schooner motored out of sight to the south. The wind seemed fair and we all expected the ship to make a quick voyage back to Kerguelen. In fact, *Patanela* had gone round South Barrier barely three miles, to Lambeth Bluff, when a howling nor'wester struck her. By 1830 she was hove to under bare poles with the log inboard and she rolled eastwards at the mercy of another storm until 0830 the next morning. Then the engine was started, foresail hoisted and by nightfall had cleared Shag Island as the ship moved north-west.

On the beach we felt suddenly dog tired and it took all our remaining energy to carry the Pyramid tent, essential sleeping and cooking equipment and a bit of food to the Base Camp site. The remaining loads were placed in a sheltered hollow on the terrace and we retired for a well-earned rest. We had landed with all our gear, safely if luckily, and had a month for accomplishing our objectives.

Patanela would return by 11 February. Before us was the immediate problem of finding a way up the mountain. Later there was scientific work to achieve and, if we had time, a circuit of the whole island.

But these were not the only problems. Already we began to think about that day in a month's time. The capsized landings, though dangerous, were over and we had come ashore with our gear whether we liked it or not—the surf threw us ashore. But how were we going to take the loads off? We would certainly not carry a loaded USR into the water—for weight reasons alone. It would have to be loaded in the water. How, with such violent surf? And would the surf be as good on the day? It could be worse and stay worse indefinitely. But on the evening of 12 January we lay back on our new air mattresses, replete with stew, gave up thinking and flaked.

Part Two:

BIG BEN

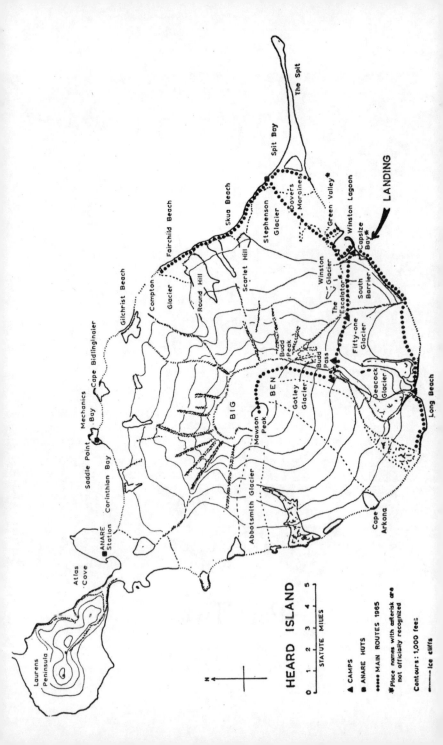

7

WHAT DOES NOT KILL YOU...

FROM THE BEGINNING COLIN REFERRED to our climb of Big Ben as unique. He said that it was the first ascent of a mountain to start below sea level. Our ducking qualified this and, on looking up at the towering ridges and leering ice cliffs, we needed no reminder that we had to climb every inch of the 9005 feet marked on the map. And there was no question of going straight up. We would have to traverse about seven miles of mountain slopes to find a suitable campsite for the final assault on Mawson Peak.

As *Patanela* laboured her way out of a storm on 13 January, we worked in windy sunshine. It was a good day for drying as we unpacked, sorted and ferried all the remaining loads from the terrace to the camp. The USR deflated, it was cached beneath a large boulder on the moraine, covered with the motor, paddles, pump, spare parts and the sail cover, well weighted with rocks. Behind it we discovered pieces of weathered planks and next day John dug excitedly into the remains of an old sealers' hut. At the camp we erected the Bechervaise tent to allow more room and soon the intervening space between the tents was littered with food, clothing and equipment. We found to our dismay that two light tents we intended for low and emergency bivouacs had not been brought ashore. The Pyramid and the Bechervaise were our sole source of shelter.

We rolled up our wet suits and waterproof trousers from the ship then, like schoolboys at Christmas, dived into the kitbags of special clothing to deck ourselves out. We intended keeping warm and dry in Heard's miserably changeable climate and a description of our dress, from underwear up, will give some idea of how we hoped to achieve this ambition. Most of us preferred long, woollen underwear though there was an odd string vest about, and over this we had heavy woollen shirts and trousers. We needed only one pair of Norwegian wool socks with the rubber vapour barrier boots. Their inner 'silver' sock and calf-high tops kept feet dry and hot when moving. One invariably pulled them off at night to let wrinkled toes steam dry of sweat. They never froze like leather boots but were not suited to climbing as we soon learned. Over the woollens we wore windproofs of ventile, all of them used before on Heard or in Antarctica. These took all the edge off the wind and I chose a red set of trousers and parka with a dashing, furlined hood. Also, each had a heavy sweater and a 'Putt Parka'.

These black, tent-like parkas sheltered the whole body to the knees in nyloprene and were designed from Col's experience in wet New Zealand and New Guinea bush. It was just as liable to rain as snow at 6,000 feet and the ventile windproofs became a sorry sight after an hour's downpour. Then, with typical vindictiveness, the weather was liable to swing southerly and freeze hard. The Putt Parka was our main line of defence against this phenomenon which had come close to killing Heard explorers in the past. Finally, we had woollen balaclavas, woollen mitts and windproof overmitts. Muffled up in this clothing, and wearing snow goggles, we could only distinguish one another at distance by colours. Warwick in black, Grahame in fawn, John in blue, Col in chalky red and myself in dark red (with fur).

For restful nights we had full-length Lilos, Himalayan down jackets and Everest sleeping bags. For cooking we had self-pricking, single-burner primuses with side tanks, ordinary billies and a pressure cooker that was mainly used for storing films. Kerosene was carried in plastic bottles, the rum in a smaller one, and under nearby rocks we stashed Foster's lager and four bottles of McCallum's whisky. The food was mediocre as only light-weight rations can be. Our main meat supply was freeze-dried in foil packets and though we had a delectable variety of sausage, beef mince and curried mince we usually threw them altogether in a hoosh since we could not tell the difference. The other ingredient of the hoosh was potato powder.

This was the food we took up the mountain, with hard biscuits and butter, cheese, porridge, chocolate, sugar, milk powder, tea, coffee, cocoa, marzipan and rum.

Climbing equipment was standard New Zealand alpine gear. Warwick, Grahame and John used the new, light Austrian ice axes but Col and I stuck to our own heavy, guide models which had served us well for years. Ropes were nylon, borrowed with much of the other gear from the NZ Alpine Club, except for my heavyweight perlon which had been to the top of New Guinea's highest peak. I had a nostalgic fondness for this and my axe and everyone had something, however small, that had been with him on expeditions in other parts of the world. It was a curious assemblage of gear which held the stories of many frights and delights, successes and failures: the down jackets had been used in the Barun Valley, Nepal in 1954; the sleeping bags in Peru, 1962; one sleeping bag had been used on Fuch's Trans-Antarctic Expedition; two axes had been used on New Guinea expeditions, 1961, 1962; there were windproofs from Heard 1963, boots from the Southern Alps, a balaclava from the Karakoram, 1958 and a flag from Alaska, 1956. This was the pennant of the Parachute Regiment Mountaineering Club to which Warwick had belonged when he made his first expedition. Apart from this we had two new flags, Australian and New Zealand ensigns, which Col and I had been given to take to the summit—if we got there.

Apart from all the paraphernalia mentioned above we had to carry tent brushes, tent pegs, ice screws, shovels, snow saws, spare clothing, cameras (two still colour, one still black and white, two movie), film, spoons, plastic jugs, pot scrapers, spongers, crevasse ladder, prussik loops, rope slings, spare rope, snow cream, medical kit, crevasse thermometers, notebooks, crampons, piton hammer, pliers, wire, toilet paper, matches, meta fuel, cigarettes, cigars, waist ties, the Pyramid's bamboo poles which measured ten feet, and 100 polythene marker poles, each six feet long. After careful consideration, Warwick allowed us each to take one book. Ironically, Grahame took poems by Frost and I carried a novel by Snow.

Our attempt on Big Ben became more of a siege than a climb. After their narrow escape in 1963, Grahame had no trouble convincing Warwick that a solid camp, where we could sit safely through a three-week blizzard, was a minimum prerequisite for the ascent. There was Grahame's sound, meticulous planning behind each item of equipment but I hoped the expedition did not become bogged down from sheer inertia. Warwick felt it was doing that right from the start and complained about our slowness in moving up the mountain. But we needed time to find our land legs, sort the mountain of gear and gradually regain climbing fitness lost during the long voyage.

There was an occasional snap and squabble as we took time to readjust our thoughts. Warwick decided that to make full use of daylight we would move on to Heard Triple Summertime. Our watches were moved forward three hours so that nightfall was not until after midnight, and dawn came at four. We went to bed at midnight and got up at eight or nine instead of retiring at nine and getting up at five or six which is the usual mountain pattern. Peeved, I argued strongly against it but could make no headway against Warwick's paradoxical viewpoint which reasoned that the new times enabled one to live with normal civilized meal hours, thus more mental comfort; and then that they made him feel as though he was on an expedition.

In 1963, Grahame's expedition found that the best route to the main crater of Big Ben lay over the upper reaches of the Gotley Glacier. They had reached this after a climb up the Fifty-One Glacier and a traverse through a pass at 4000 feet now known as Budd Pass. From there Grahame, with Warwick and Jon Stephenson, climbed to the crater at over 7000 feet and pitched a camp. This was snowed under and they descended to Long Beach in a blizzard, lucky to save their lives. From a technical point of view, Budd Pass and the Gotley offered the best route. But in view of the '63 lesson it was felt that a strong camp at the pass was preferable to a high camp with nothing behind us. The weather there was likely not to be as severe and retreat would be easier. It was assumed that we could ascend the final 5000 feet and return in one day. In retrospect, this assumption seems over-ambitious and we relied a great deal on luck with the daily weather.

To reach the Pass from our Base Camp, now known as Poly Gully as dirty polythene bags flew around in the wind, we would have to cross the South Barrier. At about 3000 feet its spurs sharpened and we needed a pass that gave access through the final ridge and down its western cliffs to the Fifty-One Glacier. Then we could make a gentle traverse across to join the '63 route. So far so good. Then we realised that this course would take us up to 3000 feet, down to 2000 and up to 4000 over a seven-mile meander of rock, snow and ice.

The total load of food and equipment came to close on half a ton! I have never been a good load carrier, assiduously following a policy of carrying as little as possible on a climbing trip. Whenever I looked at the huge mound of gear in Poly Gully, I found the only way I could cope with the prospect of carrying it all was to find some kind of mental distraction each time it entered my head. Also, I was consoled by the knowledge that the four others detested the prospect almost as much as I did—and that it had to be done if we wished to climb Big Ben safely and with a modicum of comfort.

Warwick was impatient and restless. He seemed to sort his personal and filming gear faster than the rest of us and then would not pause before he reconnoitred the first part of our route. His tall and bulky, dark-haired figure strode up the gully and disappeared as he climbed through the boulders. Later we picked him out on the skyline as he examined the snowslope and came back to report that this was the only route which offered easy access to the broad regions on the South Barrier. He took a bundle of 20 orange marker poles and dumped them at the edge of the snow as if to say: 'Right! We've started. Now let's get up as quickly as possible!'

On 14 January we began. We each took a package of 12-man-day rations weighing 28 pounds. They were packed on the assumption, for some reason, that six men would be on Heard with the result that we had rations not divisible by five. With packs and climbing gear the loads came to 50 pounds and it was more than enough as we laboured over the first steep scree slope. This was the most annoying part of the whole climb: 300 feet of loose, shifting rock calculated to upset one's balance and temper. Panting and red-faced we negotiated

Colin and Grahame with big loads on South Barrier snow, Poly Gully below

boulders slippery with grit and flopped down by the snow to strap on crampons. A cold, blustery wind cooled us off and the weather over the Barrier seemed none too good as streamers of cloud shot over our heads. The crampons were heavy-duty ten-pointers. We each had a pair of these, a complete reserve set and half a dozen lighter pairs of crampons from the NZ Alpine Club. In 1963 broken crampon rings had been a pest. But on this trip, with 15 pairs between us, we broke only one.

The snow was deceptively steep but with deep steps from Colin and new, spiky crampons on our boots, we made hay of the 200-foot traverse and moved on to an easier slope above. We took in our first view, looking out to Winston Lagoon with lumps of brash ice from the glacier floating like white ducks. The black slag heaps of Dovers Moraine lay beyond with the delicious green of a narrow ablation valley unvisited by man. Further still was the Spit, Spit Bay and Scarlet Hill overlooking Skua Beach. Grahame remarked that the Spit lagoon, dry in 1963, was full again. But I lost interest rapidly in a desolate scene fringed by grey sea and, despite aching shoulders, was eager to see what lay over the next false crest.

The South Barrier was the highest unglaciated area of any extent on the island. Guarded by bluffs or sea cliffs on all sides save the north, where the Winston Glacier ran down its flank, it was a typical volcanic plateau of scoria and small lava flows. Not that it was flat but, compared to its huge 1000-foot sea cliffs, it rose gently from their crest to the beginning of an alpine ridge 2000 feet higher. There were gullies and hollows, bumps, corrugations and a few low cones above the general level that revealed an active volcanic past. The hues were mainly brown but this was relieved by splashes of bright red rock and a multitude of soft pastels where white, yellow and green mosses and lichens clung to the rough, cindery pebbles. All the deeper hollows were filled with snow and in our first view the ultimate ridge, before the Fifty-One Glacier, was disguised in mist.

With our new Summertime, we had not left camp until after lunch. So it was three o'clock before we plodded up to a prominent cone we christened Red Crater and sidled its abominable flank. Scoria ran beneath our boots, we often slid to our knees and it was a thankful band that regained the snow but wondered where to go next. Before us were steeper snowslopes leading to the final ridge. But the cloud revealed no clues for a pass and we climbed on in desultory fashion, Col and John forging ahead in a bout of one-upmanship.

With my twisted knee giving sharp, painful twinges, I crawled up the last steep snow and collapsed where the rest had dumped their packs. I looked up. Grahame and Warwick climbed and chatted their way over a snow dome on the ridge and with a sigh I made to follow them. On the crest of the ridge both the sheer cliffs dropping to the Fifty-One, and a malevolent wind, became obvious. We bent in its bitter force, as rain threatened to empty from the thick scud, and lost all hope of seeing across the glacier to the 4000-foot pass. The three of us encountered John and Col on their way back to collect forgotten parkas, and they gloomily remarked that there were no likely routes off the Barrier. Surely not an impasse this early in our climb?

The only regular smoker in the party, I suffered frustration after frustration. I lit up as Col and John disappeared while Warwick and Grahame pooled their hoard of Heard memories and decided what to do next. But I barely turned my back to the wet wind and inhaled before they moved off. I flung the cigarette away rather than be left behind, and stumbled after them, casting a jaundiced eye at the shattered rock falling to our left. Impatiently Warwick strode ahead as the ridge narrowed and I joined Grahame as he passed two prominent dykes, standing up like intact walls among a scene of ruins. We stopped together, walked over a little saddle and descended a short way to peer over the edge. The dykes ran straight down, parallel and without a break to the Fifty-One. Between them was an even slope of scree that merged with the snow, several hundred feet below, with no obstacle or crevasse. We yelled to Warwick and went down.

Our ice axes made valuable props as gingerly we trod the steep, loose slope, testing the stability of the rocks. Grahame's vapour-barrier boots seemed to take a course in opposition to his feet and I smugly followed in leather climbing boots. But there was plenty of time for last laughs. In quarter of an hour we reached the bottom and Grahame celebrated our arrival at the Fifty-One in a typical mountaineer's rude fashion. We could see glimpses of the main pass and the ice ahead seemed to offer no problems. We climbed back as Warwick kicked down pebbles and affirmed that the gully offered the most practicable route. To one side we examined a cave—an ideal dump site—but were too tired to face the task of humping the loads down over the sliding scree. Col arrived and we had our gully christened. Obviously, with its moveable surface and distinct sides, it should be called the Escalator. The cave was the Toyshop and the ridge Emporium. As Col's face glowed with satisfaction at the names I reflected that this Emporium differed from most stores in that its one-way escalator went down and not up.

The weather was worsening, the day growing old and loads were scattered along the ridge. We found a hole near the crest for a temporary dump and began the tiresome task of retrieving the packs. We tried a different route out of the wind but this entailed only hard work over icy snow. Grahame went for a slide down a steep slope and we decided to stick to the ridge. Almost in a stupor from tiredness and cold I followed him as he tried to stay in the lee. But the increasing wind would not give us peace and I cried out in fury as it struck equally hard from all points of the compass; roaring over the rock in sudden willywaws, throwing one's balance awry and pelting drift snow into one's eyes. I was soaked from the knees down and only the voluminous Putt Parka kept the rest of my clothes dry. Grahame became entangled in a steep gully and, fuming, I balanced on nicks cut in ice above a long fall, frantically wondering from which direction the gale would blow next. Bedraggled we joined the others, rid ourselves of the food packs and took a short rest. A few minutes later I threw away another half-smoked cigarette as the others plunged down the snow for home and was soon glad to leave the swirl of cloud and flying snow.

That first long day exhausted us and revealed how unfit and lacking in co-ordination we were. But a good feed, a warm bag and a tot of rum will cure most ills and Warwick's drive did the rest. Over 15 and 16 January we ferried more loads up the South Barrier. The route to the Escalator was straightened out, marked with cairns decorated by fluorescent strips, and our fitness improved beyond measure. It must be admitted, however, that Warwick's push, which degenerated at times to sheer impatience, almost overtook our rising curve of physical acclimatisation.

There was no question about it. 'Tomorrow (the 17th) we move up and establish a higher camp. If we don't move soon we'll develop a bad case of Base Camp-itis and won't leave ourselves time for the final climb.' There were frowns and groans but we realised the fundamental justness of Warwick's urgency. After all, we had come a long way at great effort and expense to climb the mountain and aches, pains and personal irritations had to be put aside for the main task in hand. We did not have much time, there were many other jobs to do, and Lord knew what obstacles lay in wait higher up.

In twilight at one o'clock in the morning I sat on a rock outside the Pyramid and brought my diary up to date. A single candle burned inside creating a small orange glow in the cold darkness, and the elephant seals continued to grunt and snort. There was a trilling chatter from the penguin rookery and thin whistles as prions dashed past in a white flutter. All around, the azorella mounds were riddled with their burrows and only at night was it safe for them to come home and tend their chicks, hidden from the scavenging eye of the skua. As I wrote I had mixed thoughts. I was ambitious to climb Big Ben—for the achievement itself—but I had found no love for Heard Island: a hostile place, cold in its climate and very demeanour. The violent surf and wind formed a bass continuo and I wondered why we had pitted ourselves so determinedly against the power of such a mountain. I shivered in the thick cover of my down jacket.

Before we left Base, Warwick sealed messages in tins, both at the USR dump and in the dump of food and supplies remaining at Poly Gully. If we disappeared at least a search party would know where to look. He was eager to be off, since we planned for a camp on the Fifty-One, but I lagged behind, placing more boulders on the strip of Verylite which covered the dump. I kicked some empty tins into a hole, took a last look round and sat down. The final pack loads were in the vicinity of eighty to a hundred pounds and the only way one could transfer the pack from the ground to one's back was by going to it and not expecting to lift it and remain in balance. My pack was propped on a small shelf and I braced my back against it, fitting my arms through the straps. Then I grabbed my ice axe, jammed it firmly into the ground, took a firm grip of the head and rose to my feet with a grunt. A pause to shift the load into a favourable position. Then the beginning of a slow, regular plod up the uninviting talus slope, concentrating on the next step ahead to avoid discouragement at the sight of the distance to go. I was lucky. I had a bundle of twenty marker poles on top of everything else but Grahame nobly took the Pyramid poles and Col the tent, bulky and weighing forty pounds dry. Warwick had an unknown quantity of movie equipment but at least it consisted of one Bolex turret lens camera, a small fifty-foot magazine camera, a tripod and about 2000 feet of 16mm film.

The snowslope was in bad condition after several trips. The steps were sloppy and insecure while the marker poles prodded the steep slope and threw us off balance. Methodically, as calves ached, we drove the axes in ahead, moving carefully up while holding them firmly; axe out of snow, in again, move up to it, rest, out of snow, in again. Above, we plodded slowly up the familiar, monotonous scoria. I trailed behind but thought: We've picked a good day for it anyway. The sun was brilliant, the wind a cold zephyr, Big Ben clear and silent as though astounded at the sudden peace. The upper South Barrier looked like any alpine ridge on a good summer's day. There were no spirals of drift but there were no avalanches either, impressions of melting snow or heat shimmering off the blinding snowfields. There was an intrinsic cold and rarely did this relent, unfreeze the balustrades of ice and let them tumble to the gentler fields below.

It was warm enough on the Winston snowfield below the Escalator. My leather boots became saturated in soft snow, despite proofed overboots, and we splashed through wide areas of blue and glistening melt streams. We never decided whether the basin below the Escalator was glaciated or not. There were no obvious crevasses and we always crossed it unroped. The Fifty-One was a different proposition altogether. There were bad areas of bursting pressure domes; long, thin, horizontal crevasses running hundreds of yards and an aura of insecure ice about the whole landscape.

We negotiated the Escalator one by one, to avoid kicking rocks on each other's heads, and then sat in assorted painful positions at its foot to strap on crampons and rope up for the first time. As we stepped out across the initial sharp slope of the glacier, Col discovered that crampons were not designed for vapour-barrier boots. They slid round the rubber and the only safe means of locomotion was to go forward with one's feet pointing up the slope.

Fortunately for Col's peace of mind we travelled only a short distance to a section of glacier that seemed safe from crevasses, avalanche and rockfall. There was one pile of debris that showed an occasional avalanche could force its way across the bergschrund*, but we hoped a line of crevasses above would catch any fall coming our way. Grahame and Warwick paced around the proposed campsite, tied to a rope, and pronounced us on safe ground. Then we bent to the task of digging. Under Grahame's expert supervision we sawed the snow into rectangular blocks and shovelled these out until we were left with a flat, entrenched platform. The Pyramid was erected on this and its generous outside flaps weighted down with the blocks. The tent guys were tied to ice axes or pegs buried like deadmen, and we had a secure haven once more. The Pyramid was a tried and trusty design, used on most Antarctic journeys and was known to stand up to the worst blizzards. It gave a sense of security when compared to a normal alpine tent but one could still come to grief in one, as Robert Falcon Scott demonstrated.

In the peak of the tent, below the leather sockets for the poles, was a small sleeve ventilator. Below this was the only entrance, another sleeve which Warwick swore was only eighteen inches wide despite its six-foot length. Whatever the exact measurements, it was long and narrow. Warwick and Col, in their bulk, always found it awkward to negotiate and it began to prove an effective deterrent to going outside. Never quite sure what the best technique was for get-

---

* Gap between a glacier and the steep mountainside.

Grahame takes a break during the lift across the Fifty-One Glacier

ting in and out, we tried it head first, feet first, lying straight using our elbows for progress or with knees bent, though this latter course generally ended in disaster. Warwick persisted in a belligerent approach to the problem and rather than insinuate his wide six foot three down the tunnel, which was against his nature, he preferred to battle unceasingly against the tyrant as if in the hope that it would surrender one day and expand. His bull-in-the-china-shop technique almost ended in hysterics that first night on the glacier. He battled his way out for some minutes and then shouted in fury that there seemed to be no end to the bloody thing. The mouth had been tied in a knot to stop draughts.

We laid out the Pyramid floor, blew up the air mattresses and stretched back to rest as Grahame prepared the evening stew. Warwick scribbled in his diary, made notes on filming and sketched out a plan for the following days. Col bent earnestly and silently to the task of crampon modification. With pliers and wire he improved the heel fitting then sat back with a sigh to admire his handiwork. That done he wormed into his sleeping bag, lay immobile on his back and stared at the tent peak. Colin did not read, write or photograph on an expedition and had developed the happy knack of finding rest and relaxation in contemplation, not of his navel since it was too cold, but of the orange tent fabric as it flapped and buffeted in the wind.

According to a careful, prearranged formula, Grahame served us each with a jug of hot coffee before the meal. John sat up brightly with a familiar 'Beauty boy!' and we all stirred gladly to take hold of the hot plastic measuring beakers which we used as plate, bowl and mug. There was comfort in the warmth as the temperature dropped and the coffee proved a stimulant to conversation. But no pearls of wisdom were dropped and we rambled on about climbing techniques, weather and details until Warwick laid out the plan for the next forty-eight hours. John lit up an obnoxious cigar after dinner and then we began the ritual which was to mark the end of every day on the mountain.

Warwick produced a small marzipan bar for each of us and Grahame lovingly poured us a capful each from our plastic bottle of rum. A chew of marzipan, a capful of rum and we were ready for sleep.

The rum was so strong that it could be constantly diluted with snow. Though it grew weaker, the flavour improved and, like something from a fairy tale, the level in the bottle never dropped.

The next morning we crawled through the sleeve to find a bright day with an invigorating wind. At eight it was still freezing and there was no desire to delay in fitting crampons and tying ropes so that we could move off and warm up. Col, Grahame and John went off towards Budd Pass with marker poles. The programme was that they would find and mark a safe route through the crevasses while Warwick and I went back to the Toyshop and brought down all the loads to the camp. With the route established and the loads together we could make a double carry the next day and set up camp at the pass for the final climb.

The rope of three moved off briskly, without packs for a change, while Warwick and I retraced the few hundred yards to the foot of the Escalator. As Warwick noted, we spent a 'galling morning' bringing the loads down 300 feet from the cave to the glacier. The loose scree, partly cemented by drift, gave no sure footing and our struggle with kitbags, food packets and lightly-bound marker poles created a cold, hellish frustration. Loads tipped out of control when we tried to roll them, a bundle of poles slid quickly down the steep slope, and only by a quirk of the terrain were they stopped short of oblivion in a crevasse. The heavy polythene bags containing food were ripped by the sharp rocks. Ankles twisted, heels were jarred and all the time fine waves of drift snow came sweeping across the glacier with a nor'wester and hurtled up the Escalator in rising swirls. Drift blown with scree dust into our faces finally soured any vestiges of good humour.

By two o'clock we had everything down to the glacier and one load back to camp. We paused for a hot drink, surprised at the sound of voices when the other three returned. They bundled in to join us, blowing on cold hands, brushed snow from their trousers and told us what happened. They encountered the same annoying drift swirls and, after finding a way through the first crevasse maze, were halted at the foot of the pass by thickening mist. An attempt to continue resulted in circling to cross their own tracks. They gave up any further effort as dangerous and futile. But Grahame and Col were confident that the final approaches were clear and we could continue as planned.

The whole glacier became enveloped in cloud. The wind rose and as we dumped the last loads the drift rattled against the tent. The weather changed rapidly before and could do so again, generally for the worse and Warwick knew that every minute of fine weather had to be used. The final double carry would involve several hours and we had to start as soon as the cloud broke. Each hour one of us checked the weather but at ten we abandoned this for sleep though Col undertook to wake at four the next morning. He woke promptly and after a deliberate walk outside announced a clear sky. 'A perfect alpine dawn!' he called. The rest of us sat up in various stages of torpor then pushed down Warwick's porridge and coffee before dressing.

When I shook my crampons free of snow I found the sky over the sea was black and the distant surf beat hardly against the moraine. But above was perfectly clear, save for high cloud, and for the first time we could survey the ice cliffs in their entirety. Grahame looked knowingly at Warwick and said: 'What do you think? Do we try her now or wait?' Grahame was obsessed with the idea that Big Ben was trying to catch us, lure us higher with good weather, trap us and cause another retreat as in 1963. He constantly implied that the good spells of weather we encountered could not last. A fast attempt then, while the weather was calm and the mountain unprepared, might reap the success that could be denied later by blizzards. It was a tempting opportunity: a crisp, fast climb in crampons without packs, then back early to the beach to repose in our victory. But it was a long way. There were another 6000 feet, miles of glacier and the risk of benightment in a storm that would spell disaster.

Warwick opined that we were not ready for such an extended effort, physically or mentally. We would stick to the plan and establish the Pass Camp. We moved off with the first load at a fast clip, crampons biting crisply into the early morning hardness of the snow. Colin led with Grahame behind John who was in the middle of the three-man rope. Warwick and myself as tail-end Charlie followed.

We forged on without pause, moving from one marker pole to another, detouring round the bigger crevasses, striding over the small ones. Occasionally we slowed to probe an uncertain surface with our ice axes. With it pronounced safe, or the position of a new hole discovered, we carried on and soon reached the double poles that marked the limit of the previous day's exploration.

Now we could see Budd Peak's hair-raising south-west ridge, the unprepossessing heap of Peak 4100 directly above the pass and a wide scatter of rocks on the glacier from its north wall. The slope steepened rapidly as we climbed. The last hundred feet to the crest of the pass were devoid of snow and the bare blue ice mutely told of the perpetual wind that funnelled through the gap. My ankles barely stood the strain as we climbed over the angled, knobbly ice, my whole weight and load balanced on the crampon points which merely nicked the surface. The crampons had to be placed firmly and squarely on the ice, whatever the angle, and it was not until we reached the top that I was relieved of the disjointing pressure on my ankles.

Before us was the vast, impressive waste of the Gotley Glacier, merging into the distant Abbotsmith. At the coast we saw a green splash on Cape Arkona but the remainder of the westerly view was white, with shadows of grey and blue. We all glanced up, eager to see Mawson Peak, but the cloud had come and there was no view above 6000 feet. It was bitterly cold as we cached our loads beneath a rock overhang. Nearby, where the ridge fell to the iced pass, was a large windscoop in the glacier. Its depth was testimony to the wind's strength and here, two years before, Warwick and Grahame had almost been buried alive in a snow cave dug in its side. A suggestion that we use it for our camp was curtly dismissed by Warwick and we selected a site on a gentle slope of the Gotley. One more load and the lift would be finished. With frost the spur we descended quickly from the pass.

The transformation as we left the bare ice for snow was almost unbelievable. Above there was a keen, cutting wind and grey skies. Below the sun shone through white woolly cloud that paradoxically dropped new snow on our tracks. There was not a breath of wind and soon we became overheated, the thin cloud intensifying the sun. The snow underfoot became wet and soft, sticking and filling the space between crampon points. It caked in soggy layers to our boots, like gluey mud, and we stumbled and slipped as our grip was lost. After the tiring carry and cold, the still heat was enervating and we plodded back to the camp feeling like wet rags.

With the weather so still, Warwick was adamant that we take everything that remained and force ourselves along to reach the pass again before a change. The loads looked enormous but I had no energy to demur as I flopped against a pack and waited while Warwick prepared a meal. The heat was almost tropical and he stripped off to the waist to sunbathe while tending the primus. We ate lethargically, postponing the inevitable, but at two o'clock a move could not be denied any longer. We struck the tent. The packs did not bear thinking about but it was not until I manoeuvred mine to my shoulders that I realised the full weight. Our spring balance was lost but, since there was no doubt the packs were heavier than anything we had carried to date, they were all a hundred pounds or more.

The first half hour was tolerable. But when we passed into thick cloud again, and pushed on without rest, the pack became Sinbad's Old Man of the Sea and my legs like jelly. I seemed to lose all control over my movements, save for a simple stagger. Snow plastered my goggles, I could barely see as it melted and ran down the perspex and then they misted up inside from tears that involuntarily streamed down my cheeks. I went on, pulled by the tight rope from Warwick; the wind rose, the cloud thickened and snow pelted into our faces. I had no more energy to step over the simplest crevasses, tripped on their lips and fell three times, flat on my face in the snow. This offered the only respite in an agonising rush that became increasingly blind. But the rest was hardly worth the effort needed to regain my footing.

Grahame wrote that our fatigue and heavy loads created a lack of safety and increased the danger immeasurably should someone fall down a crevasse. Under ideal conditions it was hard enough for a man to help himself out of a crevasse. Exhausted, in bad weather, with a huge load it would have been impossible. As we trudged and staggered on I hoped that Grahame in front knew where we were going. We were in an almost complete white out: white cloud, white snow merging with no relief. But sometimes I would feel a click as the bundle of poles on my pack pushed against one in the snow. Colin changed packs with me but soon we came to a halt and I sagged onto my ice axe.

Vaguely I heard Grahame saying, compass in hand, that we were virtually lost and any further movement was foolish. Drift snow spun past, the wind slapped us and snow that melted on our cheeks ran to our straggling beards, then froze. We dropped the packs and picked up the shovels and saws. As we moved around to dig a tent platform our dark figures in the total whiteness seemed disembodied, floating in a world of snowy unreality.

8

...MAKES YOU STRONGER

I WROTE,'TODAY WE SHACK UP as a sou'wester blows relentless-ly—a curious storm since we only receive it in eddies and gusts. Sometimes it is entirely quiet, the tent is still, there is not a suggestion of wind, and all one can hear if the others are asleep is the distant roar of wind bellowing over the pass. The wind will suddenly return and hit the tent with snow and drift, causing the whole structure to flap violently, shaking down particles of rime like a shower of fine snow. We seem to be iced up both inside and out though drift is accumulating only on the leeward sides with a tendency to scour on the windward. The ventilator has a beard of ice hanging from it and the sleeve entrance is quickly filling with snow like a distended bladder.'

Lying there, waiting for the storm to abate, Grahame still worried. Nearly all our kerosene had been taken to the pass and we only had enough to last a day or two. He wondered what would happen if a long blizzard set in. Would we struggle up to the pass to get some, or go back to Base? Then he recalled that supplies had been left at Long Beach in '63. He broached the possibility of making a trip to the beach if upwards movement was impossible. It was a straight-forward journey down the Fifty-One. 'We must not be fooled into expecting the weather to improve as we did last time. Or we'll end up the same way: a disorderly retreat at the last minute.' The spectre of the 1963 failure continued to rear its ugly head. It was disquieting and annoying even if it did prevent over-confidence and ensure a safe, methodical advance. I thought, a trip to Long Beach for extra supplies before we're down to our uppers would not be too bad.

There was a bottle of untouched Negrita rum to pick up.

A delicate tension imbued the forced camp. We had been caught with our pants down in the strange situation of having our main supplies up the mountain, and not down which has been the case with many expedition crises in the past. At the Toyshop we had cached the Bechervaise tent and primus but no food or fuel. This was our emergency backstop, affording at least some shelter in a precipitous retreat. Poly Gully with its luxuries seemed a long way off. But with Long Beach as a last resort, our worries about food and safety seemed unfounded. The chief problem was time. We could retreat safely but we could not afford the time to retreat and return, with still enough time in hand to climb the peak. It was 20 January and we had already been on Heard eight of the prescribed twenty-eight days. Delay and disorganisation were the threats to our ambitions.

On the morning of the 21st our gloom was banished as we crawled out into new snow and squinted in the sun. The sky was still black and sullen out to sea but there seemed to be time for us to regain the pass. Our windproofs dried quickly but I found that my leather boots had finally lost the competition with rubber. They were saturated on pitching the camp and during the storm had frozen solid. It would take hours to make them pliant and as the others bustled me along I glumly resorted to the sloppy vapour barrier boots. The tent was well cemented with drift but we speedily dug it out and divided the equipment into two loads. We discovered that our camp was below the last rise to the foot of the pass slopes, although the scene had changed dramatically. Much of the bare rock was enveloped in new snow and the spikes and towers seemed decorated with icing sugar. The marker poles were still visible, some leaning under the weight of rime, and we climbed up to rejoin the old route. The pass crest was still bare but the snow below was deep and in avalanche condition. We kept high above the main slope and the perfect, symmetrical cone of Mawson Peak came into view. The steep, even slopes rising to the summit 5000 feet higher seemed quite unattainable and we were sobered as the expanding scene revealed the distance to climb.

Grahame, as next cook on the roster, stayed with the Pyramid while the rest of us went back for the final loads. There had been some difficulty carving a platform since the snow at the campsite lay in sugary layers. A lack of impeding wind enabled us to work steadily, however, but there was no time to admire the view. The sky looked in a bellicose mood again and we could not afford smoko until all the loads were up. We ploughed quickly down to the forced campsite which formed a yellowed blot on the virgin-white landscape, covered with empty packets and paper that clung to our crampons like litter to a park keeper's stick.

We returned at a fast, unrelenting pace that saw us to the pass just as the weather closed in. The wind whistled over, making balance a test of nerves. In new boots I was anxious to take my time. But Warwick drove on without pause, almost dragging me behind, and by the time we crossed the crest I was groggy and gasping from exhaustion. It was raining. As my windproofs became soaked in a heavy downpour I swore in disgust. What a foul island with a foul mountain and foul weather! If it rained all the time we could plan for it—or if it snowed or froze or anything. But the unpredictable cycle of rain, snow, high temperatures, low temperatures, wind and brief sun left one in a constant puzzle and in danger of being caught out in Heard's infuriating quick change act.

The sun went down and the bad weather paused. Warwick and Grahame left the comfort of their sleeping bags and went out to photograph as Mawson Peak revealed itself again and seemed astonishingly close in the fading light. The rest of us lay back reading or smoking, ignoring Grahame's persistent calls: 'Come out and see the view. The summit's absolutely clear!' Then the inevitable, pessimistic closing note: 'You may not get the chance to see it like this again!' Some rude remarks were passed in undertone but, responding to the call of nature rather than Grahame's exhortations, I quickly scrambled into the open. It took so much time and trouble to dress for a trip outside that I braved the cold and snow in long woolly underpants and bare feet. Hopping vigorously around the Pyramid I concurred with their sublimated opinion of the view and then cursed as the ubiquitous cameras appeared and I was told to 'Hold it!'

The weather worsened again during the night and we awoke to an opaque whiteness, a steady wind and drift snow finally securing the tent. After the rain and relative warmth the fabric had become wet and the overnight freeze formed sheets of ice that cracked alarmingly as we leant against the walls. This was unavoidable since the Pyramid was designed as a three-man tent. Five fitted and though there was discomfort at times, the combined heat of bodies squeezed together kept us cosy and warm. We lay across the tent, facing the entrance. Since the Pyramid was eight feet square there was room for the Lilos and about two feet of space between them and the wall. In the left hand part of this space we kept the stove, billies, jugs and food bags. At the right were shovels, saws, boots and spare pieces of equipment. The space before the sleeve was left vacant and the floor rolled back so that anyone entering could shed wet clothes and boots without encroaching on it. An advantage of the Pyramid was that one could stand upright at the centre so that dressing was accomplished without spreading oneself over somebody's legs or body.

We rotated sleeping positions so that each man took his turn as cook, lying opposite the stove. It also ensured that we all took turns at sleeping in the outside positions—the worst of all since there we pressed against the cold wall and rime on the fabric. That night I was on the right, outside, mattress but could look-forward to the two best positions (inside before the cook) on the following nights. When I was in the centre Col slept on my right and Warwick on my left. Agreeable company, save that Warwick invariably found his air mattress too narrow and unconsciously encroached on two of my four tubes during the night. If I wished to sleep on my side, my slight 10 stone wedged warmly between two bodies of 14 stone, I could not have better sleeping partners. But lying on my back was often impossible until I discovered the trick of bolstering the side of my mattress to stop Warwick rolling.

The tent platform was not quite flat. In the confusing blankness of snow it is a clever man who can expertly cut a perfectly flat ledge out of a slope without a spirit level. Often tilts in tent platforms are not discovered until sleeping positions are tried when a gentle rush of blood to the head will cause sensitive humans to

Three of the climbing party on the Ascent Glacier, Budd Pass below

seek a more comfortable angle. This discomfort can be relieved by simple movement but no-one has yet discovered how to instil Lilos with a useful sense of inertia. The heat of our bodies penetrated through the mattresses and floor, melted the snow and smoothed out corrugations caused by the digging. This provided a polished surface and the mattresses imperceptibly inched their way towards the entrance. We woke in the morning to find our feet in dirty pots or boots and vigorous rearrangement was necessary to sort ourselves back into a manageable heap. The allusion was inevitable. Encased in the cocoons of dark-green sleeping bags, jammed together, a few snorts and grunts were only required to make us the highest elephant seals on the island.

The weather forced another day of uncomfortable rest on 22 January. I reflected that this expedition consisted of either intense activity or intense inactivity. The previous day we had strained ourselves to the utmost, snatching a break in the weather to establish the assault camp. From the evening of the 21st until well into the 23rd we lay flat on our backs, turning or sitting up when we grew stiff or numb, and barely poked our noses outside the tent. Not that there were any complaints. We could rest with easy consciences after the heavy lift over the South Barrier and the comforting knowledge that we no longer had to carry loads up. In future they would be going down. But this thought always provoked the remembrance that before we could go down we still had to reach the summit.

Surrounded by the orange tent fabric, with no window, it was difficult to decide whether the sky was clear or still blanketed in drift and cloud. The mixture of snow and mist was relatively bright and often in our orange glow we wondered nervously if the sun was shining and we should be up and on our way. Grahame, the most anxious, and the most willing to sacrifice the warmth of his bag for the sake of our objective, often untwisted the sleeve, spread it open and peered outside. Then, the blue-white glare of the blank landscape broke the suffusion of orange light like an empty television screen, and there were cries of discomfort as a cold blast of air cut through the warm fug we had built up inside.

Sooner or later the conversation worked its way round to the weather and what it was going to do. Grahame talked of three-week blizzards while Warwick was anxious to make use of even the smallest break. He wished to keep us moving so that we did not descend into mental lethargy and lose our opportunities by slow reaction. He talked of getting up at eight or nine that evening if necessary and marking the first few hundred yards up the mountain. I snuggled deeper into my bag and thought: *Que sera, sera.*

We had supplies for three weeks, though through miscalculation, only enough kerosene for about two. If necessary we could economise and make this last and our problem lay not in lack of supplies or a safe camp, but still in time. We could not stay longer than three weeks anyway since *Patanela* was due back after that time. It seemed unlikely that we would need three weeks but the weather was completely unpredictable. Then we needed time to fulfil our scientific and film responsibilities at sea level. As the wind blew without diminishing, the distressing thought occurred that we might sit here in a storm without reaching the top and leave ourselves no time for all our other aims. What a fiasco that would be! Warwick constantly sought the opportunity to move and still found time to film indoors and keep our spirits up. He sang bawdy ditties in competition with Colin, cracked jokes, stimulated conversation but tempered any over-seriousness with a Goonish flavour. Eccles, Neddie Seagoon and Bluebottle were our constant imaginary companions and kept our cramped lie-up in lighter perspective. Some people think that a group of men, forced into close proximity under difficult conditions, and with such an idealistic aim as climbing a mountain, will dream beautiful dreams and rise to fine, intellectual discussion. But in reality there is little room for such things since they probe too deeply into each individual's character, his personal beliefs and prejudices. The end result can be conflict, lack of co-operation and ruination of close teamwork. Humour, tolerance and selflessness were the most important criteria for success.

In the evening, when it was clear we could not move that day, Warwick initiated the writing of a rough poem which is the sole record I have of any combined artistic effort. It was designed to draw out our thoughts as we lay back waiting for sleep, staring at the patterns formed by ice on the outside of the tent.

WARWICK:

'What do you think?' a young man asked of me
'As you lie back looking yet not seeing with such glassy stare?'

JOHN:

The world outside is dead and
Wind crackles out
On the skin of the tent.

COLIN:

Wherein all that is sordid and living is pent,
By the thin synthetic wall that holds back purity and death.

ME:

So we dreamt of rum
On a glacial sea
And the darkling hum
As the rocks sang ho and hee
To the breaking wave
And boats that turned in their grave.

GRAHAME:

Deterred by a tiresome tunnel
And the sandy rattle of drift
We lie here and stare at the red-striped poles,
While outside—who knows?—the summit stands clear
And our only chance silently passes.

As Warwick said later, we should have sloshed Grahame for being so practical.

With so little physical activity we slept lightly. Warwick tossed and turned, sometimes mumbling in a strange dream of claustropho-bia. It seemed inexplicable until I remembered the great windscoop below us and the terrible memory that he must have of struggling through a hole in the snow cave as the drift tried to fill it up. He and Grahame had come close to death. Now they returned to the scene of a struggle for existence in another throw against a pernicious Big Ben. I woke at two-thirty as first light shaped the sleeping figures and watched with half-closed eyes as Grahame struggled with the sleeve and went outside. He returned quickly, climbed into his bag quietly and I went back to sleep, secure in the knowledge that we could not make an early start.

At four-thirty Warwick did the same but the visibility was nil, snow falling, though the wind had slackened off. Heat generated by the stove for the evening meal had disappeared long since and our breaths rose in clouds of vapour. We had breakfast but when noon came and the prospect of lunch John, as cook, and in charge of ra-tions, decided that we should make do with coffee and a couple of biscuits. Though he felt we should conserve supplies, an argument ensued that Warwick finally resolved with another look outside. 'The sun's shining up there somewhere and the cloud's thinner. We'll have some good tucker and go and have a look. Even if we only pole across the pass crevasses we'll be on our feet again with a bit of forward motion.'

Stiff and tottering, we stumbled in the snow, walking again for the first time in forty-four hours. The packs and ropes were half bur-ied in snow, the ice axes and tent fantastically adorned with frets and spicules of ice like frozen pennants. My windproofs were still soaked from the rain and frozen stiff until body heat and a fresh wind dried them out. Col felt the cold badly, stamping round the tent until he had generated enough warmth to bang his pack free of snow and sort his equipment. Apart from climbing gear we took forty marker poles and bivouac kit. This consisted of spare clothing, a nylon sheet, food, a shovel and saw and full primus in case we were caught in a storm and forced to dig a snow cave. With this kit we could expect to sur-vive in relative comfort for forty-eight hours.

Visibility was only a hundred yards but occasionally the thin cloud parted over the pass and we caught a glimpse of the Fifty-One and the eastern ice cliffs. The crater rim was clear in the distance with blue sky above. It looked promising and as soon as we had persuaded our numb fingers to tie the ropes we set out in the same order as before. Crampons were unnecessary in the deep, new snow and we made good progress to the poles over the windscoop. Our first requirement was to find a way through the bad crevasses near the pass. From there we would climb at a steady angle, close to the western side of the ridge rising to Budd Peak, with the main, broken Gotley Glacier on our left. The slope, which Grahame called the Ascent Glacier, gave direct and unbroken access to the main crater edge. From its head a short, steep slope would take us over the lip and onto the wide plateau inside the crater. Then a short, flat walk would lead us to the bottom of the final 1500-foot cone of Mawson Peak. Technically, the climb was straightforward. Success depended on the weather allowing us enough time to climb 5000 feet over a horizontal distance of three miles—and return.

Grahame led off into the crevasses with a compass but the cloud was so thick that he returned initially and told Warwick that it was both difficult and dangerous to try and find a way under the present conditions. Warwick demurred and persuaded him to have another try. He pushed on, Col planted poles at regular intervals and the camp disappeared. The cloud was so thick that I, as fifth man, could barely see Grahame 200 feet ahead. He followed a compass course but found it impossible to look at the compass and for holes in the snow at the same time. John took over the compass and kept Grahame on a straight course with a whistle: one blast for moving left, two meant his direction was correct and three that he should move right.

We felt, rather than saw, the sheer rock face on our right as we moved steadily forward. With surprising ease we wound our way through the blue maws in the ice and began to climb gently over unbroken snow. By that stage we were warmed up, dry, stiffness gone and we enjoyed the hard exercise of climbing again. The sun became more apparent, the snow brightened, the cloud thinned and suddenly we broke through the thick rolls of vapour spreading out to sea and gloried in brilliant sunshine. The whole upper mountain was clear and we moved in an elevated world separated sharply from the tumble of sea and rocks below. The southern face of Mawson Peak was littered with unstable seracs[*] that discounted it as an ascent route. But the eastern profile of the cone was even and almost free from corrugations. It led down to the plateau and seemed the obvious way up.

Fitting snow goggles as the glare hurt our eyes, we were delighted to see white smoke rolling off the summit. The peak was still active as a volcano! We were suddenly full of ideas as to what lay inside the small crater: a big hole, a lake, hot springs, gas vents and the dangers of ice associated with heat that might stop us reaching the very top. On our other hand Budd Peak's ridge was horrific; slabs of steep ice, vertical rock walls surmounted by fancy flutes and honeycombs of ice. There was a constant wind swerving over the top with spurts of drift and a noise like a far-off, roaring primus. We climbed on slowly, placing marker poles and photographing.

Grahame stopped to lower thermometers down crevasses in his survey to establish if the glaciers were polar or temperate. The new snow covered many crevasses and careful probing was required to make the way safe. Higher up John relieved Grahame of the hard work of plugging deep steps. A few minutes later he paused at the sight of a suspicious hollow, found a crevasse with his axe and went slowly forward, packing the snow with his boots while Colin knelt behind, belaying the rope round his deeply embedded axe. Grahame waited on the lower side of another crevasse while Warwick and I on a separate rope stamped round impatiently further down the slope. I plunged my axe in the snow and bent over to shift the pack on my back, watching John's progress. He probed ahead and called back to Colin that the way was clear. Col released the rope leading to John and turned to take Grahame's until he was safely up to him. Then John just disappeared.

There was no sound and I was astounded that in the blink of an eyelid a man had vanished, leaving behind a dark crack in the

---

[*]   Pinnacles of ice.

snow. The rope from Colin ran out a short way, but he felt no tug and did not know of John's disappearance until I yelled: 'Hey Col! John's gone!' Quickly he transferred his attention from Grahame and lashed the dead rope to his axe. Feeling that someone should go to his aid, since John responded to none of our calls, I moved forward. But Col had to stay put holding the rope, Grahame could not move for the danger of the lower crevasse and Warwick pulled out his movie camera. John could not have fallen far since the rope had not run out more than a few feet. But I swore heartily at the others' inaction and received some black looks for my trouble.

Thankfully, John's waving ice axe appeared and his gloved hand as he thrashed away at the loose snow on the crevasse edge. Soon his head appeared and, as he hauled himself out with a pull from Colin, the cameras whirred and clicked. Covered in soft snow John muttered that he had only fallen through the crevasse lid and landed in a featherbed of snow on a ledge eight feet lower. With nothing below that, I congratulated him on a lucky landing.

Our climbing and rope techniques were not co-ordinated. We halted at each slight sign of danger and made slow progress, probing at every opportunity. This was aggravated by our holding the hidden crevasses in nervous awe rather than confident respect, and the chances of an accident increased. Further up we stopped to eat, wandered in all directions for photographs without belays, and found on moving off that we had been within feet of another big hole.

We stopped at eight o'clock in the evening at 7000 feet at the foot of the final steep slope to the crater rim. We had found and established a safe route and could return to camp with the satisfaction of knowing the first 3000 feet at first hand. Beyond that point the route was obvious and all we needed was one good day for the climb. In increasing wind and greying skies we made fast time down the glacier. With memories of John's fall we held the ropes tightly but in astonishment I watched as he disappeared again. It was the same crevasse but he fell in at a point several yards to one side of the old hole. The same thing had happened, the same ledge was there eight feet down but this time Warwick and I were quickly to the scene to haul him out if necessary.

When we came to the pass it was noticeable that its funnelling effect collected more cloud than elsewhere. This warned us not to lie up, deterred at the sight of fog from the tent, since it might be clear higher. There was an enchanting picture of quilting cloud drifting over an Antarctic ridge with green moraines and white brash ice on a sullen sea. The drift hissed past and occasionally there were whirling snow devils spinning against the delicate, pale watercolour of blue ice and a snowy sky fading into the late evening. Warwick and I reached the tent first and crawled inside to find rime hard on the walls, Lilos frozen to the floor and icy to the touch.

We made a hot drink, changed and pulled on sleeping bags but the others did not return save when Grahame stood outside and asked me to pass out some ice screws. Over an hour later, in almost total darkness, they came in and said that they had encountered trouble with yet another crevasse. Most of the food packages were cached in the overhang above the tent and a short climb, crossing two crevasses, was necessary to reach it. Col and John climbed up, cut packages out of the ice, then slid them down to Grahame. Two packages slid into his arms but the third, as it careered quickly towards him, stopped short as another crevasse opened up and received it into its grinning jaws. Grahame attached our folding ladder to ice screws and climbed down, twenty feet, and successfully recovered the food: quite a day for crevasses.

We finished our dinner at two o'clock in the morning of 24 January as a lone candle twinkled off the stars of rime. Fortunately the weather later that day did not encourage another climb and we slept long and hard in the hope of a good day on the 25th. The wind battered the tent, twisted the poles and thoroughly showered us with rime. It dusted our bags, melted on their warmth and slowly but surely wet them through. The mattresses were wet from condensation, our clothing was wet and only our down jackets created a reasonable heat. In an effort to keep dry Col and I made use of our flags. They were full-size ensigns, six feet long, and the bunting made a good cover for our bags. Though John had brought a sleeping bag cover we lay back smugly as Warwick and Grahame tried to combat the rime with spare clothing. Col, in his habit of lying on his back,

Climbing the upper reaches of the Gotley Glacier, Mawson Peak beyond

legs and arms straight, bag pulled up to his chin and yellow balaclava pulled down like a helmet, looked strangely like a warrior lying in state beneath the red, white and blue Australian flag.

Discussions that day included recriminations about our slow climbing and poor safety techniques. Grahame wrote that he was disgusted at our attitude towards crevasses and snow bridges. We were too cautious and timid since 'the glacier was as good a piece of country as anywhere on Heard.'

'At times I feel that Mawson Peak is beyond the reach of this party but doubtless some learning will occur.' On the same day I wrote that there was a lack of drive in our approach to the climb and also opined: 'I shan't be at all surprised if we don't get up this mountain.' Nothing was wrong with our techniques and we all had experience on mountains all over the world. But we had never climbed together before and it is well known that it takes time to build up an efficient climbing team. Practice and work together is as important in mountaineering as in any other sport. There had been no time or opportunity for this before reaching Big Ben. This lack, plus the aura of danger and hostility that surrounded us from constant stories of the near disaster in 1963, caused us to fumble in our approach. There was no need to spell out, either, that there were only five human beings on the island—us—and we had no recourse to help from anyone, no radio contact with the outside world and *Patanela* was 300 miles away at Kerguelen.

We decided that when we climbed again we would all tie on one rope. This gave immense security since if one fell down there were four others to hold him. With this security, the route mostly marked and a distinct knowledge of the crevasse pattern and danger we could climb quickly and not waste vital time hesitating at the lips of crevasses.

As the 24th drew on we took turns reading poems out of Grahame's volume of Robert Frost, John read a book on chess and I went into the world of Cambridge dons with C. P. Snow as Col peered over my shoulder. Later John and I played cards, then Warwick showed us how to win, new jokes were remembered, old ones retold and there were puns and songs. I offended Warwick by writing a rude remark in the quarter-inch rime on the wall before we turned over for sleep at nine o'clock. I was cook for the next day and I gave Col a jaundiced look when he promised to wake me at two-thirty. We did not fall asleep immediately. One could sense others thinking in the freezing twilight and, for a while, John crooned Australian ballads and one of Sophia Loren's sexy songs that stuck in his mind: *Boom-diddy-boom- diddy-boom-diddy-boom-diddy-boom, diddy-boom-diddy boom boom boom*, and I slipped into sleep, hoping for another rest day on the morrow.

After fitful sleep I was not in the best of tempers when Col took a brief look at the weather and woke me to cook breakfast at three o'clock. There was a numbing, dark cold about the tent, barely alleviated by the single candle which required three matches to light. The others lay smothered and silent, apparently asleep, but I knew that they were half awake (as I was always) enjoying the sound of someone else cooking while they were warm and inactive. Bad-tempered at this, and with the candle, I found then that my mattress and Warwick's projected into the cooking area, covering the stove and billies. As usual mine was half covered by Warwick so that it was with sadistic delight that I pulled it hard and he promptly fell into the gap. He woke with a start and we rearranged the mattresses to suit us both.

The primus started very easily but by the time I melted the first snow for porridge it was apparent that I would need more for coffee. In furious irritation I wrestled with the frozen sleeve, forcing and pushing it into reasonable shape, and dragged myself through its stiff envelope. It was a snowed-up world outside where all seemed to be cloud with a vestige of light improving the luminosity of the glacier. Crawling out on hands and knees, my fingers plunging into drift snow like freezing, sifted flour, I hastily stood up, looked around with half-opened eyes, relieved myself and bent to pick up a snow block. Pushing it inside, I followed quickly, warmed my fingers over the stove and searched for food from the pile in the corner.

Everything was packed in triple polythene bags and as I burrowed amongst them, old bags and new bags, there seemed little chance of finding anything to eat. With a loud oath that the best thing for

John (L) and the Author, with Mawson peak behind

breakfast would be poly bags, I finally discovered the porridge. Then, as my feet froze, the breakfast slowly cooked. I smoked three cigarettes and added salt, butter, sugar and milk to the thickening porridge: a nice, creamy brew. With satisfaction I shoved Warwick and Col and placed a jug of steaming food into their hands as they sat up sleepily, evincing pleasant surprise at the sight of my efforts. Later I felt more human drinking hot coffee with a piece of Grahame's Christmas cake. We talked inconsequentially and, for a change, no-one said anything about the weather, which was curiously still.

At five-thirty, in unspoken agreement, we pulled on socks and boots, windproofs, adjusted balaclavas and goggles, fastened waist ties, tucked gloves, cameras and personal oddments into pockets and followed each other in quick succession through the sleeve. The packs had to be dug out again and there was little talk as each man was preoccupied in sorting his own gear and combating the cold.

There seemed to be no question of whether we should start or not, despite the mist. Then suddenly it broke and there was Mawson Peak, the glaciers, the ridge and all, clear and shining in the frost, the white light of dawn with a crystal sky and old moon in the east. Everyone was heartened by the sight and Warwick felt instinctively that this might be the day.

Five on one rope created problems. Knots were tied in the wrong places, too much spare rope was wrapped round the shoulders of one man, prussik loops became snarled up in karabiners and Warwick almost spat in reply when I shouted 'Giddyap! Mush!' at six-thirty and he led off to promptly put his foot in a crevasse. It was agreed that stops should be kept to a minimum. In good army style we climbed for fifty minutes, rested for ten and each of us took a turn at ploughing the trail. We soon grew used to five tied together and, once rhythm was established, felt comforted that we were all together and directly responsible for each other's safety.

The temperature was about 18°F and our feet were cold even in vapour barrier boots. My right hand, firmly gripping the ice axe, became numb in spite of two pairs of gloves and I was forced to change hands frequently to restore circulation. Unfortunately the Budd Peak ridge barred any sunlight from our route. While the summit became brilliant we could climb without goggles and prolonged exercise was our only means of keeping warm. Initially there were thick banks of woolly cloud beneath us but we had little time or inclination to watch as the rising sun rimmed them with red and sketched the ridge pinnacles into a black and white silhouette.

We went on steadily, first Warwick plugging steps, then myself, then John, and Col took over to lead from shadow to sunlight as we reached the limit of our reconnaissance on the 23rd. Col sat down, coughing badly, and explained that a whiff of sulphurous fumes had affected his breathing following an accident he had sustained in a chemical factory. But he entertained no question of stopping and forced himself along for the rest of the day without pause. We adjusted goggles but when I went to apply sun cream, the tube snapped in half, frozen solid. We strapped on crampons, picked up marker poles and Grahame led up the steep slope to the crater. The sky was blue with no streaks of threatening wind cloud, and below the angrier clouds had gone to leave little puffs over a calm sea. I looked at Warwick, pointed to the sky and summit, then grimaced. This looked like it.

The others were in a grim mood as we cramponned to the edge of Big Ben's crater. My jocular remarks were ill received but I felt no worry save that we might get within a few hundred feet of the top, retreat in bad weather, and then have to grind back up those long, monotonous slopes in a second attempt. There was a keen wind at the edge and we stumbled over sastrugi* and ribs of ice, seeking a way down low ice cliffs to the plateau. This was a wide plain of nothing. Bumps and mushrooms of ice formed the peaks on the opposite side, two miles away. Budd Peak on our right, that had looked so impressive from below, became merely an extension of the crater rim with bulges of weathered ice still moaning in the wind.

We planted poles at regular intervals, dropped down to the

---

*   Wind-formed wave-like ridges in hard snow.

plateau and made a beeline for the summit cone. Stopping at the Gotley Glacier bergschrund we ate a mouthful of chocolate and Grahame lowered another thermometer. It was twelve-thirty and the end of Grahame's spell in the lead. Before we moved off Col said: 'I think Grahame should lead all the way unless he finds deep snow and wants a rest.' Warwick nodded: 'I heartily agree.' Of all of us, this was Grahame's mountain. When he first visited the island in 1954, the challenge of Big Ben loomed in his thoughts; he saw it again during a voyage to Antarctica and in 1963 had been so close to success with his own expedition. When the lead was relinquished to him he found it a very moving moment. As we went forward, left the plateau and began to rise... 'I knew that at last I was climbing that endless snow slope that I've climbed, in one disguise or another, in my dreams for eleven years.'

There was a threat in the air. The wind direction had changed to north west. A pall of grey rapidly spread across the sky and the question of whether we would make it or not, before the weather closed in, began to raise its ugly head. We dumped most of the marker poles at the bergschrund, broke the rest in half, and climbed steadily up the thirty-degree slope of the cone. The snow was in perfect condition to kick firm steps and we went straight up under a watery sun.

Budd Peak, at 7600 feet, dropped beneath us and we felt a sense of elation, treading the highest ground on the island. The sea was muffled in storm clouds and there was nothing to see but the white waste of glaciers. Grahame looked tired at times but he ploughed ahead while Warwick filmed assiduously. At about 8500 feet we came to a large crevasse stretching across the slope and Grahame had to force a dangerous route across an unstable snow bridge to reach the upper lip. Above he cut steps in bare ice. Then we moved over a bumpy surface as the slope eased, and found a break in the edge of the cone. Passing formations like ice cauliflowers, we climbed awkwardly over giant ice feathers on the active crater's edge—'like candelabras up to a foot long'. To the left, steam gushed from a vent in the ice; brown silica deposits stained the ground below. We manoeuvred along the edge until Grahame reached the apex of a slight rise. He signalled to Warwick that we had reached the top. So had the cloud and nor'wester. A gush of mist swept over the summit to join the steam and soon there was nothing but a thick, cold fog and rising wind.

9

ENTR'ACTE

It was three o'clock and the wind swept drift into our faces at twenty knots. Clustered together, we shook hands, and photographed each other and the large flags as they flapped almost out of control. Looking through the viewfinder at the group of heavily-clothed figures against a blank background I remarked that they looked like Scott's party at the South Pole. Col gruffly replied: 'We'll end up the same way too if we don't get off this bloody mountain soon!' But we had to make some effort to examine the active crater before we left. Nobody had seen it before and no-one was likely to see it again.

The crater was a valley about twenty feet deep, seventy-five feet wide and 250 long. The brown silica deposits were prominent, looking like rocks, steam drifted over them and hot water bubbled from holes at the side. Grahame, John and Col untied from Warwick and myself in order to climb down but the sides were so steep and unstable that they quickly retreated. The effect of heat on the ice meant that it was liable to give way under the least weight, and a tumble into something scalding and obnoxious would be the reward. After a brief discussion we decided to leave immediately, before the weather worsened. We had the bivouac kit but we were not anxious to spend a night out near the top of Big Ben.

The others readjusted ropes and moved off. As they stretched out in line I hastily pulled my New Zealand flag on to the snow and staked it out with pieces of marker pole. The rope tightened and I followed quickly. For a few hours, until the wind ripped it away, the splash of red, white and blue would be the only mark that men had

At the summit.
L-R: John Crick, Grahame Budd, the Author and Colin Putt

been on the virgin peak.

Our way down was identified by half marker poles but with the poor visibility and increasing drift there was every likelihood that we would miss them and lose ourselves. Snow began to fall, melting quickly on our windproofs, and we saw the signs of a typical weather cycle. A 'warm' nor'wester with the temperature only just on freezing at 9000 feet; snow melting on our warm bodies, turning to rain lower down, saturating us. Then, if we did not reach camp in time, the wind would swing to south-west, dropping the temperature, freezing us to the marrow. We did not dwell on the consequences.

Grahame led, past the cauliflowers, off the ice feathers, following the little fingers of orange shining in the drift. We negotiated the ice steps, half covered in new snow, and crossed the crevasse. Then, instead of the zigzag we had followed in ascending, Grahame went straight down and my calls were swallowed by the wind. A crampon came off Col's boot and while he bent to strap it back, Grahame cast around for the correct route. I suggested left but he told Warwick that we should veer slightly right in an effort to find more poles.

We moved off again, down, down and at least we knew from the angle that we were still on the cone. Lower, when we began to wonder if we would come out above the huge ice cliffs of the Gotley, Grahame glimpsed a leering ice face to his right and straightened out the descent. We plunged on, warm if anxious and abruptly came to the foot of the cone. To our left was the bergschrund—and the bundle of marker poles upright in the snow. With a sigh of relief we traversed up to it and took a well-deserved rest.

We were not out of the wood. We still had to find our way off the plateau though we felt confident of feeling our way back to camp once we reached the lower glacier. Since we had eaten little after breakfast twelve hours earlier, we forced down cheese, chocolate, biscuits and butter. I took a bite of dehydrated meat and vegetable bar which repeated on me all the way down. Grahame recovered his thermometer and led off again, following a compass course. With ease we found the poles at the crater edge and cramponned over, a wet wind lashing at our exposed cheeks. By that stage we all had Putt Parkas over the windproofs in an effort to combat the moisture.

At 7000 feet we emerged on to the regular slope of the glacier and descended below the belly of the cloud into a heavy downpour. As I took over the lead from Grahame, the snow became slushy from the rain. The crevasses began to bare their teeth and snow bridges we used on the ascent were on the brink of collapse.

I fell to the snow with a thump and looked down to find my legs hanging in a crevasse, my rump wedged against the lip. Narrow at the top, the crevasse opened into a huge bell and I was thankful for Warwick's tight rope. Confident after success, and at the sight of the Pyramid, we took an almost straight course down the glacier, taking the crevasses as they came. Warwick disappeared for a few minutes, we all continued to put feet or legs through and we seemed to be going up and down like the head of a sewing machine. But the rope was always tight, our reaction sharp and one was never in danger of falling more than a few feet.

The glacier at the pass was bare and blue from rain and wind. We tried to cross this zone without crampons but after skating sideways and backwards out of control, we sat down and strapped them on. We now knew why the ice was always bare at the crest of the pass. An irregular 40-knot wind tore across, pushing us off balance, making progress both difficult and dangerous. Halfway across the blue ice, Warwick lost a crampon and our descent ended on a note of comedy as he appeared to play hopscotch before reaching snow again.

Near the tent we moved out of the wind but it continued to roar across the ridge above. Waterfalls were blown up, down, sideways and backwards in the thaw. Water and soft snow streamed off the rock and the level of snow around the tent had dropped, leaving piles of rubbish on mounds of unmelted snow. The temperature was over 40°F, the tent almost free of ice, and we were able to collect water for cooking from the windscoop. Sunburnt, tired, saturated but happy we crawled into the sleeping bags at eight-thirty. There was no jubilation, only satisfied relief, but John kept on singing 'What a mighty day!' We drank great quantities of tea and coffee but ate little and went to sleep exhausted after a bar of rum fudge and a triple tot of real rum. Putting our watches back to normal time, we stole three extra hours of sleep.

All through the night of 25/26 January a violent sou'wester blew, the temperature fell as predicted and Big Ben seemed to batter at our tent in fury at being conquered. There was no question of moving down next day for the weather was bad and we were too tired to undertake more prolonged activity, especially with mountainous packs. The day was given over to unrestricted eating, an analysis of the climb and plans for the remaining fortnight on the island. In that time Warwick wished to complete his movie film; Colin to make a survey of the whole South Barrier region; Grahame a biological survey; me a comprehensive insect collection, while John would assist Colin and make collections of lichens and soil samples.

Warwick also wanted to collect algae and botanical specimens, John to investigate sealers' remains and Colin to collect rocks. We hoped to take photographs, monochrome and colour, of everything, including some to show glacial retreat and, apart from all this, to make a circuit of the island and make preparations to leave on 11 February: quite a programme.

After discussion we agreed that, although there was time for the circuit, it would have a detrimental effect on the rest of the work which was largely sedentary. Instead, Warwick decided that we would go back to Poly Gully in one carry, taking one day only, as soon as the weather cleared. A day there, then with Grahame and I he would go to Spit Bay, returning four days later. A further day would be spent at Base when it was hoped that Col's survey would be completed and all could go round the coast to Long Beach. Warwick and I would stay there while the others went up the west coast in a general survey, all returning to Poly Gully by 9 February.

Now the nasty part was over we looked forward to warmer, more congenial surroundings at sea level. There we could become absorbed in our own fields of work, and have time for mental rest and solitude before the long voyage home. Though most of us were a little self-satisfied over our achievement, Warwick entertained a dark foreboding that we would come to grief at the last minute. He felt that Big Ben had let us off lightly and that sooner or later we would pay the price for success. Grahame developed a similar train of thought: 'Things have worked in our favour often. What is the price?' It was a morbid preoccupation which had the smell of a death wish. I was influenced and my distinct dislike of Heard Island turned to a hate of its hostile environment, where one could never journey for more than two or three hours without tying on a rope.

The ice was all around while over it all blew a bitter wind, and a freezing sea threshed at its foot. The most apt poem in Grahame's volume of Robert Frost was *Fire and Ice*:

> Some say the world will end in fire,
> Some say in ice.
> From what I've tasted of desire
> I hold with those who favour fire.
> But if we had to perish twice,
> I think I know enough of hate
> To say that for destruction ice
> Is also great
> And would suffice.

Though fearing its power, Warwick was fascinated by Heard's challenge to existence; John found the place exciting, as might be expected on his first expedition, and Colin was non-committal. To Grahame it was a 'special island'. If anyone had a right to call Heard his own, he had. After four visits and meticulous study he knew probably more about Heard than anyone alive. He had been on one of the only two circuits of the island, knew all its nooks and crannies, its animals, and now had climbed its mountain. He seemed to hold it in the palm of his hand, the cup of his mind and though I could never see the 'specialness' of Heard through his eyes I was not eager to break his image. For we all have some place that is special and dear to us.

On 27 January the weather was still poor. With the mist, the wind and the cold we lacked resolve and wished to put off the hard, miserable work entailed in reaching Base. Rime continued to shower our sleeping bags and they became wet through. The down balled up in the box quilting and rolled into lumps in the corners. I could see light through the fabric and all that lay between me and the cold were the nylon and my damp clothes. Our feet were permanently cold so that we resorted to vigorous 'bicycling' exercises to the accompaniment of nonsense songs. Conversation meandered while Colin wrote a summary of our vulcanological findings at the summit. Grahame, as scientific officer, began to feel guilty about our short stay at the top—that no time was spent in serious scientific investigation—and curiously labelled the climb a strangled triumph.

The most uncomfortable part of being confined to the tent in a blizzard lay in controlling and serving the needs of nature. The narrow, frozen sleeve, half blocked by drift was an additional deterrent to going outside and the problem became a major preoccupation. We used an empty tin for urine that could be tipped through the sleeve, without moving far from the sleeping bag. But major relief demanded a trip into the snow. After several hours of procrastination, one was forced to yield to the physical pressure, and there followed the distasteful job of dressing to go out. The damp warmth of a bag was forsaken for damp trousers, slimy boots, a Putt Parka covered in moisture and, perhaps, Grahame's foul-weather suit trousers which took on the role of shining armour against the drift.

'Out, out damned spot!' Warwick cried and I crawled down the sleeve, shuddering at the clammy, dank touch of the waterproofs. Outside, I squinted without snow goggles, and lurched drunkenly away from the Pyramid, unable to judge the surface of the snow in the white out.

Stopping, I removed my overmitts, lowered two pairs of trousers and endured a few minutes of pain as the wind viciously swept drift, biting and stinging at my bare flesh. I stood up, found that my overmitts had disappeared and scrambled back to my bed with frozen fingers. Chortling with satisfaction, I regained warmth, cajoled the others as they lay in varying stages of discomfort, knowing that I was secure for another 24 hours.

Sheathed in ice again, the tent walls presented peculiar, striated patterns, like the veins of a leaf. The rime inside was a quarter inch thick. On the last two nights at the camp I drew the outside positions and my patience was sorely tried as the heaviest showers of rime fell on me as I endeavoured to complete my diary. The wall shook constantly and once billowed sharply inwards and effectively stubbed out my cigarette. Col took over the left outside position on the afternoon of the 27th and I shall never forget the pained expression on his face as shower after shower of rime fell down his shirt collar or spread across his cheeks in a delicate torture.

It grew dark quickly through the cloud and ice and we lit a candle to watch it shine off the rime and, when it flickered, a shimmer ran across the walls like the movement of tiny jewels. It was a magic, glittering world above the increasingly squalid jumble of sleeping bags, poly bags, clothes, empty food packets and cigarette butts.

When darkness finally set in, Grahame suggested we sing songs and started off with a roundelay derived from old England. We sang it in parts with crescendos and diminuendos until the harmony of our voices carried us away from thoughts of discomfort and cold. 'Heigh ho! Nobody at home! Meat nor drink nor money have I none, still-I-will-be-ha-a-ppy! Heigh ho! Nobody at home!...'

The wind fell overnight and John was up at three preparing another early breakfast. It was ferociously cold and with wet clothes the only solution was movement and hard work. There was plenty of that for it took hours to clear and strike the tent. After a week the Pyramid flaps were frozen hard into the glacier and we dug and hacked until our backs ached and the cemented blocks were cut away. Tent pegs were buried several feet deep and we were forced to dig deep pits to free the guys. Normally the tent, without pegs, poles or floor, weighed about 40 pounds but the skin of ice nearly doubled the load. We scraped away as much as we could, pulling icicles from the ventilator, though first we removed ice pennants up to eighteen inches long that flew from our axes.

We dumped surplus food, emptied kerosene from the bottles, left anything to reduce the load we faced in the carry down. The sight of rubbish blowing round us, and the dirty, stained snow, gave the final impetus in our desire to leave. At least we should try and reach our old camp at the other side of the Fifty-One. There was never any consideration of this in Warwick's mind, and he was determined to sleep in Poly Gully that night. Grahame nobly volunteered to carry the Pyramid. Still coated in ice—it formed as quickly as we scraped it away—the tent would not fold into a reasonable size. It was an enormous load to take on top of his personal gear, cameras and scientific equipment.

Warwick led us over the pass, staggering under our packs, still as a five-man rope. The bare ice at the crest tested our balance and strength to the utmost. It was almost with relief that I felt the rope tighten behind me and turned to find Grahame sitting on the ice, unable to stand under the tent. For some agonising minutes I stood, ankles bent sharply to keep my crampons gripping the ice, while Col and John helped Grahame to his feet and guided him to the basin of the windscoop. We all followed, dropped our packs, and threw out more equipment in an effort to make the loads manageable.

Grahame's personal gear was split between us and it was sad to see spare ice axes, boots and thermometers scattered in the snow, beginning a shift to oblivion in the wind. Warwick fairly dragged us away from the windscoop. The precipitous retreat of 1963 still preyed on his mind. At that time, Grahame had slipped on the same bare ice, lost his gloves and suffered frostbite. I almost fell over as Warwick started off again like a spirited horse and I hauled hard at the rope to rein him in.

Below the ice, we encountered the same conditions as a week before. The wind disappeared, the snow became soft and thick cloud caused us to become overheated. The visibility was poor so that Warwick raised his snow goggles to see better and suffered a touch of snow blindness for his pains. At the bottom of the pass slope we left the cloud and Warwick fell over, apparently at the sight of the wide stretch of the Fifty-One. The warm nor'wester two days earlier had ablated much of the snow so that the glacier presented a curiously mottled surface of drift and bare ice.

Visibility increased, as did the eternal wind, and we were battered frequently by furious swirls of drift. We followed the marker poles and, since Warwick's vision seemed poor, I shouted directions to guide him from one to another. Pausing often to regain our breath, and to ease the pain in our shoulders, we still maintained good time and reached the old campsite early in the afternoon. We rested here

A photo for the sponsors. Pass Camp, L–R: Grahame, Colin, the Author

and looked over to the Escalator with dismay. Taking a load down it had been bad enough, but the climb up was a painful prospect. Col suggested a route higher, where we could climb on snow all the way. But after resuming the climb that way for some minutes we came to a nest of evil crevasses. Warwick pondered for a moment then swore that he had seen enough crevasses to last him a lifetime. With 'Better the devil we know', he turned and cramponned off towards the Escalator.

Feeling at the end of my tether, I trod awkwardly across the scree and leaned against a rock to rest. We unroped, removed crampons, and each of us made his own way up the gully. The wind battered the South Barrier, sending up clouds of drift that rode the rocks like wraiths of the storm. I lit a cigarette, taking my time for once, and waited until the others were well up before following. But we had picked the best day for ascending the Escalator. The scree was partly cemented by snow and the powerful wind jumped off the Fifty-One, roared up our backsides and pushed us on our way. Even so, the effort was excruciating. My eyes became half closed from dust and snow, and at the top I was almost retching for breath.

Plodding over the ridgetop, I found Grahame extolling his special island. There was blue sky and sunlight, while the soft green and browns of Spit Bay in the distance were a sight for sore eyes after all those white days. Descending out of the wind, the red of South Barrier's rock was only part of the warmth in colour and landscape that welcomed us back into a milder world after eleven days of aseptic ice. We trudged across the Winston snowfield without ropes, looking like tinkers with our packs adorned in billies and shovels, crampons and ropes while Colin carried the yellow and red bamboo poles. Even he dragged his feet. The last tramp over the scoria to the edge of Poly Gully seemed interminable and when we got there, to look down at the seals and azorella, Big Ben had one final trick up his sleeve.

The snowslope above Base Camp was in bad condition. In parts it had melted away to reveal bare smooth rock and overall it had hardened to a thin layer. Dog tired, we stood and watched as Warwick fastened a rope to a boulder, then lowered himself down, kicking steps. Slowly, one by one we followed him, packs like lead, and slithered over scree, loose rocks, and springy azorella to the untouched dump.

Warwick and John went ahead to open up tins of fruit and condensed milk. There was beer and whisky, a tin of corned beef, a warm floor of earth and azorella for the tent. As we put it up, its last snow and ice began to melt and the dregs of the climb flowed away. Playfully I picked up a pebble and tossed it towards an elephant seal. The small stone bounced on its slabby flank and the seal jerked into life as though it had been shot. It raised a mournful head and stared with lugubrious eyes as I tossed another. It trickled down the fat belly. The seal endeavoured to look angry and, threatening, opened its mouth wide, but relaxed as I turned away. The huge mouth slowly shut, the eyes looked troubled, closed, then the seal snorted and turned over.

We had climbed the mountain and come down safely but I felt this was very insignificant on looking round the gully and along the shore we named Capsize Bay. The surf beat as it did the day we landed and as it had done every day before and since. The prions mined in the azorella, the skuas stalked them, the penguins paraded and squabbled. The seals moulted and slept, irritated, not awed, by our presence. Though we laid claim to the land and the mountain, we were a rare, migrating species with a delicate grip on existence. They were the true children of Heard.

10

SEALS AND SEALERS

WE HAD BEEN ON HEARD ISLAND sixteen days. Though we were engrossed in our mountain, our difficulties and our success, the Skipper, Antony, Russ, Mal and Ed on *Patanela* were never far from our thoughts. The ship had passed from sight at 1700 hours on 12 January, and with no radio contact we knew nothing of *Patanela*'s voyage to Kerguelen or of what happened on her arrival. With no knowledge of her whereabouts it was natural that occasional, horrible thoughts entered our minds. She might have come to grief and we would not know for weeks. We knew that the ship could not be in more capable hands, but five was a small crew for a sixty-three-foot schooner in the Southern Ocean.

In fact, after clearing Heard and its storm on 13 January, the ship encountered mediocre, cloudy weather in a largely uneventful voyage which brought them to the main French base at Port aux Francais three days later. The base of 120 men gave them a great welcome and the five's first entry to the dining hall was met with cheers and stamping feet. Over the following two days they were royally entertained and shown over the well-equipped station which catered for a dozen research projects. Much of the work was undertaken by French national servicemen, among them students from the Sorbonne University who welcomed the opportunity to spend most of their two years' training in extra curricular field research at Kerguelen. Port aux Francais was relieved twice yearly by a ship from Marseilles that called in at the tropical island of Reunion en route and engaged local labour for domestic work at the base. During winter there were only 60 men on the island but at midsummer this was doubled as the old wintering party waited to be taken home after the relief ship's second visit.

The *Patanela* party visited a sealing factory, fully equipped but never used. It was derelict under the care of a wan French Vicomte who was tired of his profitless occupation and asked for a berth on *Patanela* to seek his fortune in Australia. They inspected a fine Catholic chapel overlooking the base that was built by personnel since the war; were entertained by the commandant and almost everyone else in their private huts; then went on a tour of the scientific huts and a bewildering array of equipment. The Skipper remarked that, 'With little science and less French', he finally understood as much about the research programme as the depressed, moulting King penguins that wandered round the station.

Antony spoke fluent French from study at the Sorbonne, the Skipper knew more of the language than he cared to admit, Russ eventually remembered a lot of his schoolboy French and the others picked up the more important words and phrases. The Skipper had once said that if an Englishman could not make himself understood in the first place, he should speak louder and more slowly (in English) so that any fool must understand. Mal went one better. It was said that he never learnt more than Bonjour! and Merci! but at the end of the visit spoke loudly and slowly in English with a perfect French accent! On 18 January they took *Patanela* to Port Jeanne d'Arc. This was at the south-west extremity of Baie de Morbihan, the huge bay where Port aux Francais lay. With them went two French workers on holiday and a Breton fisherman in naval service who acted as pilot. He took them through a complex of islands, peninsulas, channels and reefs, avoiding an indefinite area of minefields, laid during the War by the RAN* to deter German raiders. They called at Île Longue where the pilot went ashore to service generators in a sheep-shearing shed. Many sheep were run on Kerguelen in the past but, after their depredations to the vegetation, numbers had been restricted to regions near the base and they were mainly useful in providing fresh meat for its personnel. And for us, since we were

---

* Royal Australian Navy

generously given a whole carcase.

At Port Jeanne d'Arc there was an abandoned whaling station. Like a ghost town the flensing platforms, factory buildings and dormitories looked as if they had been left in a hurry at the behest of some strange calamity. Full-sized whaleboats were lined up on the shore, rotting, backs broken, and little remained of a 200-foot jetty. It had been abandoned for 35 years but carvings, scrawled names, little monuments and graves on a hill told the story of what was once a thriving French whaling community. The Frenchmen slept ashore in one of the old buildings and the next day a versatile Alouette came to take the Breton pilot back to Port aux Francais.

Although an official letter from Paris denied them the right to any land expeditions on Kerguelen, the *Patanela* party found no local obstruction to their proposal for short trips into the hills. On 20 January Russ, Mal and Ed went off with Claude and Jacques to visit the Mont Ross area, two days' walk to the west from Port Jeanne d'Arc. They encountered a delightfully mixed scenery of hills and bays, rivers, islands, mountains and snow, in pointed contrast to the severe landscape of Heard. Halfway to the Mont Ross basin they spent the night in a deep cave which had been improved by previous French visitors to form an ideal mountain hut. Dry and sheltered, they fed on ravioli and sampled the French army rations which catered for the jaded appetite rather than a rumbling belly. That day on Heard, we sat in the blizzard on the Fifty-One Glacier, sampling monotonous stew and hard biscuits while, on Kerguelen, they relished nougat, fruit bar, cheese, sardines, orangeade, coffee and *Eau de Vie*—a small bottle of Cognac without which no French army ration is complete.

On 21 January they entered the glacial region and photographed fine views of Mont Ross, 6430 feet, the highest, and unclimbed, peak of Kerguelen. It is the highest point on an old crater rim, 2600 feet lower than Mawson Peak, but a far more difficult climbing problem with knife-edge ridges, sheer ice faces and a needle summit. The party spent a miserable night in tents which filtered the rain and returned to the whaling station next day. A landing barge from Port aux Francais called to pick up the Frenchmen and dropped two more who went with Antony and Mal on the same walk.

Patanela stayed at Port Jeanne d'Arc until 1 February when she returned to Port aux Francais for final resupply and arrangements before leaving for Heard again. Various repairs were made to the ship, Mal collected insects and Russ kept up his bird log. In a succession of culinary delights, well lubricated by Louzoù, they experimented with fresh mussels and chestnut conserve, and Mal discovered a hidden talent for baking fresh bread and buns. Ed carved a chess set and the game became a major preoccupation, culminating in an eighteen-hour marathon on a day of bad weather.

The journey back to Port aux Francais on the afternoon of 1 February involved only a few hours of motoring; but they found on arrival that a strong westerly prevented them from obtaining a secure anchorage. The Skipper took *Patanela* to the west and sought a lee behind Pointe Molloy five miles away. First soundings revealed deep water but eventually the anchor held in the shelter of low cliffs. Anchor watches were kept in the mediocre weather and Russ paced the deck until 0130 when Mal relieved him.

Ed, as ship's cook, was sleeping in Warwick's bunk by the stove and the fo'c'sle was closed for the duration. He said that as soon as he was woken by the bumping at 0330, he rolled out of his bunk in a flash. As *Patanela*'s hull banged again with the reverberation that every seaman fears, the sound of steel on rock, he dived into the engine-room and pressed the starter. The Skipper climbed up on deck as the others scrambled out in bare feet and shirtsleeves. Ed pressed the red button once, twice, and nothing happened! Never before had the Rolls-Royce missed firing twice. With his heart in his mouth he pressed a third time and the familiar rumble filled the engine room. The Skipper stood by the wheel while Antony, Russ and Mal struggled with an anchor fouled with kelp. The night was black as pitch, blowing a furious snowstorm with a wind measured by the French meteorologists as force eleven—sixty knots.

The anchor was raised and cleared with an axe, and at slow ahead the Skipper took the ship away from the invisible rocks. As the dawn broke feebly in the east, Ed swung the lead and they tried five times to anchor in a better lee. Time after time the anchor dragged until finally at 0600 it held and they could rest. It was a nightmare night

Wrecked schooner, Kerguelen *(Malcolm Hay)*

and a shock after the days of tranquillity and leisure. Within a few days the Skipper had to consider leaving for Heard, in order to keep the rendezvous on 11 February. But no-one knew to what extent *Patanela*'s hull had been damaged from the grounding. Before leaving for Heard, and the long voyage to Australia, the state of the hull would have to be ascertained and any damage repaired.

*   *   **   *   *

Warwick's diary for 29 January reads 'Pottering. Tide marking by Colin and Grahame who seem to want to render getting wet in the surf into an understandable science with probably the same results; John ruminates on his idealism; Phil insectivorates and I sort film, doing nothing.' Big Ben was climbed but only a fortnight remained before we had to achieve the equally important object of rejoining *Patanela*. Col and Grahame felt that a study of the tides, and the surf at different states of the tide, might reveal a safe and calm period for take-off. They laid rocks at intervals up the beach and since Col was working round the South Barrier, sleeping in Poly Gully, he had a continued opportunity to measure the tide levels. They walked along the lagoon spit, examining the beach there, and found a bundle of marker poles washed up after being thrown overboard when the ship left. To Col these were a gift from the sea since he could use them for marking his survey base line at the end of the spit.

The beaches under Cape Lockyer were also examined and one of Col's typical bright ideas came to light when he noticed a flat rock jutting from the boulders. It seemed an ideal jetty and loading platform but increased surf over the following days soon showed it an impractical choice. There was nothing very positive we could decide on for the take off. So much depended on the state of the weather and surf the day the ship arrived. The initial problem lay in launching the USR but we guessed that this could be achieved by good timing, as on 12 January. The over-riding problem involved loading the USR. We would not make a fast and efficient getaway if we tried to carry half a ton through the surf for we simply did not have enough manpower. This left us with the unpalatable prospect of loading the USR after launching. Since this was fraught with difficulties, we hedged around the subject and Warwick wisely suggested we forget about the problem until nearer the day and get on with our other tasks.

On 30 January, Warwick, Grahame and I filled our packs for a four-day trip to Spit Bay. The Pyramid stayed at Poly Gully and since the Bechervaise, virtually unused, was still cached at the Toyshop, we decided to make do with the small Spit Hut for accommodation. This had no angled roof and had been made from a huge packing case used in 1947 when a Supermarine Walrus amphibian was taken to Heard for survey photography. The 'plane made one flight before it was wrecked in a storm but its case still survived in the form of a handy refuge.

The weather was fine so that Col and John accompanied us as far as the Winston Glacier for filming. Warwick had covered most of the ascent but needed close-up shots of climbing technique, to fill out the picture. We scrambled over the moraine north of camp and descended to the shores of Winston Lagoon. A few Gentoo penguins occupied a small beach, elephant seals bathed ponderously in the water and Grahame was happy to find a single juvenile King penguin.

Since World War II they had been rare on the island but, two years before, he found signs that they were recolonising. One of the main parts of his biological survey was to make a count of the Kings, and also fur seals which had become scarce following sealing depredations.

Heard Island's early history is one of slaughter. Discovered in 1833 by British sealer, Peter Kemp, it was kept a trade secret and virtually no-one knew of its existence until Captain John Heard, in the barque *Oriental* out of Boston, rediscovered the island 20 years later and initiated the first landing in 1855. There followed 20 years of annual visits by sealers, mostly American, who decimated the population of fur and elephant seals. They took King penguins too, for their blubber and colourful skins. After twenty years the slaughter became unprofitable but, when they left, enough animals had survived, at sea or in migrating to safer islands, to regenerate substantially by 1907. Sealing began again but had finished by 1930 when world depression curtailed many enterprises, the Kerguelen whaling station included.

The sealers were hard men, with no regard for or knowledge of the balance of nature, but the courage and hardship entailed in their work made us feel molly-coddled in comparison. Square-rigged sailing ships beat all the way down from Massachusetts or Connecticut to an island only half charted, with innumerable unknown dangers. Lying offshore at Atlas Cove or Spit Bay, whalers were put over the side and, with stout oarsmen and a wily coxswain, they sliced through the surf to land a shore party who stayed to work the whole summer. They were given timber and nails, trypots and lances, the rough, heavy gear for work and survival, with a little food and rum. The sealers built their own huts and ovens, lived largely off the land—seal meat and penguin breasts—and spent months labouring in the cold with poor clothing until their hands became gnarled and broken.

In March the ships returned and there followed the dangerous task of transferring huge barrels of oil and skins from the beach, before the long voyage home. Sometimes the ships did not come back. Wrecked elsewhere, or engaged on more pressing business, the barques left sealer colonies to winter over on an island already two-thirds covered in ice. In winter nearly all the seals and birds migrated and the men were forced to traverse glaciers, plough through snow in leather shoes, to hunt stray elephant seals that were too lazy to leave. Often they survived, often they did not, and in many corners of Heard there are old graves which point to the sealers' hardships, death from exposure, malnutrition and, probably, vicious fights which broke out among small groups of tough men living under confining conditions.

Atlas Cove once had several big sailing ships anchored in its roads, a sight never seen this century. But the spiralling storms, which were such a bane to us, meant destruction to them. Without engines, a skipper had to be canny, able to raise anchor at the first smell of a nor'wester and beat out to sea, leaving men and stores behind at the shore, regardless of the situation. They beat out to sea, sometimes never to sail back, either wrecked or because the skipper deemed it too dangerous to return. Wooden masts and spars still litter Heard's coastline. There is the story of a great ship caught at anchor during a storm in Corinthian Bay. Unable to tack safely away, the ship was dashed against the hundred-foot ice cliffs where the Challenger Glacier met the sea. As it began to break up against the ice, a daring seaman shinned up the mast and walked out on a yard-arm. With a plain axe to cut steps he jumped off the yardarm on to the ice, trailed a rope behind him and brought many others to safety before the ship sank.

As we walked over the Winston Glacier, clad with our fine boots, crampons, ice axes, nylon ropes, down clothing in our packs, I could not help but feel admiration for the hard men of a hundred years before. They had no knowledge of biology and the precious cycle of animal life, and almost destroyed it, but neither did they have science to help their enterprises or temper their difficulties. Above us was a vast mound of ice called Big Ben and this, named after some long-gone giant of a sealer, was the most appropriate name and monument on the island.

Above the snout of the Winston Glacier we roped up and, to Warwick's instructions, walked, climbed, chopped steps and ma-noeuvred for the benefit of his movie camera. While he changed film we sat down and photographed ourselves. The glacier sloped away from our feet and a hundred yards further stopped abruptly and fell in cliffs to the lagoon.

Beyond lay the spit, the sea, and above a line of curly waves, clouds moving across the sky like a team of white serpents. Winston Lagoon was covered in lumps of floating ice, brash which had calved from the glacier snout. Throughout the day there were rumbles and roars, sometimes like gunshots, as ice split from the cliffs and fell into the water. Once we watched, open mouthed, as a pillar about a hundred feet high and twenty wide subsided like the collapsing wall of a tall building. It fell slowly, following a deep rending crack, then the water erupted as if a depth charge had been detonated and the great chunks of breaking ice sank, only to bob up like plastic toys in a bath. Waves washed out over the lagoon and soon there were more lumps of ice to litter the beaches like frozen swans.

At noon, Col and John thankfully left the filming behind and

Gentoo Penguin with chick

went back to Poly Gully before scaling the South Barrier to begin the survey. Warwick, Grahame and I checked our knots and prepared to find a way through the leering maze of seracs and corrugations at the northern side of the glacier. Rocky bluffs squeezed the steep ice as it fell from the slopes of Big Ben, causing a knot of fissures and folds and an awkward climbing problem. Fortunately the ice was old and bare so there were no concealed crevasses. We could see all the pitfalls and dangers. Warwick led and he chose to engage in a rock climb on ice as we tiptoed along narrow arêtes, slithered à cheval and climbed around towers on the side points of crampons. We cut steps if the going became too difficult and within half an hour we left the last teetering block to scramble over mud and moraine. In the distance we saw the red and blue figures of Col and John as they waited to see we were safely across before returning to Base.

On the beach at the head of the lagoon we stopped for lunch and provoked a leopard seal to action. Uncommon on Heard, one lay slothfully at the edge of the water. As large as a medium-sized elephant seal, the spots explained its name and a serpentine head filled with curling teeth gave it something else in common with its jungle brother. It reacted sluggishly to Grahame's waving ice axe, eyes and nose suppurating with a repulsive marine disease to which they are prone. But in the sea they are deadly, attacking and tearing at any animal, as vicious as a shark: the one seal we feared in our surf landings.

We followed the beach round, beneath bluffs streaming with waterfalls, negotiated the awkward boulders of the north shore then struck up the first rise of Dovers Moraine. Old ice provided the core for hills of scree and rubble, left by the retreating Stephenson Glacier, and we watched our footing on the steeper slopes to avoid a nasty slip. Topping the first line of hills flanking Winston Lagoon, we looked down into the head of a new valley. Within the last few years the ice had retreated so fast that the glacier melt streams created wide flats in the moraine. Down to the right we glimpsed green. There, towards the sea was a river valley occupied by plants and animals but never visited or named by man. We determined to call in on the way back.

Crossing the flats, where the scum of green and orange algae filled

The Author jumping a crevasse on the Winston Glacier

quiet side pools, we gained easily the old ice of Stephenson Glacier. It sloped gently to the scree and there was no trouble in ascending to clear the rubble and begin a long traverse to the northern end of Dovers Moraine and Spit Bay. Now it was a perfect day with clear skies, sun and no wind, so that it seemed like summer in the Southern Alps. After the past climb it appeared slightly ridiculous to tramp over an easy, uncrevassed glacier in shirtsleeves. Occasionally there were deep, bottomless melt holes, roaring with hidden water, and one moulin, a glacial stream, with overhanging sides. We jumped across, anxious not to tumble down to the freezing torrent rushing over its slippery bed.

Scarlet Hill became prominent, then the Nunatak and eventually Round Hill with Shag Island in the background. But the greatest view of all was that of Big Ben. It remained clear all day—a huge rectangular block of ice and rock. Beyond the wide, rolling sweep of Stephenson Glacier, the white volcano seemed a distant, separate, inaccessible island, especially in the late-afternoon haze or from behind moraine hummocks when it appeared like an ethereal backdrop. Drift spumed off exposed ridgetops in twisting columns as though a thousand fires were burning.

It was a great relief to know that we had finished with Big Ben. I began to feel a sense of proportion about the island after the rush and tussle with the mountain at close quarters. Now we could stand back and view it objectively, in the warmth of the lower altitudes and the green of the beaches. We stopped to admire frost flowers and crystals forming in a pool and realised that the temperature was close to freezing near the surface of the glacier. Still in shirtsleeves we understood what a difference the wind and wet snow made to comfort. With our packs weighing almost half their mountain weight, we strolled towards a calm, evening sea.

We overshot the moraine route to Spit Hut and came to the beach by the lagoon of Stephenson Glacier. This had retreated too in common with other Heard, and world, glaciers. Ten years earlier there had been ice cliffs in the sea. When the sea and its rocks came into full view we discovered with delight that fur seals were playing 'king of the castle'. A bull sat poised on the peak of a rock when suddenly a cow leapt from the water, nipped and nudged him with a splash into the sea. There was a tumble in the water, then the cow jumped out on to the rock, the bull challenged her and they continued to slither and gambol in vying for an elevated position.

Along the beach we passed shags and Rockhopper penguins. The birds sat among the rocks and watched us with far more interest than fear. A white Gentoo caused amusement when it refused to move from our path and brayed aggressively when I scratched it behind the ear. We crossed a stream and came to the hut positioned at the top of the steep, bouldery beach. It was surrounded by a Gentoo colony and elephant seals and we received a shock on the other side when a full-grown fur seal asserted its squatting rights, harrumphing and growling in an imperious stance. They were like overgrown dogs, barking, growling and scratching their lice-infested fur. When they drew themselves up on their fore flippers, looked down their nose, whiskers twitching, I was reminded of circus seals I had not seen since youth. Since they were aggressive and fast moving, we watched our step on the following days when wandering through the tussocks. Measuring up to five feet long, they moved much faster than we could walk and if one was cornered unexpectedly, a shame-faced run was the only wise action.

The hut was about ten feet wide by twelve feet long and eight feet high, lined with sheet iron. The roof was flat, however, a certainty to leak in Heard's climate, and eventually we rigged a 'humpy' inside when it began to rain. It was a real refuge, stocked with food, fuel, kerosene heaters, stoves and lamp, blankets, sleeping bags and covers so that anyone in distress could make themselves warm and comfortable. Most of the tinned food had rusted through over the years but there were ANARE rations from the 1963 expedition, and the odd tin of jam or corned beef turned up trumps. All the fuel was secure in drums and with the old canvas tents we were able to build an effective second roof inside. The hut was erected in 1950 and a Lilliput magazine dated 1949 with the builders' names carved on the door created a touch of nostalgia. It was seldom visited but Grahame had been there five times and assumed a rather proprietorial air as we rearranged the stores to

Warwick with trypots, Spit Bay *(Grahame Budd)*

spread our Lilos and sleeping bags.

In the still, starlit evening we lit the pressure lamp and tried a meal of pemmican and ANARE biscuits spread with apricot jam. Warwick grimaced unappreciatively but I was eager to try for the first time the concentrated meat extract which had supported so many explorers in the past. Later I hung the lamp outside against a white sheet. In other parts of the world many flying insects, as well as moths, are attracted to light. From all previous reports it appeared that no flying insects existed on Heard—undoubtedly deterred by the wind and lack of high vegetation. But there was no harm in trying since, like every collector, I harboured the secret hope of finding a new species. Three beetles crawled up from the wall of the hut, prions fluttered past the lamp like moths and a Gentoo, disturbed from a catnap, paraded back and forth, squinting at the strange glow; but there was nothing else. We slept with the door ajar but rain came in the early morning and only then did we stretch out the old tents, fumbling in the dark.

The new day dawned dreary and grey with a strong nor'wester and the earlier calm sea was flailing the boulders on the shore. It seemed a bad day for any activity but by nine the cloud broke and the morning developed into an unbelievably warm afternoon.Later, as I collected insects, I almost fell asleep on the springy azorella. The sun beat down and brought a fit of drowsiness I hardly thought possible on Heard. The physical strain of the previous fortnight drained away and I almost began to grow fond of the island. West of the sandy Spit were acres of vegetation—azorella hummocks, patches of thick Kerguelen Cabbage, tussock intermingled with rare grasses and moss. Beyond were the dun moraines and, ever present, the suspended white mass of the great, table mountain.

Warwick and Grahame wandered away to the southern beach of the Spit, counting fur seals and King penguins and filming animals and the remains of sealers' huts. I enjoyed solitude in my insect collecting and found, to my surprise and satisfaction, that a rare wingless moth thought to finish its life cycle by the end of January was still prolific at Spit Bay. Wingless flies hopped on the bare ground between the tussocks; primitive, flightless beetles crawled through the azorella, small spiders chased springtails under rocks while the birds' nests crawled with ticks, mites and fleas. It was a good day for the insects and they hopped and jumped in the sun. Fur seals lay curled up on hummocks sunbathing while the elephant seals found the heat another easy excuse to lie in torpid heaps.

Along the beach were a line of old barrels, split and half covered in sand. Wood lay scattered amongst the pebbles and I followed a trail of broken iron to the remains of a factory hut. The walls and roof were gone but the stout timber deck was still firm to tread. On one side was a furnace, built from red bricks, try-pots for reducing seal blubber to useful oil and a hand press for crushing carcases. Its box was filled with sand, a stack of rusted barrel hoops lay against the ruined chimney and an old fire rake lying at my feet seemed a good souvenir. Around the deck were lances, nails, rods, rivets, an old shoe and innumerable pieces of unidentifiable iron.

Over by the beach lay a huge spar with brass fittings, the mast or yardarm of a long-wrecked barque. Everywhere one travelled at Spit Bay there were wreckage and remnants of the past, beaches littered with history, and unknowing, unconcerned seals.

The Spit wriggled its way out to sea, a blasted heap of sand and tussock littered with the carcases of dead elephant seal pups which had not survived the breeding season. Giant petrels ('Nellies'), Dominican gulls and skuas hovered around for carrion but the gruesome body of a dead petrel in the tussock lay unmolested. Inland from the sand were wide fields of tussock and azorella, worn into hummocks and hollows by the heavy elephants. Prime bulls, the beachmasters, weighed up to four tons but these had gone to sea after mating and the hundreds we saw moulting were cows and young bulls. All around were the characteristic grunts and bellows, screams and barks, snarls, the sudden shifting of ponderous bodies as they jostled for comfortable positions. Occasionally a pyramid of shaking flesh appeared as two bulls rose up on their flippers and butted each other in anger.

For a change of scenery and bathing, the elephants travelled from

King Penguins

the azorella to the Spit Lagoon or the beach. The journey was exhausting. The seals shuffled along furiously for several yards, a terrible effort with so much weight to shift and only flippers and tail to
provide motive power. Regularly they flopped exhausted, chin on the
sand, then raised their heads to gauge the remaining distance with a
look that seemed to say:'God help me. Not that far surely!' Then off
they slummocked again.

On our second day at Spit Bay, while Warwick and Grahame
made an excursion to Fairchild Beach, I visited the colony of sixty
King penguins they found the day before. These penguins are second
in size only to the Emperors which inhabit Antarctica. Up to three
feet high they parade slowly and majestically, never hurrying or rushing away in startled flight at the sight of humans like other penguins.

Aloof and disdainful they strut like silky sergeant majors, long,
graceful beaks tipped slightly in the air, and one could imagine a
swagger stick tucked beneath their stiff, vestigial wings. Glossy grey
and white, a velvet green adorns their throats, almost iridescent, and
a flash of orange on the black head and white breast gives the final
regal touch. While other penguins bray and chatter, the Kings open
their black beaks to emit an entrancing call like the jazzy sound of a
saxophone with a loose reed.

They lose their dignity and beauty when moulting or when in
the juvenile state. Colours are pale, down fluffs round the neck or
clumps of sprouting feathers make them tattered and torn. On the
beach they parade with decorum and a sense of superiority but at
home in the tussock colony, they squabble and nag each other in an
unremitting display of bad temper. The Gentoos often squabble too
but generally with their chicks and fledglings, chasing them away or
being chased by them in search of food. But it was disappointing to
see the imperious Kings as'human' as the rest.

Grahame and Warwick's return from Fairchild Beach on 1 February rounded off a successful sojourn at the Spit. Including later addi-
tions, Grahame counted over 300 fur seals between Winston Lagoon
and Fairchild and 120 King penguins, half as many again breeding
than in the 1963 count. There was no doubt that both species were
firmly re-establishing themselves on the lee side of the island where

Moulting Elephant Seal wallow

better weather and increasing vegetation encouraged new colonies. I had made a good catch of insects and Warwick seemed pleased with the extent of his filming. Although another nor'wester blew, it was with regret that we made preparations to leave the next day to return to the vagaries of Poly Gully and the dooming surf.

During the night the canvas tent sagged in the hut and Warwick disturbed our sleep with his old dream of claustrophobia. But at seven Grahame shook us gently and woke us with his pleasant habit of serving coffee and fruit cake before breakfast. It was still raining, a skua stood outside the door waiting for scraps, its feathers ruffled by the wind, and we reluctantly stowed our sleeping bags in the packs. We left everything as we found it, adding a shovel to the refuge equipment, covered the stores and scribbled a note on the wall. We wired the door, jammed a copper rivet in the crack and walked up the stream behind the hut. Here we passed a group of fur seals and Warwick almost trod on a bull, sending us into brief flight until circumspectly we retraced our route.

We found direct access through the moraine to Spit Glacier and tramped back over the same route with icy, southern snow showers lashing in our faces. With no encouragement to stop we made good time to the flats of the new valley. Warwick collected algae from the upper pools but when we tried to follow the stream to the sea we found it disappeared beneath old ice and we were forced to scramble over moraine hills. The dead moraine ended abruptly and we suddenly entered the main valley. There were river terraces below and rolling hills covered in verdant vegetation. The slopes were gentle with few rocks and a depth of green that made it the most idyllic spot we had seen on Heard.

We lit the stove at the entrance of a prion burrow, relaxed on the soft azorella and had a picnic lunch. Arguing whether we should call it Hidden Valley or Green Valley, we settled on the latter under pressure from Grahame's sense of ownership. There were two hours available for exploration and again, while the other two wandered off to count animals, I slowly walked to the beach, looking for insects. We met at three o'clock and climbed over to the lagoon to find a great wallow of elephant seals and two leopards.

The end of the lagoon spit was only 200 yards away but the rough, freezing water between decreed that we must walk round and over the Winston Glacier once more.

The lagoon shore made for difficult walking. Boulders and brash ice bordered old ice, treacherously covered in a thin skin of scree, and we stumbled and fell many times. Finally I fell between two rocks and jarred my right knee, the one I twisted and damaged in the landing. Limping, I followed the others and we all looked up at a sudden roar. We swallowed hard and watched as a huge serac fell down the bluffs to the beach at the lagoon's head, split into a thousand pieces and flew across the sand. Walking through the litter of ice fragments ten minutes later we were thankful we had timed our movement well.

A thin pall of rain drifted over the lagoon as we climbed to the glacier and a rainbow curved over the water when we roped and strapped on crampons. Finding an easier route through the jumble of seracs and crevasses, we soon made our way to the southern shore.

Warwick stood in a resigned stance as a block fell off a dead tower of ice and trundled to his feet. Both he and Grahame fell down in the moraine, and we were all happy to surmount the last rise and look down at the orange tents in Poly Gully. Col and John greeted us with a 'Welcome' mat inside the sleeve entrance but we looked mystified at the new tent pitched on the azorella. It was small, green and its sleeve entrance looked suspiciously like the Australian ensign. With time on his hands during bad weather, Col made the new tent which he called 'Sad Sack'. If we all travelled to Long Beach, he was determined that we need not carry the heavy Pyramid. The Bechervaise, which they had retrieved from the Toyshop, and the 'Sad Sack' would do. We regaled them with stories of the King penguins, fur seals and sealers' remains; they told a familiar tale of bad weather on the South Barrier, and we all lay back to discuss the last round.

II

THE VICIOUS CIRCLE

JOHN FELT GLOOMY AFTER CONFINEMENT to Poly Gully and the South Barrier region. Our original plans for a circuit of the island, later an examination of the little-known west coast, had been abandoned for lack of time so that his chances of exploring further were considerably diminished. Warwick was determined, however, that we make an excursion to Long Beach and thought that a quick foray up the west coast might still be on the cards. Colin had failed again, on 3 February, to strike good visibility for completion of his survey so, with typical good-natured resignation he persuaded a cautious Warwick that he should stay alone at Base so that the map might be finished. The rest of us could go to Long Beach.

D-Day with *Patanela* was only a week off. Our next ambition, now that climbing was successful and scientific work close to completion, was to leave Heard Island safely and enjoy a fast sail home. Warwick wrote: 'Note that general attitude is take it easy and stay alive.' It seemed as though Heard, in diabolical form, was determined to trip us up before we left. Colin, more than anyone, was concerned with the risks of a take off through the surf, and he tried to derive some consoling information from his observation of the tide markers. At this time, south-westerlies began to dominate the weather, and they whipped the surf into frightening proportions. Then, on 4 February, they effectively stopped us from rounding the South Barrier cliffs for the journey to Long Beach.

The four of us found that our packs still weighed fifty to sixty pounds though we carried no food or fuel. We relied on the expectation that the dump left at the Beach in 1963 by Grahame's party was

still intact. Depressed once more by the weight on my back, I sauntered after Warwick, Grahame and John as they made their way
down the Gully. The knee I had twisted in the capsize was feeling
spongy and useless and neither Grahame nor I fancied my chances
of boulder hopping along the cliffs.

The wind was so strong that even the skuas did not fly. A dozen
or more huddled behind the shelter of sparse tussock at the edge
of the beach and ducked their heads out of sight as sheets of sand
flew past. The stinging sand bit into our cheeks, sought the corners
of our eyes and caused us to stagger as vision was impaired. At the
end of the beach, surf lashed into the rocks and we ran from one to
another as the sea sucked it away for another battering cascade. The
flying sand, dangerous surf and high wind convinced Warwick that
a safe journey to Long Beach was hardly a moot point. John had
forged ahead but, with some spirited yells into the gale, we recalled
him and trudged back to camp. We would try again another day.

Colin was back already from another attempt to keep his survey stations. On the Barrier, he was blown about so severely that
he was forced to crawl on hands and knees over the scoria. Would
the weather never let us be? The climb back to Base had finally
convinced me that my knee would not stand up to another awkward journey with a heavy load. Grahame prescribed rest and, although one side of my nature felt disgruntled at being unable to
collect insects at Long Beach, the other was gratified at the prospect
of solitary meanders round Poly Gully. On 5 February there was
still wind with showers of sago snow. But Warwick, Grahame and
John set off on another attempt to negotiate South Barrier and did
not return.

Colin was unable to complete his survey until 8 February; three
days of foul weather forced him down again and again. Time began
to run out and in one final bid for success he decided to camp alone
on the desert of the Barrier and snatch any break in the clouds for
his final observations. The Bechervaise tent had been taken to Long
Beach so he had to make do with the 'Sad Sack'. He carried this up
with supplies and pitched it at nearly 2000 feet. As he might have
expected, the sky cleared as soon as he had set up the camp, and he

was able to climb to the ridge, take his final stations and return to Base that evening with everything done.

On the same day I took advantage of the sudden good weather and made my longest collecting excursion. Following Col's footsteps in the old snow above camp, I climbed on to the South Barrier and made my way quickly to the prominent cinder cone above. Almost all our route cairns had toppled in the wind and the scoria was liberally spattered with drift snow promising an early autumn. Poly Gully, with its revealed vegetation and occasional patches of snow, would have seemed in the grip of winter anywhere else. But here it was late summer and I imagined the white acres of winter when there was nothing but snow and rock or beaches washed black by the sea. Then nearly all the birds would be gone and only a few seals would remain who thought themselves fat enough to withstand six months of deep cold.

I passed forlorn 'Sad Sack' and saw Colin's red figure on the skyline as he bent to his survey table. Mist smothered the cinder cone as I turned pebbles to find beetles and pulled their larvae from scattered lumps of moss. I lay flat on my stomach and became so absorbed in the work that I failed to notice the cloud lift. When I stood up, a sweeping view hung beneath a blue sky and for the last time I saw the ice cliffs of Big Ben in sunshine. For a while there was no wind, the sun beat down and heat waves shimmered over the red-brown rocks already nurtured in fire.

Later I descended by a different route and made my way to a gully which cut through the sea cliffs. The contrast was amazing. At first I was on the South Barrier—rough rock, scoria with pads of moss, washings of lichen, drifts of snow; a new, cold wind, fresh cloud and a rising mountain of silence and ice. But a few steps further and I rounded a boulder to look over the cliff to the beach. The silence turned to noise, the bare rock to movement and colour: death to life, unmoving hardness to a vivid assertion of rights to life.

From the top to the sea, the cliffs were teeming with Macaroni penguins, Rockhopper penguins, skuas, sheath-bills, giant petrels, prions, cape pigeons and seals, all among the terraces and fields of azorella, tussock and Kerguelen Cabbage. Emanating from them was a cacophony of calls: the counterpoint of skuas' alarm against the seals' nasal contentment and rumbling torpor, the bray of the Macaroni ensemble, and beneath all the pounding bass of surf.

The animals climbed to the limit of vegetation. There were prion burrows even in the topmost azorella hummocks and above these a skua occasionally sauntered past, ever on the watch for a quick meal. Above the skuas was nothing, save the expression of men in piles of disturbed stones, bits of paper, melted footprints in drifted snow; microbes on the move since banished by the inhospitable wind and the fear of permanent prison on a mountain that would never be a home but merely a test of strength.

I developed a grudging admiration for the heavy-bodied skuas— though their predatory nature was objectionable or, on a broader scale, the whole vicious circle with which they were associated. Never before as on Heard Island had I seen such a blatant, unrelieved picture of dog eat dog, kill thy neighbour for thine own sake. The skuas in Poly Gully that February lived in territories along the steep, well-vegetated stream slopes under the cliffs. There were many pairs with fledglings that scurried furtively through the azorella, displaying an incredible capacity for concealment behind the low hummocks.

Their parents always screamed shrilly whenever we approached the nests, raising their magnificent wings in alarm. One adult bird stood on a prominent observation point while the other soared above ready to attack. If a fledgling seemed in danger, it would dive bomb in a disconcerting manner, swooping over one's head so that we resorted to a wild thrashing of the air with our ice axes. Their nests did not seem worthy of defence. They were nothing but springy hollows in the azorella littered with the remains of prions and other unfortunate birds.

The skuas soon recognised that we sometimes stirred up other sections of the bird community and created the opportunity for easy hunting. Often, as I dug around the vegetation in pursuit of insects, I looked up to find a skua only a stone's throw away, waiting and watching with his beady eye. Once I excavated a prion's burrow and turned with a start to find a skua at my elbow, nonchalantly awaiting its turn to dig for a defenceless chick.

They struck a discordant note with their cold calculation. Along the Winston Lagoon spit, I battled into a headwind after examining seal carcases and experienced the strange sensation of an alien presence. I paused in my preoccupation with drifting sand and awkward stones to find a skua hovering a few feet above and behind my head. I felt the tinge of doom that one associates with lurid tales of birds that attack humans. Quickly, I swung my axe and caught it with a thump on the side. The skua flew off, soundlessly, showing no distress or concern. Of all the birds on Heard Island, they seemed to demonstrate the best group reaction and defence. When I approached a group in the tussock, one sharply pecked a sleeping companion to warn it of my approach. Though they had the virtue of open brotherhood, they proved a deadly Gestapo to the poor prion underground.

From the top of the South Barrier cliffs, I climbed down a steep gully to the beach. The greater part of the boulder-strewn slopes was colonised by Macaroni penguins, with a few subdued Rockhoppers in obscure corners. The Macaroni is the dominant penguin on Heard, far overshadowing Rockhoppers, Kings and even Gentoos which occupy the tussock and wallow areas. Their very assertiveness and self-confidence explains why they take over, in tens of thousands, the lion's share of unglaciated land each summer. On South Barrier they noised their dominance abroad from a rookery that rose nearly 2000 feet. Short (up to two feet high), with a compressed, orange bill and quills raked back from its forehead like windswept eyebrows, each male defended a family territory within the close-packed rookery.

The notable feature of Macaroni calls is braying. A male substantiates its claim to a nesting site by facing a trespasser and braying like a little donkey while rolling its head back and forth, beak in the air, covering about 240 degrees in an arc. The trespasser does the same, its rippling call lasting about a minute. Then they both pause, blow mucous down their nostrils, shake it off and swallow hard as if to say: 'Wow! That was hard work!' As I walked through the rookery, most of the Macaronis withdrew from my path but some con-

Macaroni Penguin colony, Long Beach

tested my right to walk through their territory, pecked at my legs and brayed 'Git off my property!' There were many fledglings in the rookery, crowded together, and I was loath to upset them in my passage. But they tumbled out of the way, sometimes bouncing down the rocky slopes in somersaults when their inadequate webbed feet lost their grip. It seemed, however, that with short, powerful legs and vestigial wings, there was nothing to break, while the feathers and blubber were a good insurance against bruising.

The 'Macs' had minor related colonies up and down the beach so that there was a constant procession of birds along the sand by the water. A memory that will always remain with me is that of the identical scene of our arrival and departure, the unchanging cycle that proclaimed us intruders. When we landed, there were Macaronis and Gentoos to greet us, to stop and curiously investigate. When we left there were Macaronis and Gentoos to see us off, to watch these strange creatures entering the water. When we had gone there were only our leavings for them to mull over in the winter snows and winds.

I moved out of the main Macaroni colony and made the rest of my descent via a much-used carriageway. Dozens of 'Macs' hopped laboriously up the slope, from one rock to the next, a foot at a time. It was almost pathetic as I looked back and saw the tiny figures, nearly at the top, making the final effort to reach their nests. The ones up there had come off second best in the competition for sites. To reach the sea for fishing, to feed themselves and their chicks, they had to make the tiresome journey each day, down and up 1500 feet.

At the bottom, two skuas were busy attacking a weakened fledgling. In anger I tossed a boulder at them and then found that I had to dispatch their victim with my ice axe. Its head was already half eaten away. The carnage was all around, the predators weeding out the weaker animals for butchering. If the scene seemed a vicious circle it did, at least, create a healthy natural cycle. The birds that were left were the strongest, capable of surviving the winter to breed vigorously the next spring.

While the penguins ducked and dived under the breaking surf, the biggest villain of all was busily employed in feeding on the beach.

A giant petrel, or Nelly, had just killed another Gentoo. It tore into the carcase with a heavy vicious beak, oblivious of its surroundings. Gentoos that had escaped stood by unconcerned, probably satisfied that the Nelly was sated for another day. I approached the ugly, horrible bird, almost as big as a Wandering Albatross, and waved my ice axe.

With a cowardly look over its shoulder, it raised its wings in alarm and staggered up the beach. It had eaten so much that it could only waddle. Despite strenuous efforts as I ran after it, the Nelly could not take off and only after disgorging some of its meal did it limp into the air over the sea. The Nelly was the Gentoos' bogey man. The dreamy creatures were disturbed often as the dirty hunter waddled into a colony, obscene with bristling neck feathers and pale, malevolent eyes. Like a sheepdog, it herded the penguins through the tussock until a straggler was captured by a blow on the head.

The third member of the villainous trio was the sheathbill or Paddy. Small, white, fluttering and hen-like, it was the only true land bird on Heard Island and stayed throughout the year—scavenging. It seemed an inconsequential and stupid bird with a nasty streak as it tripped around, beak covered in excreta, to peck among Nelly leftovers; even to pick at a small bare patch of flesh at the tip of a sleeping seal's flipper. The Nellies, skuas and Paddies sifted through the island's population of birds and seals with the more refined assistance of Dominican gulls. They were the scavengers, the garbage men, the killers, the parasites of the great society. The Nellies and skuas left in the winter when pickings were lean but there was always enough refuse to support a small population of gulls and sheathbills.

Almost all the penguins went in the winter, leaving reduced numbers of Gentoos, the albatrosses, the petrels and prions. Then the cycle was at its lowest ebb, with the rare flutter of wings and snort of a seal, until the spring came and the first renewing arc of the vicious circle. The life principle on Heard was that, whatever you were, you either lived strongly or died. There was no in-between, or very little time for it. Sick penguins were quickly picked off—even straggling skuas. A clean organic mechanism ensured life remained uncluttered; the oil in it was blood from slaughter, a constant excision.

With the exception of the fine spell on 8 February, the weather remained obnoxious. The continuous sou'westers and their willy-waws, marching and spinning round Cape Lockyer, whipped up big seas. On the worst days, four rollers broke in unison, extending half a mile out to sea. Inshore the surf flung boulders across the beach and snatched at the low terrace behind. Rocks crashed from it as the sea undermined the base while the penguins huddled in crevices for protection. Colin checked and tested both outboard motor and assault craft. He declared them fit for action but I preferred not to dwell on the problems of our take-off into the hostile sea.

The other three arrived back from Long Beach in the late afternoon of 9 February. In good spirits, they had completed the scientific and filming objectives. The coastal route was travelled safely, despite the terrors of a windscoop, between South Barrier and the Fifty-One Glacier, that funnelled winds up to a hundred miles an hour. On 5 February willy-waws had knocked them about as they climbed over the boulders. Sand and spray were blown violently in their faces while they were like troops under fire in the windscoop with stones flying everywhere. The Fifty-One provided easy going after that and the Long Beach dump was reached at 4pm. Here there was nostalgia for Warwick and Grahame. The supplies they left behind in 1963, after their painful retreat from Big Ben, were still largely intact. The memories of a makeshift camp, frostbite and the following forced march to the base at Atlas Cove were all too vivid.

Long Beach, more exposed to the shifting westerlies, gave the trio an uncomfortable time of pouring rain and wind, wet nights and frustrating days when it was difficult to film and even collect. There were fits of depression like the one that provoked Grahame to write that the grey days felt like 'the withering fag end of the expedition'. Even he remarked to Warwick that he had seen enough of Heard and a thirty-day stay was sufficient. During a particularly bad spell, as they lay up in the Bechervaise tent, Warwick wrote: 'One has some pleasant chats during such enforced idleness and it is worth considering that it is not given to many to share a "warmish" tent with good companions, good tucker, a view of the surf through the entrance and the calls of penguins all round. It would be foolish and unimaginative not to feel such experiences and they are the meat of expeditions, making up for the harder bits.' The treasure of half a bottle of Negrita rum, cached in the '63 dump, helped to while away cold evenings, and eventually enough sun came to allow completion of filming, survey photography and biological work. The journey back on 9 February was easier and late that day we lay in the Pyramid, together again, to face our last problem on the island.

Warwick: 'Nice cup of tea and now for plans. Westerly still strong. Wonder where *Patanela* is?' On the morning of 10 February we woke late and spent a great deal of time over breakfast, which developed into three courses after Grahame's ritual of coffee and cake on awakening. The thought of sorting all the debris and packing up was abhorrent. Everyone was eager to raise irrelevant topics for discussion, postponing the work we could not avoid. I lay in my sleeping bag, half propped against a pack, my lap filled with vials of insects for packing. Warwick cocked a quizzical eye at flightless beetles and repulsive ticks while Grahame began to scribble furiously in his diary between answering questions on fur seals and King penguins. Colin, always irritated at unnecessary delay, struggled through the sleeve for the umpteenth time and stumped away for his morning relief. The burble of conversation continued at nine o'clock until, suddenly, Col's astounded shout drowned us out. 'Hey! Here's *Patanela*!' Prostrate under a mound of vials I cursed as Warwick lurched across the Lilos and scrabbled for the radio. The aerial poked everywhere and finally, when we both disentangled ourselves, we tumbled out to join the others. Sure enough, *Patanela* lay bobbing gently a mile offshore as if she had been there all the time. She pulled at the anchor cable and vaguely we could discern a minute figure in the ratlines. We were caught with our pants down, a day early. As Warwick fumed over the unresponsive radio, I vigorously waved a red flag. A rain shower swept past and my eyes dropped to the surf below.

*   *   *

On the ship's safe return to Port aux Francais, Russ had dived overboard clad in wet suit and aqualung to examine *Patanela*'s hull.

Elephant Seals

Bumping on rocks is not conducive to sweet dreams and everyone was anxious to know what damage had been sustained. Half an hour in cold water and kelp produced a negative answer. There was nothing obviously wrong with the hull and we could continue with minds at rest. We did, all the way home, where we discovered that increased difficulty in steering was caused by loosened bolts in the rudder attachment.

4 February was the last day at Kerguelen. The Skipper was keen to get away, allowing himself a full week in which to make the rendezvous. On the evening of the 3rd, the crew were dined by the base personnel, shown some films and Antony presented a picture of sartorial elegance by wearing a grey lounge suit and old school tie which he had jealously guarded in the cray tank since Sydney. Yet, despite good intentions, *Patanela* did not leave as planned. Gale-force winds gave a trying time at the buoy and it was felt that any misjudgement in slipping the cable would put the ship on the beach. The risk was not taken and double watches stood through the following night until a more settled dawn.

Patanela was motored out in the forenoon of 5 February, left the Baie de Morbihan under foresail and staysail, into a brief lee as Mont Ross and the mountains revealed themselves for the last time. During the night, the barometer dropped, the westerly freshened and the ship rattled along at five and a half knots under only two sails. In the first twenty-four hours she covered half the distance to Heard. With the lugubrious prospect of arriving four days early in a storm, and the rising seas about them, the Skipper hove to for 40 hours. It was a difficult time for the five in charge of the ship.

Watches were arranged so that single watch was kept during the day and a normal double watch at night. Everyone was violently seasick after the secluded days at Kerguelen and life was a tossing misery. The seas became enormous and even while hove to, the Skipper ordered that two stand in the charthouse in case a port was stove in.

By dawn on 8 February the wind and seas had moderated and sail was hoisted once more. The sun made a belated appearance and good progress was maintained until the night, when rough seas, squalls and a morose barometer precipitated another six hours hove to. First, bleary light on 9 February brought the forbidding black shapes of the McDonald Islands into view. Heard came into sight at 1100 and with the strong sou'westerly behind her, *Patanela* raced along towards the north coast. At 1400 the sails were lowered after several big 'uns came aboard and Russ relates: 'We "sailed" around Red Island under bare poles at about 3 knots with long waves following—the largest I have seen this voyage. Willy-waws were whistling along the coast of Laurens Peninsula and the air was thick with Nellies, prions and pintados.' The roller-coaster swell carried the ship round the island until the fury of the westerly was lost in the lee of the east coast. Malcolm wrote: 'Hell what a relief it is to suddenly stop being thrown about.' Anchorage was sought in favoured Spit Bay and the night was spent in the atmosphere of uneasy peace we had experienced there before. Tea and toast preceded weighing the anchor at 0600 on 10 February and by 0900 they had motored round the Spit to stand off Poly Gully. The orange tents were prominent but the lack of activity seemed mysterious. Until Colin emerged to make his startled discovery, thoughts of mishap were entertained rather than suggestions of a lazy breakfast in bed.

As the rain intensified and the surf bared its white teeth I thought: What are we going to do? *Patanela* was a day early and I felt irritated at being unfairly caught napping. It was a rotten day for getting off, and there was all the packing up to do. On the other hand, the sooner *Patanela* showed her heels to the fickle vortex of storms, the better. We might sooner leave our unbecoming prison, too.

By 0945 Warwick and Ed were talking to each other by radio. Our state of readiness was announced and the Skipper was informed that we could not attempt to take off until 1400 when we hoped our gear would be packed and the surf more prepossessing. Warwick continued his conversation in formal radio jargon and only wasted breath on take-off arrangements, strangely disregarding the obvious question that was on everybody's lips aboard ship. Finally, Ed asked point blank: 'Did you climb the mountain?' Warwick was not to be carried away by the poignancy of the moment and replied: 'All aims have been achieved.' This laconic understatement stemmed, not from a desire to appear stoutly modest, but from the pressure of the moment. The task of getting off the island had been thrust hard into our laps without that precious extra day to adjust our thoughts or to allow mild resignation to take the place of some of our undoubted fears. Dry in the mouth and reluctant, I struggled into my wet suit. I hoped that something might postpone the evil moment but it became slowly apparent, from Warwick's determination and Grahame's eagerness, that every effort would be made to get off that day.

Packing seemed an interminable job made doubly frustrating by the pressure of a deadline. Everything had to be stowed in order of priority. Exposed film, scientific collections and records, valuable optical equipment had to go. Of secondary importance were bags of valuable personal gear. Then there was all the climbing and camping equipment, much of it on loan. Altogether there was one full boat load. The problem finally stared us in the face. How were we going to carry the loaded USR into the water or, alternatively, load it in the water? The only feasible plan required launching the craft empty, save for two men who would motor beyond the surf break, secure it with our small fisherman's anchor and motor back as close to the shore as was safe. A line to the shore would be used for hauling loads, after they had been tossed over the surf by the remaining three men. But a moderate sea was essential for the success of this plan. The surf still dumped heavily that morning and our only hope was high tide which might improve the conditions.

Warwick maintained hourly radio contact and kept the Skipper informed of our progress. The take-off time was postponed and postponed as the surf seemed to promise calm conditions in the evening. The Skipper agreed to wait until 1730, with a last radio schedule at 1700, but then he would have to seek an anchorage for the night. 'We'll come back tomorrow but won't promise any more.' Maybe it would be better tomorrow—this lack of wind might be the end of the sou'wester. Colin thought this was the case and made no bones about his doubts of a safe departure that day. In my reluctance, I mentally supported him then quailed at the prospect if the weather did not continue to improve. We might be stuck for a fortnight, and where would *Patanela* go then? It was an agonising dilemma that intensified as the day grew old.

Could we go? Should we go? Could we wait? Arguments, discussions, perusal of the sea filled every spare moment between packing and radio schedules. Little of our situation was conveyed to the ship's party, for our activities appeared curiously lethargic and distant.

Their view of the surf was unimpressive and it was hard to imagine the great barrier that seemed to separate us from safety. Grahame, in typical vein, was eager to make an attempt, Colin was doubtful, John non-committal and myself hardly in the forum with my jaundiced, non-swimmer's appreciation. During the early stages, Warwick understandably sat on the fence. With him rested the final decision.

Principally, our safety had to be assured and the problem lay in securing that as well as transporting the equipment. Much of it was not ours. Equipment loaned by the NZ Alpine Club was of great value and had been used all over the world on expeditions. Our consciences were stricken by the thought of abandoning it on that miserable, god-forsaken beach. And our pride was stung by the thought of a shame-faced retreat, a faint-hearted escape, like an army throwing away its arms.

We worked all day, packing and ferrying the loads down to the terrace above the beach. All food and surplus supplies were dumped unceremoniously and we decided to leave the tents erected until the last minute, in case of a postponement. John cooked up a huge stew at midday and we stuffed this down, aware that this might be our only chance to eat for many long, strenuous hours.

By mid-afternoon all the loads were down, the radio re-established at the terrace and a red flag ready for signalling. We wore our wet suits, Putt parkas, sailing-suit trousers, vapour barrier boots and partly-inflated life jackets. The surf had gone down a little but the sky was leaden, and optimistic views of the weather were leavened with more doubts. Stiff, uncomfortable and frankly afraid, I stood by the radio, staring glumly at *Patanela*. Warwick paced up and down, hands behind his back and head bent as Grahame or Colin opened a new line of attack on the problem. I looked up at a skua floating past. Oh to have wings! By 1630 it was clear that the surf would be just good enough to take off safely with top priority loads lashed into the

Skuas

assault craft.

But there was no question of offshore loading if we meant to go that afternoon. The problem was now clear cut, the dilemma sharply defined. There now remained two definite alternatives: we could probably get ourselves and vital gear off safely and quickly that afternoon or we could wait and place ourselves in the dubious hands of a new day. These cut and dried alternatives were never discussed. They simply emerged through the plethora of anxieties and half- answered questions. Warwick saw them clearly and, as the last radio schedule approached, decided where our true course lay. He turned and summarily said: 'We'll give it a go.' Lives were more important than the salvage of equipment. We would not risk waiting or offshore loading, purely on its account.

At 1700, Ed came up on the radio and Warwick told him that we would attempt to take off within the following half hour. The red flag indicating action was raised and he added: 'Keep a sharp look out for us in case anything goes wrong.' But we were on our own.

The radio was left where it was and we manhandled the craft off the shelf and on to the beach. The point we chose was above the wallow of elephant seals and we almost ran into them. They reared up at the sight of the strange apparition rushing down and bounced away, hugely and slowly, with the slight aid of their flippers, jaws gaping with ineffectual threats. We pulled up short, lumbered further up the beach with the assault craft and set it down beyond the reach of the water. Colin brought down the motor and the rest of us collected the two heavy packs of priority gear. Here was the film, the photographs, the survey data, soil samples, lichen and botanical specimens, rock samples, insects, algae. They were all packed tightly in polythene bags and air mattresses cut in half, along with diaries, records, cameras and smaller items of valuable equipment. A third bulky but light bag contained essential clothing we could not replace on *Patanela*.

The three loads were lashed into the craft, the rest left in a row on the shelf. There was talk of coming back for them if the weather was fine the next day. Small comfort hoping for that and I felt a sharp pang as I saw my ice axe tangled with the rest. It had gone a long way with me and was almost a talisman: I had fallen safely down Mount Cook and tramped across New Guinea with it. Many mountains had felt its spike, not least Big Ben, and it was painful to dump it in such a peremptory manner. Again I was reminded of the parallel. I was like a soldier throwing away his rifle.

This was one of many thoughts mixed with fear as I stood beside the craft and waited. The loads were lashed, the paddles stowed, motor checked and mounted. Warwick was port bowman with myself behind at the stern. Grahame was starboard bowman with Colin at the stern and John in between. Anxious, restless, cold or eager, we shuffled around in the rain, black sand clinging to boots and boat. Final procedure was discussed. Grahame was to give the orders. He decided that we should watch the surf pattern for a while to arrive at correct timing. When he gave the word go, we would run with the raft as far as possible, until we hit the steep shelf dropping beneath our feet, then leap aboard and paddle furiously. As soon as we had sufficient depth for the propeller—which was almost immediately—Colin would start the motor. As someone remarked: 'We'll be away on a fast camel.' The minutes dragged horribly as the big surf came and went. We stared out to sea, watching the size of the rollers, and it became clear that a relatively calm period followed a clutch of two or three big breakers. We should take advantage of that, though it was sometimes difficult to pick the third nasty dumper. Warwick ran round the assault craft to keep warm, joking to relieve the tension; Grahame made regular, precise comments on the surf; John was still and Colin flapped his arms as he stared worriedly at the ship. I slouched under the tug of the tight, wet-suit hood, my hand firmly gripping the rear handle of the boat.

There came a short order: 'Forward.' We moved up. 'Hold it!' A breaker snarled in, thrashed at the sand and ran up towards us, floating the bows. Suddenly the sea flattened and there was Grahame's 'Let's go!' Once we were on our way, all fear and agitation was gone. We ran, heads down, hauling hard at the bulky craft. Dimly I saw Warwick jump in ahead and immediately followed suit. Grabbing a paddle, I made to dig it in the water but, before I could, a surprise dumper lifted the bows into the air and for a breathless moment we hung on the point of balance. Then the bows dropped hard down and Warwick and I began to paddle.

Colin's yells stopped us short. 'Warwick! Paddle on the other side! The other side!' He was on board beside the motor but Grahame and John were still in the water, out of their depth. Our one-sided paddling had slewed the craft round and we were almost broadside on to the surf. I moved over with Warwick but could not paddle because of John's body. Incredibly, we bobbed on a surfless sea. Warwick hauled John by the seat of his pants as they climbed in and we all bent to the task as our charmed life seemed to run out. Grahame called the stroke, the boat straightened out and we moved sluggishly out to sea. Impetuously I yelled: 'Let her go Col!' He quickly pulled the start toggle and the Johnson roared into life. With gasps and sighs of relief we shipped the paddles.

A moment later we were working again as the motor spluttered and threatened to stall. The swell rushed past and broke a few yards behind the boat. Any drift and we would be dashed back on to the beach. But the motor continued to fire spasmodically, mostly on one cylinder, and we painfully crabbed out from the shore. We edged diagonally across the rising waves and Grahame exhorted Col to keep the boat straight. Feeling like an ant on a leaf crossing a raging river, I crouched over the loads and gauged the distance to the ship. The weather was making one of its rapid changes for the worse. Thick clouds poured round South Barrier and *Patanela* often disappeared for long seconds in the increasing swell.

In no mood to take photographs, I let Warwick cut the waterproof camera from my neck and he began to photograph our bedraggled escape. Wet, cold but slightly elated, I looked over his shoulder as the yellow hull came nearer. The island was almost covered in cloud but the orange tents and red flag stood out like neon signs to mark the pivot of our adventure. The motor laboured on and soon we could make out details of the ship. Five figures lined the rail and, carried by the wind, we heard a ragged and no doubt obscene cheer which we answered with thumbs up. Sickly, we manoeuvred to the lee side of the ship and, as she rolled, our rubber sponson squashed firmly into the familiar yellow steel. We were back.

Thankfully I swung over the rail to receive handshakes and congratulations. The deck seemed incredibly firm, the rigging strong and orderly, the whole ship gave an unmistakable aura of security. We took the loads from Warwick and Colin who then edged the assault craft round to the davit on the windward side. It bucked and swung and Colin fumed as everyone clustered over the rail to lift the motor. There was confusion and awkwardness until it was suspended and rapidly swung inboard. The craft was pulled to the bows and dragged over the rail. The wind lifted it up, forcing us to hang like deadweights to prevent it being blown away.

Finally it was on the deck and with childish delight I loosened the valves and rolled over the boat to deflate it. Russ showed a resigned grin as someone pointed to a vague shape bobbing in the water astern. It was the Zodiac, or its remains. Despite all Russ's attentions and repairs, our 'rescue' craft had given up the ghost and was dumped once it was seen we were safely off the beach. Soon the assault craft looked like a shrivelled elephant seal.

As news was passed around, I stood up, my legs suddenly weak, and looked down to find my parka smothered in green shark repellent which had leaked from the Mae West. Someone said 'Go below' and we went below to find a cheerful Ed with steaming mugs of tea. I gulped it down, the Skipper swung into the charthouse, Colin and Russ staggered down with the motor and I made a sudden dash for the deck as my stomach heaved. Excited and relieved, the occasion almost made me sick but a few gasps of the south-westerly and my stomach was appeased. I do not remember looking back at Heard Island. The devil was behind us and I had no desire to renew acquaintance. At 1815 the anchor was weighed, foresail and staysail hoisted and we laid course for home with a new storm behind us.

The Skipper would not let the shore party stand watch that first night. The next day, as I went to make my first log entry on the return voyage, I read his entry for the afternoon of 10 February. Our fears, anxieties, effort, success and elation were described in typically laconic terms: 'Shore party came off, minus kit. Got anchor. Course south.'

END

Inevitably, the return voyage was an anticlimax. After three months of moving from one vital goal to the next—Albany, 40°S, Kerguelen, Heard Island, Big Ben and safe departure—there only remained the business of going home. We suddenly seemed tired, lacking in purpose and our main preoccupations were sleep, calculation of the beer supplies, attempts to eat the mountain of fruit cake that remained in the deep freeze, and dreams of parties and reunion with loved ones. There was much self-analysis, wise afterthoughts and regrets that some things were not achieved, others partially, and it began to seem that most things we did achieve could have been done better. But these searchings, these analyses, were of little importance. It is said that nothing succeeds like success; so we had succeeded and no-one would seriously question our means to that end.

The westerlies on our port quarter lent wings to our heels and we covered the 2250 miles to Albany in less than eighteen days. All but the last three of these were under sail and the most memorable day was 15 February when we found that we had averaged over 6 knots for the previous twenty-four hours with little assistance from the mainsail. With reduced stores and fuel, *Patanela* responded to a fair wind as she was wont and the long, return reach across the South Indian Ocean gave the best sailing of the whole voyage. The late summer moderated the Roaring Forties and though we had strong winds and high seas, there never seemed the threat of an all-destroying gale. Slowly the temperature rose. Our energies and interest returned with the shedding of clothes. The initial days saw a simple, monotonous routine of watchkeeping, eating and sleeping but the sun saw us stir to the tasks set by 'debriefing'.

Remaining equipment was listed and accounted for. Some had

to be returned to sponsors, the rest sold to clear our final overdraft. The job of listing added further to the 'end-of-expedition-depression' and it was distasteful to begin dismantling our hard-won enterprise while we still had two or three thousand miles to sail. But it would save chaos in Sydney when everyone would be eager to leave and have done with the tedious after-expedition chores. Apart from this, some of us had to start writing. Newspapers, magazines in Australia, New Zealand and England all had claims on our time. Now that we had done what we said we would do, we had an obligation to tell everyone about it. Part of our obligation was mercenary but not all of it. Our altruistic aim had been to demonstrate that successful private expeditions were still possible from Australia, and that adventurous enterprise should be a keynote in a growing nation.

We had a particular obligation to *The Australian* newspaper which had been one of our two main sponsors. Its philanthropic £3000 donation could only be rewarded by a few articles, photographs and, most important of all, the scoop news of our success. Our earnest desire to give the latter led to no little embarrassment. Ed's radio communications with Australia were always haphazard due to our limited aerial capacity. Although he was in morse contact with some station every day of the voyage, this was often Mawson on the Antarctic Continent and it was usually easier to pick up Singapore or Hong Kong than Sydney or Perth. When *Patanela* sailed from Kerguelen for the rendezvous, Ed spoke to Mawson every day. There was a natural desire on their part to hear of happenings on Heard and whether the whole party was safe or not. But until we sent the news to Canberra we could not communicate with anyone else for fear of a news leak. For days Ed transmitted with no response from the north. Stations came in loud and clear on the receiver but he could not make himself heard. One evening, as he was about to give up again, Cape Town suddenly replied to his call. The brief news release was sent. But before it reached *The Australian*, the telecommunications system required that it be sent to London and then back to Sydney!

For a fortnight the wind whipped us along and the occasional wave came to swamp the decks when we slipped slightly beam on to the following sea. We made too much northing and a more easterly course increased the risk of gybing and demanded more attention to the helm. The wheel proved more recalcitrant after the bump at Kerguelen and the chains and cogs rumbled unceasingly as we spun and pulled when *Patanela* sideslipped down a wave and the booms jerked and thumped back into position. John won the wooden spoon when he gybed the foresail and its kicker ripped the starboard rail from the bulwarks.

But watchkeeping was not hard work any more. We now had a sum of experience and, since Colin also stood watch and the Skipper took his turn at the wheel, our hours on deck were noticeably shortened. A minor competition began to see whose watch reaped the most miles and we hardly believed the log when one three-hour watch totalled twenty-four miles. We began to understand why the Forties had been a favourite clipper route.

St Valentine's Day was the Skipper's sixty-seventh birthday and in a toast that evening we expressed something of the admiration and respect we held for him. Whatever reservations we may have had at the beginning were long gone in recognition of a fortitude and inner strength that are not given to many. He fractured his thumb on the second day of the return voyage but the success of the expedition and his final identification with a well-found ship gave rise to high spirits which such discomforts could never subdue. We now had the full benefit of his dry humour in delicious, quaint stories and side remarks. As we hoisted the mainsail in an effort to make more way with a light breeze, 'the good ship leapt gallantly forward'.

Finer weather brought a need for washes and haircuts. For only the second time on the whole voyage, on 26 February the sea and sun combined to make conditions ideal for swimming. Russ, Grahame and John swam ahead of the ship for the benefit of Mal's movie camera and Warwick, after swimming off at sharp right angles, suddenly realised to his horror that the ship was still moving under sail. Mid ocean is not a place to feel abandoned. Mal then rigged the unused staysail boom over the port side and perched on the end to film the ship under way, receiving rude comments for his pains apart from efforts by the helmsmen to dip him in the sea.

The start of our final three days' motoring into Albany was marked by the end of our beer. The last empty can was thrown overboard at sunset to the accompaniment of a grim salute and the mournful strains of 'A Ship With No Beer'. There were untapped reserves of gin and whisky but, as Russ remarked, one can of beer per day had not promoted any tolerance to alcohol. The new sundown session of two or three pink gins was in the best nautical tradition but seemed likely to impair the smooth running of the ship. One was reminded of the Skipper's story of two oldish huntsmen who enjoyed several bottles of port after a successful day's hunt. 'What is it like outside?' said one to the other. His companion rose and, on opening a cupboard by mistake, replied, 'It's as black as pitch and smells of cheese.'

The night of 27–28 February was full of anticipation and apprehension. At sunset we knew we lay only a hundred miles off the Australian coast, and the worries of landfall and shipping lanes beset us for the first time in three months. Our navigation lights were switched on again and we found the starboard light not working. But fortune favoured the brave and we did not encounter any ships at all though we were near Australia's busy southwest corner. The Skipper stayed up nearly all night and his watch was rewarded just after two o'clock in the morning when the Eclipse Island light came into sight flashing groups of three.

I came on deck with Grahame at 0500 to relieve John and Colin. Col swung below quickly for a couple of hours sleep before breakfast but John stood in the bows, staring at the colour of Australia. There was a smell of eucalyptus and smoke. The red and brown bars that swelled with the sunrise spoke of dust and heat and burning and land; a hot, dry land that was an antidote to our memories of the previous months: there was more than cold water to the earth. We watched with pleasure, as the thick land smell filled our nostrils, while the horizon bars expanded and the heart colour of blood burgeoned into an early orange, sucking a diamond Jupiter into a hellish swirl of dust. The sun was hot when full daylight finally revealed a hazy coast.

The Skipper relaxed when the course was clear and took tea and cake at 0600: yet another perfect landfall. We motored on over the continental shelf with a line trolling and, in repetition of our first arrival at Albany, we caught tuna and ate them fried in butter as we watched a freighter slip into King George Sound.

Conscious that we would encounter people other than ourselves, we bathed, tugged at our straggling hair and beards, put on passably clean clothes and tidied the decks. As we came abreast of Breaksea Island we wondered what our reception would be. Our arrival was forewarned by radio but a sudden manoeuvre in the Sound must have provoked old doubts about our seamanship. I hauled in the logline until it was an inextricable jumble on the deck. The Skipper left the wheel to instruct me in streaming the line in reverse to unravel the kinks, until there was a shout of alarm from Antony as *Patanela* bore towards the cliffs on the western edge of the Sound.

Apart from scraping a whale chaser, we moored cleanly at the old berth in Albany. There was a crowd of curious bystanders, friends and acquaintances with a stack of congratulatory telegrams. Cameras flashed, hands shook, smiles, laughter and a sudden snort of delight from Warwick as he read the telegram from our honorary treasurer in Sydney: 'Major Deacock, Wesfarmers, Albany, W.A. Congratulations overdraft £500 draw no cheques. Evan.' We spent just a day in Albany: enough time to send away mail, articles and photographs and to sample the delights of civilization.

We enjoyed a beer in the pubs but the rest was curiously depressing. As Colin flew away to his job in Sydney, the death knell of the expedition began to sound in earnest and one was torn between the desire to preserve its life and satisfactions as long as possible and the desire to get away quickly from its fag end and get on with a fresh task. It was a frustrating time for everyone that was alleviated only by continuing good comradeship. I sometimes think that the expedition's greatest achievement was that we spent four months together in a small ship without a row or open personal conflict.

With a vacant bunk, we took aboard Phil Wynter, an itinerant journalist who had been of great assistance to us in Albany. After a prolonged bout of seasickness he was able to help in watch-keeping and we sailed to Sydney with a full complement. We oiled at Albany in the afternoon of 1 March, then sailed off the wharf and by midnight had lost the loom of Breaksea light despite a sloppy breeze. At 0500 on 2 March we started the engine and for the remaining twelve days round the coast we spent most of our time motoring into headwinds. The Bight proved bilious and perverse in its best traditions.

After two days of rolling and pitching there was a sudden outburst of complaints against motoring in the form of doggerel verse in the log. This resulted in the hoisting of all plain sail after breakfast on 4 March but there was an admonishing note from the Skipper on the log's flyleaf:

> That the log should be written in seamanlike prose
> Is a rule that every seafaring man knows.
> Only a crew of jerks or worse
> Will mar this book with any more verse.

We sailed for over a day with a favourable westerly behind us but, in a fit of complacency, failed to see the danger signal as the barometer dropped and *Patanela* creamed along at eight knots. A squall loomed on the horizon during mid afternoon on 5 March and there was a peculiar lack of urgency in taking a reef until it was too late. As we struggled with the cringles, the squall hit with its full force. *Patanela* heeled alarmingly and it soon became impossible to tie the reef points on the mains'l. The port lazy guys gave way and there was a sudden deafening report. With fears that the sail had split, I looked up from our struggle with the mainsheet to see the starboard shroud on the foremast hanging loose. The accumulated strain of days hove to off Heard Island under foresail, days of running under foresail and staysail only and this final squall had taken its toll. The masthead fitting had snapped. The mainsail was handed altogether and with the foresail useless on the starboard tack we continued with staysail and jib. Then we found the jibstay slack and the staysail alone took us through a squally night at three to four knots. Then the wind died and we submitted to the clamour of the engine once more.

The next two days brought cloud and lumpy following seas that helped, with increased revs, to give us a record daily run of 190 miles. We were not only eager to get home but had to meet a deadline too.

A telegram informed us that our sponsor required our presence outside Sydney Heads at 1000 on Sunday 14 March. Only a week away, this was a presumptuous request but we were determined to meet it. Especially the Skipper who had once failed to arrive at a civic reception in his honour because of adverse winds. On 9 March we almost equalled our record with 181 miles and came into Portland Bay after dodging cray-pots and porpoises that swept past the ship in the crests of waves higher than the bulwarks.

Lawrence Rock was smothered in gannets as we left the turbulent Bight for the softer waters of the sheltered bay. An empty ocean was now behind us and from that time we did not sail for long out of sight of land. It was an incredibly still evening with a bright moon as we spent the last hours of daylight refueling, and repairing the foremast shroud. We had the luxury of a big dinner at anchor, Mal expertly baked buns and we toasted ourselves on completion of 10,000 miles of ocean cruising. With the deadline ever in our thoughts, we motored on at 2130 and the night watches were pleasant with balmy breezes and the lights of Port Fairy and Warrnambool slipping past on the port hand.

From Portland on my insect nets began to show results after weeks of emptiness. As we ran into Bass Strait I collected scores of flying insects blown off the mainland. The catch of four small nets told of myriads in the air migrating, voluntarily or involuntarily, from Victoria to Tasmania. Thistledown swept ceaselessly over the waves and, with the birds and fish, the sea became alive after the familiar vista of empty wastes.

With Port Phillip out of sight to the north, our next landfall was Wilson Promontory at the island-studded narrows of the Strait. We picked up Cape Liptrap light in the evening of 10 March and, with a confidence born of practice, passed the Promontory in the early hours of the following morning. Motoring through the narrows in company with two other vessels, we paused off South East Point to signal our position. But the lighthouse keeper was asleep for there was no response to our Aldis lamp.

The morning was slow in coming as banks of smoke filled the horizon to north and east. Ash and soot dirtied the rigging and we realised the full extent of the worst bush fires in decades. The smoke made navigation difficult and it was not until late in the morning, when we were a few miles offshore, that the low-lying land came into view once more. The sun set early, blood red high in the sky, and we bucked on in choppy head seas, looking for Gabo Island.

Gabo was rounded at noon next day and we motored close to the coast past Green Cape and Twofold Bay. With foresail and staysail to help and steady, we seemed to glide along at eight knots. Evening drew on, and we leaned back to admire the inlets and bays. Suddenly there was a rush below and Warwick switched the engine off. Clouds of steam filled the engine room and Antony, as second engineer, found that the Rolls had boiled dry. Fearing important damage to the engine, and lying half a mile off the coast in a freshening southerly, we hoisted all plain sail and made a wide reach out to sea. This meant we had to cut almost at right angles across the main shipping lane.

It was no surprise, therefore, as we lounged in the charthouse enjoying the last of our whisky, to see a liner steam over the southern horizon. Mal said it was the moon coming up, it was so decked with lights. It made a pretty, entertaining sight until Ed nervously suggested that it would pass rather close. At the time we were making a good seven knots and thoroughly enjoying one of our last spells of spirited sailing. The *Empress of Australia*, as the liner turned out to be, was making about twenty-four and was certain to cross our path before we were out of the way. Our jokes and chortles slowly changed to nervous laughs and alarm as, one by one, we all filtered up on deck to join the watch-keepers. As the liner grew in proportions we switched on our deck-lights, sure that it would alter course on seeing us. Little did we know that it was no longer always required of steam to give way to sail. As the Empress ploughed up, Ed pulled out the Aldis lamp and shone it on the mainsail. Some of us swore that she changed course at the last minute as she steamed a few hundred yards away across our bows, and it only seemed a few seconds before we saw her starboard lights. The next day, when an Italian liner came up astern, we prudently changed course. We did not want any more narrow escapes.

That was the last day of the voyage. Through the night of 13 March we watched the loom of Sydney grow brighter and brighter, a great beacon to the end of our adventure. Meeting our deadline with two hours to spare, we tacked about off Sydney Heads and then rode in, under sail for the last time, as welcoming launches came out to meet us on a warm Sunday morning. There was the bridge we had last seen on 5 November, there was the Gap, the hydrofoil ferry; there was Colin, unrecognizable without a beard, there were the Sunday yachts, the trimarans and runabouts; there was the wharf, the big city and the end.

The expedition was suddenly over. Within a week of our return, the fêting and congratulations were swallowed in the bustle of Sydney; *Patanela* was stripped and returned to her owners, and members dispersed to their old occupations. Both John and I returned quickly to New Zealand where he took up a teaching post at Ekatahuna. Mal went doctoring in northern New South Wales and Russ did the same a month later in Christchurch. Grahame returned to the School of Public Health and Tropical Medicine in Sydney, Col was thoroughly absorbed in chemical engineering once more and Warwick sought new fields for his boundless energy and zest for innovation. Ed went to the Snowy to manage a ski lodge and Antony took a post at Canberra Grammar School after we both toyed with the idea of sailing an American ketch to San Diego.

The Skipper flew from Sydney to London on 21 March and Warwick, Colin, Grahame, Antony and Russ were able to see him off. His luggage consisted of a kitbag and one small, brown suitcase and, as Russ described: 'Skipper left with sextant in one hand and star chart in the other.' No doubt he hated the flight because he could not smoke his pipe and flying made things too quick and easy. But on this occasion he needed all the time he could save. Within the following three months he had to refit his *Mischief*, find a crew and set sail for Greenland before the northern summer grew too old.

After the expedition was wound up, there were two inevitable questions: what did we really achieve, and what now? We felt that the first question could be answered very fully. Fully enough to satisfy our supporters and our consciences. Our broad object had been achieved: the sailing of a small ship 10,000 miles through the sub-Antarctic to make the first ascent of Big Ben. Our scientific objectives were largely fulfilled.

At Sea

Throughout the 'triangle' voyage—Albany-Heard Island-Albany—regular plankton and hydrology stations were kept. These contributed greatly to the knowledge of the little-known marine biology of the Southern Indian Ocean. Twice-daily meteorological observations were made. Apart from being a valuable scientific record, the accrued information was radioed to Australia whenever possible, assisting contemporary weather forecasting. Insect nets were streamed for three-quarters of the whole voyage, providing valuable information on insect migration in a scarcely-known section of the Indo-Pacific region. Apart from these three major activities, a regular log was kept of birdlife and whale sightings.

On Land

On Heard Island, survey was completed for the first detailed map of the south-east quadrant of the island. A comprehensive insect collection was made and specimens obtained from Kerguelen for comparison. A botanical collection was made, including a wide variety of lichens. Extensive zoological observations were made, including a count of fur seals and King penguins. Mineral soil samples and rock specimens were taken, crevasse temperatures were recorded and the current volcanic activity assessed. Apart from these important collections and observations there was the valuable and permanent record of 10,000 feet of 16mm film and hundreds of black and white and colour still photographs.

These were the tangible results and on face value it can be said that these were the most important. Something concrete was added to man's knowledge of the sub-Antarctic and another milestone passed in climbing Big Ben. On the other hand, they are the cold statistics of the expedition and, with no fear of being reproached, we feel that the intangible human values demonstrated were more important. If we showed that private adventurous enterprise is still important in a modern world, and stirred some minds to such an end, then this alone was sufficient justification for our voyage.

> '... If one will only dare, one can actually do the most un-likely things that may come into one's head. For the hesi-tant, the diffident, and the many amateurs overawed by the experts of this world, this demonstration can't be made too often.'

The second question of what now? was soon answered. There should be more adventures and not by us alone. Warwick was asked to talk to the Melbourne University Mountaineering Club on 'How it is done'; to the Administrative Staff College on 'How to get things done without committees' and Colin lectured to the Sydney Rock-climbers' Club on the theme of 'How do I Organize a Trip?'. These were heartening signs and the support throughout of the Sydney business community in particular had shown faith in the value of our principles.

And what happened to *Patanela*, a ship of steel and wood, ropes and sails that over the months became more than a vehicle, that pos-sessed her own identity and the affection of her crew? The Skipper left her with regret and said he would be willing to sail her to the Antarctic Continent if an expedition could be assembled.

There was talk of buying her, for a youth-sailing school and oc-casional expeditions; but impecunious explorers are ill equipped to face the problems of hard cash. *Patanela* was overhauled, scrubbed, cleaned, painted and preened then put up for sale on the wave of our publicity. But she was not a fancy yacht and she was too expensive for an offshore work-boat. So she stayed with her owners and went back to crayfishing and other jobs. But she was built with dreams of adventure and one likes to think that, after two voyages in the sub-Antarctic and still young, that she is waiting. Waiting until her strength is tested to full measure again in the wide, blue yonder.

EXPEDITION MEMBERS

GRAHAME BUDD: Grahame could be called 'Mr Heard Island'. The island and the mountain were a magnificent obsession for him and, apart from their shared drama on Big Ben in 1963, it was inconceivable that Warwick Deacock could have organised a new expedition without his taking part as scientific officer.

Born in Murwillumbah, NSW in 1930, Grahame graduated from Sydney University in 1953. He wintered at Heard Island in 1954 as medical officer and expedition leader, and at Mawson in Antarctica in 1959 as medical officer and deputy leader, undertaking long-distance, midwinter dog-sled research journeys. Elsewhere he climbed and explored with Eric Shipton in the Karakoram; made a ten-week southern journey in Adélie Land; the first known landing on the McDonald Islands; spent a year in remote parts of New Guinea, and three summers on the fireline of Australian bushfires. Much of his work and journeying entailed research into human responses to heat and cold. He has published more than a hundred scientific papers, book chapters and monographs on this subject, as well as on the history and glaciology of Heard Island deriving from his five expeditions there. He has also published on the population ecology of Antarctica's emperor penguins and Heard's king penguins and fur seals.

Grahame was Associate Professor in Environmental Health in the University of Sydney from 1979 until his retirement in 1996, and since then has been an Honorary Associate Professor in the same university. He is a Fellow of the Royal Australasian College of Physicians, holds the Queen's Polar Medal (1969), and was made a Member of the Order of Australia in 2004.

Grahame has been married to author and editor Josephine Bastian for more than 50 years, and they have three children and one grandchild.

JOHN CRICK: Born in Melbourne in 1942, John Crick had a fine education in the Australian bush and continued this when, as a teenager, he went to the Australian Outward Bound School, established at Fisherman's Point on NSW's Hawkesbury River by Warwick Deacock in 1959. John stayed on as an instructor and then made his first migration to New Zealand to 'climb/live/learn/thrive'. As the Heard Island expedition took shape, Warwick invited him along as an 'apprentice expeditioner'.

After the expedition, John followed his heart as a teacher for 20 years, specialising in drama and outdoor pursuits in New Zealand and Australia. He eventually left teaching to perform solo shows mainly for schools, interpreting folk history and ecology in plays, music and puppetry. John's outdoor pursuits continued among the mountains and rivers and for seven years he guided the Abel Tasman National Park Seal Swim as 'John the Walrus'.

Over the last 18 years, John has travelled as a 'songman-storyman' to the 'ancestor places', exploring the light and dark of Scotland; the humour, energy and healing of Australia; the ecology and lore of Aotearoa/New Zealand.

He has been married to Margo for nearly 50 years and they have two children and two grand-children.

WARWICK DEACOCK (1926–2017): In 1944, at the age of 17, Warwick Deacock did a bunk from school and joined the Royal Marines, gaining his Green Beret and a commission. Later, he served in the Middlesex Regiment, carrying the Queen's Colours at her wedding. Then he joined the Parachute Regiment and the SAS, reaching the rank of Major, and fought in colonial conflicts in Malaya and Oman before he resigned his commission. Along the way he learned to ski and climb on services expeditions to the Himalaya, Alaska and Lapland, and developed a number of creative skills.

With his wife and baby daughter, Warwick migrated to Australia in 1959 to set up the Outward Bound School and Duke of Edinburgh Award Scheme. In 1963 he found himself on Heard Island with Grahame Budd, and when he returned, he took off on a round Australia trip to research the uses of leisure. While working as a gravedigger in the Northern Territory, he hit on the plan to organise an independent expedition back to Heard Island. The amount of work involved in bringing this together might well have sent anyone else to an early grave.

Hyperactive might be the word to describe Warwick's activities after Heard. He established the Chakola Wildlife Refuge in Kangaroo Valley, south of Sydney, a non profit centre for 'creative adventure recreation'. He also established Ausventure, the world's first adventure travel company providing trekking, rafting and wildlife expedition opportunities to all parts of the world. Warwick became involved in many community conservation projects, and for all this he deservedly won medals, not least the Order of Australia Medal for services to conservation and the environment.

Warwick enjoyed marriage for 55 years to architect and explorer Antonia who died in 2012. He has two children and three grand-children.

MALCOLM HAY (1934–2021) was 30 when he joined the Heard expedition as its cinematographer after meeting Warwick Deacock at the Australian Outward Bound School. He was one of three crew, along with Grahame Budd and Russell Pardoe, who had been a medical officer at an Australian base in Antarctica.

After the expedition, Malcolm followed a long career as an orthopaedic surgeon in Perth. But, of all the expedition's members, he translated most directly the experience and example of *Patanela*'s voyage into a major community project. He had seen how an adventurous sea voyage was capable of bringing out the best in people and in 1974 he started the fund raising of four million dollars to build a sail training ship. The three-masted barquentine *Leeuwin II* was launched in 1986 and since that time has carried about 20,000, mostly young, men and women on voyages out of Fremantle, along the western coast of Australia. In 2010 in Norway, *Leeuwin II* was declared the best in the large category Sail Training Ship world wide from among 76 other ships competing for this annual award.

After his retirement in 2007, Malcolm became more involved in volunteer youth and conservation work and in 2014 was given an award for 40 years of continuous community endeavour, especially for his work with the Leeuwin Foundation.

He was been married to Rosemary for more than 50 years, and they have three children and four grand-children.

ANTONY HILL was born in Sydney in 1940. He met Warwick Deacock while he was completing his honours degree in History and French at Sydney University and became involved in Warwick's first Outward Bound course in 1959. Antony campaigned hard to be part of *Patanela*'s crew on the basis of his extensive sailing experience, including the Sydney-Hobart Race. By then he was also studying law and helped draft the charter terms and transmogrification of *Patanela* from crayfishing boat to private yacht.

Antony finally made it on board as first mate when one of the original team members cried off. The age difference between captain and first mate was probably the greatest in the history of sea voyaging because Skipper Tilman was just about old enough to be Antony's grandfather.

After the expedition, Antony had what he describes as a 'cathartic moment' when he took a temporary job as senior French mistress at Narrabeen Girls High School. This led to a 40 plus year educational career in Australia and the USA, teaching History, French, Latin, English and coaching all manner of sports and outdoor education programmes. These included leading groups of senior students on trips to Nepal, New Zealand, Indonesia and Sri Lanka, as well as Australia and the United States. He rose and rose, becoming heavily involved in state and national educational policy-making, and ended his career as headmaster of St Mark's School in Boston, USA where he still lives.

Antony has been married to Elsa for more than 40 years and they have one daughter and three foster children. Between them, they have eight grand-children.

RUSSEL PARDOE (1932–2011) qualified as a doctor in 1958, but during his undergraduate years he served with the Australian 1st Commando Regiment where he acquired skills as a paratrooper, mountaineer, frogman and pilot. His frogman role was particularly valuable when he had to make an underwater inspection of *Patanela*'s rudder in the sub-Antarctic waters of Kerguelen..

Russ was prepared for anything. As the expedition doctor, he interviewed us all, in order to be prepared for any medical complaints that might afflict us during the five months away. In the first big storm, I came down with my first bout of malaria, which had been lying in wait after my time in the Solomon Islands. Russ had the right drugs on hand.

We were confident he would cope with any medical emergency after his heroic endeavours as medical officer at Mawson in 1961 when the base mechanic suffered a cerebral haemorrhage. He communicated with a surgeon in Melbourne by Morse Code to obtain advice about what to do; he fashioned surgical equipment from dental tools; he tested his techniques on a seal; and with the assistance of the cook and two geophysicists, he drilled through the man's skull to relieve pressure and kept him alive for two months until he could be flown back to Australia. Appropriately, he was awarded the MBE.

After the expedition, Russ emigrated to the United States where he eventually became a plastic surgeon of international consequence with a reputation for outstanding expertise in treating burns. He died in California from a brain tumour in 2011, aged 78. He had been married to Silvija for almost 45 years, and they had four sons and four grand-children.

COLIN PUTT (1926 –2016) was born near Auckland in 1926, graduated in engineering and science at Canterbury University, Christchurch, and learned how to climb and survey before taking these skills to Sydney in 1950. A chemical engineer who could actually engineer anything, he oversaw the conversion of *Patanela* from a motorised crayfish boat to an ocean-going sailing schooner equipped to withstand anything the Southern Ocean could throw at her.

Before the Heard Island expedition, when he was not managing toxic gas escapes, fires and explosions at ICI chemical plants, he climbed in the Southern Alps and Switzerland and led the New Zealand expedition to attempt the first ascent of the Carstensz Pyramide in West New Guinea in 1961.

After Heard, Colin continued his engineering career but, whenever he could manage time off, he went on more seaborne expeditions, such as sailing with Skipper Bill Tilman in *Sea Breeze* to Greenland in 1970 and a Kon-Tiki style canoe voyage across the Indian Ocean. These only ended in 1988 when, sailing in the *Dick Smith Explorer* with an expedition to climb Mount Minto in the Antarctic, the vessel was capsized twice in a great storm amongst icebergs and broke her drive shaft. With makeshift repairs he managed to get the ship back to Lyttelton to repair her properly and skipper her back to Sydney. After that, nobody wanted to be taken to the Antarctic in *Dick Smith Explorer* and Colin semi-retired at the age of 62. He taught chemical engineering part time at Sydney University until his death in his ninetieth year.

Colin and Jane had been married for 66 years. They had four children, nine grandchildren and five great-grandchildren.

ED REID (1936–2011) was 28 when he joined the expedition as its radio operator. He was another who had met Warwick at Outward Bound. Ed had learned his wireless skills in the Royal Australian Navy and he needed all of them to maintain any kind of communication between a small ship in the South Indian Ocean and shore stations in South Africa and Australia.

Ed's sense of humour was unfailing. During the return voyage from Heard, when I came up with the title of *The Sea and The Snow* for this book, Ed thought this was far too tame and said that the slightly salacious title of *Big Ben and Patanela* would attract more readers. Joke or not, he could have been right.

After the expedition, Ed pursued his talents as an artist and as an alternative educator, working with aboriginal people and also, for many years, as manager of Warwick Deacock's Chakola outdoor education centre in Kangaroo Valley. Towards the end of his life, Ed gave immense support to a New South Wales coastal safety learning group for young people. When brain cancer afflicted him, he filled his times of remission with making drawings of the twelve vessels on which he had served. Ed died in the new year of 2011 aged 74.

PHILIP TEMPLE (philiptemple.com) I was born in Yorkshire in 1939, educated in London and emigrated to New Zealand in 1957. Two years later I began climbing in the Southern Alps and first met Colin Putt when he was running climbing courses for Australian climbers who were experiencing high accident rates there.

Colin led our joint expedition to West New Guinea in 1961, when we attempted to make the first ascent of the Carstensz Pyramide (one of the 'Seven Summits of the Seven Continents'). Soon after that, I accompanied Warwick Deacock on his first visit to Mount Cook, and then both Warwick and Colin helped me to join Heinrich Harrer, when we returned to the Carstensz and made the first ascent of the Pyramide in 1962. Later, I was employed by the B.P. Bishop Museum of Hawaii, collecting ectoparasites and other insects throughout New Guinea and the Solomon Islands.

After the Heard expedition, I went to the New Zealand Outward Bound School, ending up as seamanship instructor: *Patanela* and the Skipper had been the very best of mentors. Since 1972, after a spell as features editor of the *New Zealand Listener*, I have followed a career as an author of both fiction and non-fiction, often writing books about mountains and exploration. I was made an Officer of the NZ Order of Merit in 2005 for 'services to literature' and gained a LittD degree in 2007.

I am married to poet and novelist Diane Brown and, from an earlier marriage, have two children and five grand-children.

H W 'BILL' TILMAN (1898–1977) Bill Tilman fitted, better than anyone, that overworked phrase 'a legend in his own lifetime'. In the pantheon of mountaineering, he was part of that immortal duo Shipton and Tilman who, throughout the 1930s, had explored blanks on the map in the Himalaya, had made the first ascents of Mount Kenya in Africa and Nanda Devi, and had attempted Everest. Both Tilman and Eric Shipton wrote brilliant books about their pioneering endeavours that were a source of inspiration to younger mountaineers.

Bill Tilman had not only been a mountaineer. He joined the army in 1915 at the age of 17, survived the First World War as an artillery officer, and volunteered for the Second World War in his 40s, when he ended up fighting with partisans in Albania and Italy. He won the DSO and MC and Bar.

In the early 1950s, after he had led the first group to explore the Nepalese approaches to Everest, he decided he was becoming too old for high climbing and taught himself to ocean sail and navigate. In his forty-five-foot Bristol Channel pilot cutter *Mischief* he set about exploring Arctic and Antarctic waters, and by 1964 had already voyaged as far as the Kerguelen Islands, 500km from Heard.

After the Heard expedition, Bill Tilman continued his high latitude voyages in Arctic waters. Then, in his 80th year, he was invited to join an expedition to Smith Island in Antarctica when the expedition ship, en route from Rio to the Falklands, disappeared without trace. He was one of the great heroes of 20th century exploration. His fifteen books were reissued by Lodestar Books with Vertebrate Publishing from 2015 to 2017.

PATANELA (1958–1988)

Patanela was built by Bob Brinkmann in Hobart in 1958 to a design by J B Savage. After the Heard expedition, following some necessary repairs, she was handed back to her owners, Norm and Doug Hunt. She returned to the fishing life, first in Tasmania and then out of Fremantle. When Norm retired, he decided to convert her into a cruising yacht. In 1971, while this was under way, *Patanela* was gutted by fire ignited by an oxyacetylene torch. This led to a more extensive rebuild with accommodation made accessible below decks from one end of the ship to the other. The Rolls-Royce engine was replaced by a Gardner and she was painted blue instead of yellow. In 1975 Norm embarked n a protracted cruise around the world with his family, using our original set of heavyweight terylene sails which were still in good condition.

After Norm returned to Australia with *Patanela* in 1982, the Hunt brothers used her for fishing and charter work until she was sold to Perth businessman Alan Nicol in 1988. On 16 October of that year Nicol, with his wife Doreen, daughter Ronalee, skipper and commercial pilot Ken Jones, and two young sailors, John Blissett and Michael Calvin, left Fremantle in *Patanela* on a voyage to Airlie Beach, North Queensland. Nicol had fitted all the latest electronic and navigation equipment but had paid no attention to the sails. When they went to raise sail, *Patanela*'s mainsail began to come apart after more than 20 years of use, and only two headsails proved useable.

Motorsailing around Australia, *Patanela* ran short of fuel but Nicol was not able to fully top up her tanks en route because of limited funds. Both Nicol and Jones were experiencing financial problems and at Port Lincoln, South Australia, Nicol and his daughter left *Patanela* to return to Perth to deal with these. Skipper Jones decided to sail on with the others.

Off Botany Bay, south of Sydney, in the early hours of 8 November, Jones sent an incomplete radio message to say he expected to enter Port Jackson later that day; but *Patanela* was never heard from or seen again. An alarm was raised only on 18 November when *Patanela* failed to arrive at Airlie Beach. A few months later, one of the ship's lifebuoys was washed up on a beach north of Sydney, prompting all kinds of conspiracy theories. It was even suggested to police that *Patanela* had been hijacked by Norm Hunt and was being used for smuggling and piratical activities in Brazil. An absurd police investigation followed which yielded no results.

The last radio messages from *Patanela* indicated she had run out of fuel. Skipper Jones needed engine power, not just for motoring, but also to keep batteries charged for all the electronic equipment that had been fitted. When the batteries flattened, no further radio communication was possible. Barely able to make way with only headsails in light winds, *Patanela* would have been virtually dead in the water, at night without lights, and in the shipping lane for vessels approaching Sydney. Most likely, she was run down by a container ship or bulk carrier which would have scarcely registered the impact. This was the fate we narrowly avoided off that same coast in March 1965.

The expedition on its return to Sydney 14 March 1965

Back: John Crick, Russel Pardoe, Ed Reid, Colin Putt.
Middle: Grahame Budd, Philip Temple, Warwick Deacock.
Front: Antony Hill, Grahame Budd, Bill Tilman, Malcolm Hay.

The 50th anniversary expedition reunion at Adventure Books, Oamaru 10 December 2014

Back: Philip Temple, Warwick Deacock, Antony Hill, John Crick, Grahame Budd.
Front: Malcolm Hay, Colin Putt.
Photo: Colin Monteath, Hedgehog House New Zealand

ACKNOWLEDGEMENTS

MAJOR W. M. M. DEACOCK and members of the Expedition would like to extend their sincere thanks to those who made their enterprise possible: R. Abbot Esq., W. M. Adams Ltd., Aluminium Supply, Abbotts Laboratories Pty. Ltd., Anax Pty. Ltd., Ames Company Ltd., Andrews Laboratory Pty. Ltd., Astra Pharmaceuticals (Aust.) Pty. Ltd., Australian Outward Bound Memorial Foundation, Albany, W.A., William Arnott Pty. Ltd., Airdive Equipment Sporting Goods, A.W.A. Ltd., Australian Sporting Sales Pty. Ltd., Australian Gas Light Company, Australian Dairy Produce Board, Antarctic Division, J. D. Anthony, M.P., Minister for the Interior, Miss B. Archdale, Australian and New Zealand Banking Corp., Butter Marketing Board, Boots Pure Drug Co. (Aust.) Pty. Ltd., The British Drug Houses (Aust.) Pty. Ltd., Burroughs Wellcome and Co. (Aust.) Ltd., Mr. D. Brass, James Barnes Pty. Ltd., Mrs. E. Biddulph, O. D. Bisset Esq., George Brown and Co. Pty. Ltd., Berri Fruit Juices Co-op. Ltd., Byrne and Davidson Pty. Ltd., Brella N.S.W. Pty. Ltd., Balm Paints Pty. Ltd., Bells Asbestos and Engineering (Aust.) Pty. Ltd., P. Byron Esq., D. Bellwood Esq., Barratts N.S.W. Pty. Ltd., Brandt's Pty. Ltd. Lighting and Heating, British Ex-Servicemen's Club, Bishop Museum, Honolulu, Big Sister Foods Ltd., Botany Rotary Club, Barker College, Bureau of Mineral Resources, Bureau of Meteorology, Boans Ltd. W.A., Colgate Ltd. (Aust.), Commonwealth Industrial Gases Ltd., C.S.I.R.O., Cruising Yacht Club of Australia, Cottees Ltd., C.S.R. Co. Ltd., Cadbury Fry Pascall Pty. Ltd., Commercial Apiarists' Association, Concrete Constructions Pty. Ltd., F. Crago and Sons Pty. Ltd., Comalco Products Pty. Ltd., Country Women's Association of N.S.W., Coast and Mountain Walkers' Club, Dr. G. G. V. Cawley, A. Cooper Esq., The

Right Honourable Lord Casey, C.H., D.S.O., M.C., M.A., P.C., J. Cranko Esq., Cranbrook School, Sydney, Carringbah High School, N.S.W., J. Cadwalladar Esq., Carnation Co. Pty. Ltd., Coats Patons (Aust.) Ltd., Carlton and United Breweries Ltd., Clifford Love and Co. Ltd., Drug Houses of Australia Ltd., Davies Coop N.S.W. Pty. Ltd., Drew Robinsons, Dunlop Rubber (Aust.) Ltd., Dabbie Bros. Pty. Ltd., M. C. Downes Esq., David Jones Ltd., Department of Army, D. H. Deacock Esq., Department of External Affairs, Eglo Engineering Pty.Ltd., ETA Foods Pty. Ltd., Fibre-makers Ltd., Ford Motor Co. W.A., P. Fletcher Esq., Hudson Fawcett Esq., L. Frazer Esq., Fyne Meats Pty. Ltd., J. Ferguson Esq., E. Field Esq., Foster Clark (Aust.) Ltd., R. Filsen Esq., Dr. Flint, Eric J. Gray Pty. Ltd., J. Godsen Esq., Gartrell White (Cakes) Pty. Ltd., Dr. A. R. Gilchrist, J. Gerrand Esq., Gairs Pty. Ltd., I. J. Glen Esq., Gladesville R.S.L. Club, C. J. Graham Esq., M. C. Grace Esq., E. Hill Esq., E. Harrington Esq., E. Hebblewhite Esq., Sir Edmund Hillary, N. D. Hardie Esq., The Hermandad de la Costa, J. S. Hardie Esq., J. Holder Esq., Harry Peck and Co., Horlicks Limited, Holbrooks Pty. Ltd., Dr. L. C. Hibbard, J. Holly Esq., H. J. Heinz and Co. Pty. Ltd., Hardings Sports Centre, A. S. Home Pty. Ltd., Imperial Services Club, Industrial Sugar Mills Pty. Ltd., ICIANZ, Indian Ocean Biological Centre, Imperial College of Science and Technology, Ingham Rotary Club, John Shaw (Aust.) Pty. Ltd., H. Jones and Co. Pty. Ltd., H. F. Jensen Esq., Lord Mayor of Sydney, E. Jones Esq., Kellogg (Aust.) Pty. Ltd., Kraft Foods Ltd., Knox Grammar School, J. Key Esq., Kameruka Bush Walkers, Kent Photographies Pty. Ltd., K. Lewis Esq., Professor Lowenthal, C. H. Locke Esq., Light Aircraft Pty. Ltd., J. R. Love and Co. Ltd., Lederle Laboratories Division Cyanamid D.H.A. Pty. Ltd., J. E. Lewis Esq., Herman Lightfoot Esq., Leggett Rubber Industries Pty. Ltd., Minnesota Mining and Manufacturing (Aust.) Pty. Ltd., Martin and Co. (Surgical) Ltd., J. Morgan Esq., May and Baker (Aust.) Pty. Ltd., B. McGill Esq., Mido Watch Co., Mirror Newspapers Ltd., P. McGrath Esq., D. Meade Esq., Mobil Oil (Aust.), D. and J. McCallum Ltd., B. McKelvey Esq., Moulded Products (N.S.W.) Pty. Ltd., McPhersons Ltd., Thomas McPherson and Son Ltd., Mishawaka Rubber Co. Pty. Ltd. (U.S.A.), Marrickville Margarine Pty. Ltd., R. W. Miller Ltd., Mr. and Mrs. W. McNamara, Mrs. Mortimer, Melbourne University Mountaineering Club, J. Middleton Esq., Montanari Ltd., R. Miller Esq., Andrew McGee Esq., N. Martin Esq., MacDougalls Pty. Ltd., Mount Everest Foundation, Captain Norris, National Geographic Magazine, New Zealand Alpine Club, Nippon Kogatu, New Century Batteries, N.S.W. Federation of Bushwalking Clubs, Nestle Company (Aust.) Ltd., A. Newman Esq., Outboard Marine (Aust.) Pty. Ltd., Ocean Salt Pty. Ltd., Mrs. Page, Port-a-Gas Pty. Ltd., Paddy Pallin Pty. Ltd., W. M. Pettingell, O.B.E., Prestige Products, F. J. Palmer Pty. Ltd., Pan American Airways, Mrs. Pattinson, B. Quigley Esq., Mrs. N. Rootes, Rothmans of Pall Mall (Aust.) Pty. Ltd., Royal Motor Yacht Club, Sydney, Royal Geographical Society, Rolls-Royce of Australia, Reckitt and Colman Pty. Ltd., Rosella Foods Pty. Ltd., Sydney Rock Climbers' Club, Dr. J. Stephenson, Sanyo Electric Co., Dr. G. C. Scully, Swallows Biscuits Pty. Ltd., Sanitarium Health Food Co., Supreme Sound Studios, Dr. E. Sussman, Suburban Section, Y.M.C.A., G. Sample Esq., South Sydney Junior Rugby League Club, Scanlens Goblin Sweets, D. H. Small and Son Ltd., Smith and Nephew (Aust.) Pty. Ltd., Smith Kline and French Laboratories (Aust.) Ltd., M. P. Sussman Esq., Sydney Bush Walkers, San Sei Sha Co. Ltd., Skellerup Ltd. N.Z., Tarax Drinks Pty. Ltd., Trinity Grammar School, Trans Antarctic Fund, Mrs. J. A. Tuckson, United Services Institute, Vidor Engineering, W. D. and H. O. Wills (Aust.) Ltd., White Wings Pty. Ltd., Westons Biscuit Co. Pty. Ltd., D. Williams Esq., Wormald Brothers, W. P. White and Son, A. Watson Esq., F. J. Walker Ltd., Wesfarmers, Albany, W.A., Woolworths Limited.